Dervla Murphy

was born in County Waterford, Ireland, of Dublin parents. Since 1964 she has been regularly publishing descriptions of her journeys – by bicycle or on foot – in the remoter areas of four continents. She has also written about the problems of Northern Ireland, the hazards of the nuclear power industry and race relations in Britain. She still lives in County Waterford.

Dervla Murphy is the author of many travel books, including *In Ethiopia with a Mule*, *Eight Feet in the Andes*, *On a Shoestring to Coorg*, *Full Tilt* and *The Ukimwi Road*.

D1335239

DERVLA MURPHY

Where the Indus is Young

Walking to Baltistan

Flamingo
An Imprint of HarperCollinsPublishers

Flamingo
An Imprint of HarperCollins*Publishers*
77–85 Fulham Palace Road,
Hammersmith, London W6 8JB

Published by Flamingo 1995
9 8 7 6 5 4 3 2

First published in Great Britain by
Jonathan Murray (Publishers) Ltd 1977

Author photograph by Michael Brophy

ISBN 0 00 654801 6

Set in Aldus Roman

Printed in Great Britain by
HarperCollinsManufacturing Glasgow

To Diana and Jock
most steadfast of friends, in good times and bad
with deep affection

My excursion from the base at Skardu, particularly the one along the shayok, convinced me that winter, far from being an obstacle, in certain ways facilitates travel in valleys which previous visitors have found difficult if not impossible.

Giotto Dainelli

The Balti race deserve a high degree of esteem and goodwill. They are scrupulously honest, mild of manners, gentle and good-tempered, naturally amenable to discipline, capable of the hardest labour, incredibly temperate, happy with very little and invariably good-humoured.

Fillipo de Fillipi

The river is a wonder . . . compressed tight between the mountains, it flows swift and deep and strong . . . While the mountains stand over it in granitic immobility it courses forward with a power that nothing can resist for long. Centuries of millenniums pass, but without cease it flows. And so tremendous is its power it is almost terrifying to watch.

Sir Francis Younghusband

Contents

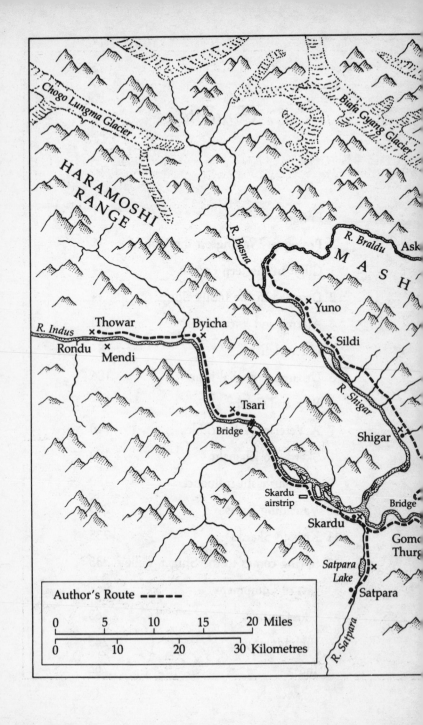

Chogo Lungma Glacier

HARAMOSHI RANGE

Biafo Gyang Glacier

R. Braldu

Ask

MASH

R. Basna

R. Indus

Thowar

Byicha

Rondu

Mendi

Yuno

Sildi

R. Shigar

Tsari

Bridge

Shigar

Skardu airstrip

Bridge

Skardu

Gomo
Thurg

Satpara Lake

Satpara

R. Satpara

Author's Route - - - -

| 0 | 5 | 10 | 15 | 20 Miles |

| 0 | 10 | 20 | 30 Kilometres |

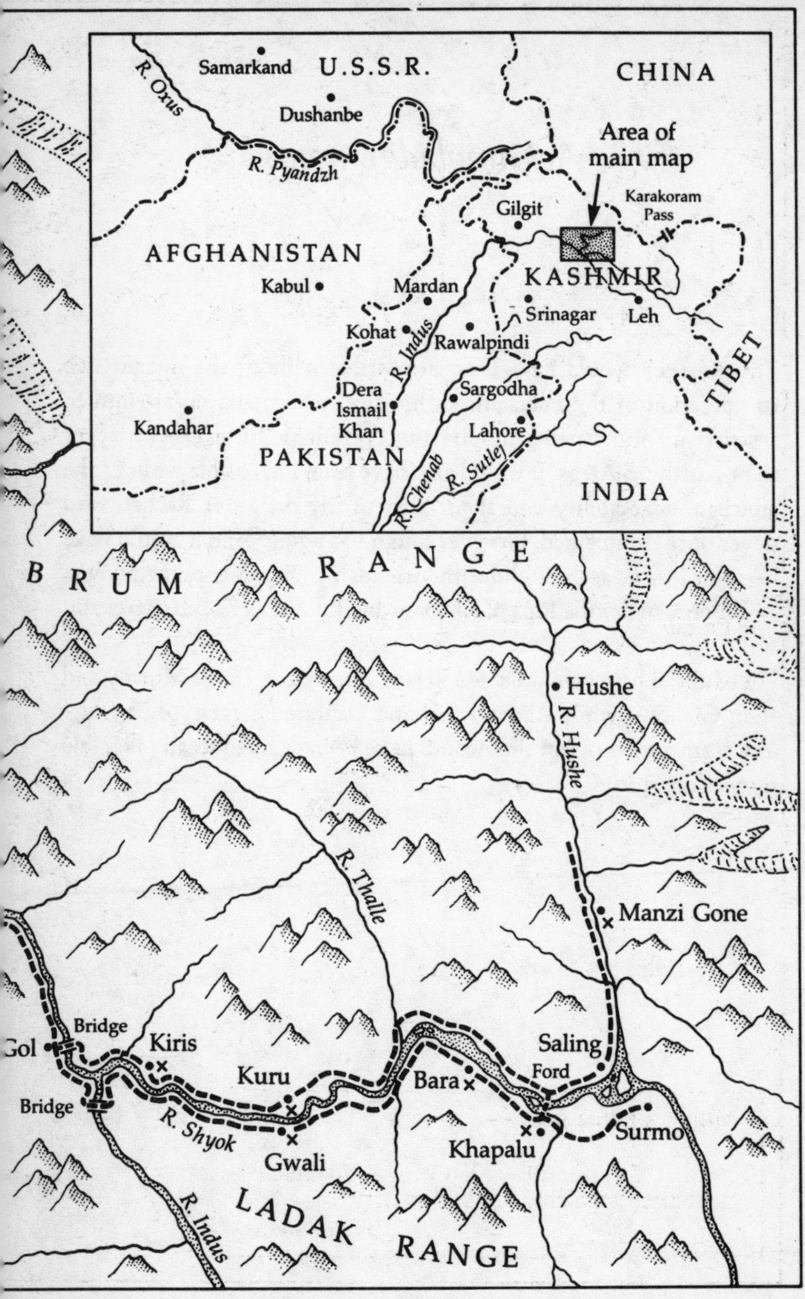
Samarkand
U.S.S.R.
CHINA
R. Oxus
Dushanbe
Area of main map
R. Pyandzh
Karakoram Pass
Gilgit
AFGHANISTAN
KASHMIR
Kabul
Mardan
Srinagar
Leh
Kohat
R. Indus
Rawalpindi
TIBET
Dera Ismail Khan
Sargodha
Kandahar
Lahore
PAKISTAN
R. Chenab
R. Sutlej
INDIA
BRUM RANGE
Hushe
R. Hushe
R. Thalle
Manzi Gone
Bridge
Gol
Kiris
Saling
Kuru
Ford
Bara
Bridge
Surmo
R. Shyok
Khapalu
Gwali
R. Indus
LADAK RANGE

Acknowledgements

This journey would have been impossible without the imaginative co-operation of the Pakistani authorities, who made no attempt to restrict my movements despite the present political sensitivity of their Northern Areas. It would also have been impossible without the stoicism, adaptability and sheer guts of my daughter Rachel, who never once complained, however tough the going. And it would have been far less pleasant without the friendship and practical help given so generously by the Raja of Khapalu and by Abbas Kazmi of Skardu.

For editorial help I am indebted to Jane Boulenger, Diana Murray and John Gibbons, while Alison Mills and Daphne Pearce typed heroically from a manuscript that would have been deemed totally illegible by weaker spirits.

Preface

In his account of the 1913–14 Italian Expedition through the Karakorams, Giotto Dainelli sowed the seed of this book: '. . . a district – Baltistan – which all the old travellers recognize as the extreme western part of Tibet . . .' At present no one has any hope of getting into Tibet proper, under acceptable conditions – and I am not sure that I would want to go there now – but the prospect of travelling through that 'extreme western part' was very attractive indeed. So I hastened off to the Pakistani Embassy in London, to seek further information.

During the previous fourteen months I had been having an intense relationship with India. This was based not merely on the writing of a travel-book about that country but on the making of a concentrated effort to achieve some degree of understanding of Hindu culture. I had spent part of the time in India and the rest of it reading, thinking, writing and feeling about India, almost to the exclusion of everything else. It had been a challenging, stimulating, exhausting, enjoyable time – and then suddenly it was over. My book was finished, and less than twenty-four hours later I entered the Pakistani Embassy.

At once, while chatting to a group of Punjabis on a dilapidated landing, I was afflicted by a mild version of what the Americans call Culture Shock. This most probably would not have affected me had there been even a week's interval between my disengagement from India and my involvement with Pakistan. As things were, the abrupt change, on several levels, was too much.

Within the preceding weeks I had often visited India House, which gives a somewhat incongruous, not to say misleading impression of elegant affluence. The Pakistani Embassy in Lowndes Square is very different. (Or was, in November 1974.) No doubt some rooms had been kept up to embassy standards, but the many corridors, hallways and stairs traversed by me were very evidently the property of a poor country. And the staff – in contrast to all those svelte, impeccably-trained Indians at India House – were so amiably clueless that they had me trotting to and fro from building to building for half-an-hour before I found the man I wanted. Yet that morning I was conscious of a wonderful feeling of relaxation, of at-homeness – an absence of barriers.

It is perilous to venture into comparisons between India and Pakistan but sometimes one has to risk offending both sides, for the sake of readers totally unfamiliar with the subcontinent.

Most Europeans find it easier to form uncomplicated friendships with Pakistanis than with Indians; we instinctively sympathize with the underdog and Pakistan has always been the underdog vis-à-vis India. At the time of Partition India inherited a well-equipped administrative capital in good working order, while the new Karachi Government scarcely had a typewriter or a telephone to its name and was operating not from Lutyens' stately buildings but from tin huts and cramped private houses. Moreover, those vast quantities of military stores which had been allocated to Pakistan under the Partition Agreements were being withheld by the new Government of India, and Field-Marshal Auchinleck's H.Q. in Delhi was abolished before it had time to supervise their distribution. Also, most ordnance factories and army schools, apart from the famous staff college at Quetta, were in India. Yet the rougher the going became, during those early years, the more guts the Pakistanis showed, though they lacked that outside support they had somewhat naively expected. India, being far more influential, got proportionately more consideration from the Big Powers.

All this naturally engenders sympathy for Pakistan. Yet our ease of communication with Pakistanis probably owes most to the obvious affinities between Christianity and Islam, though nowadays this religious factor is two-edged. Theocracies are unfashionable in the West and Pakistan initially alienated many foreigners by presenting herself as an Islamic Republic. This meant not merely that all her people were Muslim (i.e., willing to say 'There is no God but God and Mohammed is his Prophet'), but that they were fully prepared to accept the Koran, the Sunna (traditional customs) and the Sharia. The Sharia is a formidable collection of complex laws devised by theologians more than a thousand years ago and ever since guarded against change by the *Ulema*, an even less flexible institution than the Vatican. It was plainly absurd to pretend that the majority of Pakistanis fully accepted the Sharia – individuals can be selective about these laws, while remaining good Muslims – and the 1962 Constitution dropped the description 'Islamic Republic'. Since 1960 various steps have been taken of which the *Ulema* could not approve, notably President Ayub Khan's 'Muslim Family Laws Ordinance', which restricted polygamy and divorce.

Certainly the visitor is aware of no stifling conservative theocratic presence in Pakistan, which feels considerably less religion-conscious than the officially secular Republic of India. And having fairly recently visited a number of old-established Christian institutions, in both India and Pakistan, I can vouch for it that since 1947 Christian missionaries have had a much smoother ride in Pakistan than in India. I can also vouch for the fact that even the most powerful Pakistani mullahs have far less influence than the average Irish Catholic bishop.

The leaders of India's Muslim Revival, during the seventy years or so before Partition, were vigorously unorthodox reformers whose efforts to modernize Islam permanently antagonized the mullahs. While the idea of Pakistan was developing in the minds of some of these reformers, the mullahs opposed it almost unanimously – and not just because its advocates were unorthodox. Nationalism frustrates the Islamic ideal of a world in which all men are brothers, regardless of race, colour, class or occupation.

Baltistan covers an area of 10,000 square miles and was ruled from about 1840 by the Maharaja of Kashmir; therefore it is now part of the Disputed Territory between Pakistan and India. The U.N. Cease-Fire-Line forms its semi-circular north-east, east and south-east border, running from the Chinese frontier almost to the Burzil Pass and making it a very 'sensitive area'. (As one semi-inebriated Sindhi solemnly explained to me in Karachi, 'It is the reverse of an erogenous zone – it makes people hate not love.') I was therefore prepared to wage a long and probably unsuccessful battle for a Balti permit. The Indians, I knew, allowed no foreigners anywhere near their Himalayan frontier and why should the Pakistanis be any more accommodating?

When I eventually found the relevant office in the embassy and made my request a cheerful gentleman behind a wide desk beamed at me and said, 'You require no visa or permit for our Northern Areas. If you hold a valid Irish passport you may travel anywhere you like in Pakistan for as long as you like.'

'*No permit?*' I echoed, dazed. 'Are you *sure?*'

'Quite sure,' replied the cheerful gentleman. 'We have nothing to hide. Every traveller is welcome to every part of Pakistan. According to U.N. regulations you must keep ten miles away from the Cease-Fire-Line. Otherwise there are no restrictions.' He pulled open a drawer and handed me a large glossy brochure in glorious techni-color. It was entitled 'Gilgit–Hunza–Skardu' and my heart sank. Was I too late? Had even Baltistan, of which Skardu is the capital, been dragged somehow on to the beaten tourist track? But I need not have worried. The Pakistan Tourism Development Corporation is a young organization, as yet more given to promise than performance. Its information about Baltistan may be accurate by 1984 but was a mere Ministry of Tourism dream in 1974. Baltistan is still one of the least developed inhabited areas of Asia.

The P.T.D.C. also failed to give reliable advice about the approaches to the Northern Areas. According to their brochure, 'A new 302-mile, all-weather road now connects Gilgit with Saidu Sharif in the Swat Valley'. On the basis of this information I planned, before leaving London, to buy a riding-pony for my daughter in Saidu and trek into Baltistan from there, turning off the new Indus Highway near the confluence of the Indus and Gilgit rivers. But in Pindi my plan was thwarted; otherwise I might not have lived to tell this tale. Towards the end of December several thousand people were killed and a forty-mile stretch of the Indus Highway was demolished by the Swat earthquake.

When we left for Pakistan Rachel was not yet six and some eyebrows were raised at my taking such a small child into the Karakorams for the winter. But she was no amateur, even then, having spent four months in South India during the previous winter, undergoing her Asian initiation. Had that journey not been so successful, from her point of view, I would never have contemplated taking her to Baltistan. Our daily life there was obviously not going to be entirely devoid of hardship, and our style of travelling would demand a high level of endurance – by six-year-old standards – while there would be few playmates for a foreign child. But I already knew that Rachel is a natural stoic, and a muscular and vigorous little person, well able to walk ten or twelve miles a day without flagging. Moreover, as an only child she is accustomed to amusing herself for hours on end, and, though by temperament gregarious, she had then the extra-ordinary powers of adaptability common to most six-year-olds.

To me it seems that the five-to-seven-year-old stage is ideal for travelling rough with small children. Under-fives are not physically mature enough for exposure to the unavoidable health hazards, while over-sevens tend to be much less philosophical in their reactions to the inconveniences and strange customs of far-flungery. By the age of eight, children have developed their own (usually strong) views about how they wish life to be, and are no longer happy automatically to follow the parental leader. This is how it should be. I have accepted that our next joint journey – if there is one – must be something that appeals equally to Rachel and to me, rather than something imposed on Rachel by me.

On the morning of 22 November we boarded our Aeroflot plane for Karachi. Although neither of us was using our full free baggage allowance we seemed to be diabolically burdened; the essential equipment for two people who hope to survive a winter in the Karakorams cannot but seem heavy if one is obsessed about travelling light. A list of this equipment is given on page 261.

17 July 1975

Prologue: Waiting on the Wings

The large notice over the reception desk in Rawalpindi's fashionable Flashman's Hotel was exactly as I had remembered it from 1963: 'Visitors are requested to leave their weapons at the desk before entering the restaurant.' Those are the little touches that make one feel spiritually back in Pathan-land, though Pindi itself belongs to the Punjab and the Frontier Province lies west of the Indus.

The Pakistan Tourism Development Corporation has its head office at Flashman's, presided over by the Director of Tourism – a tall, youngish Pathan with auburn hair, green eyes and no great interest in people who want to do untouristical things like spending a winter in Baltistan. However, he courteously explained that the Indus Highway had been closed to foreigners months ago because of Chinese pressure and that we would have to fly to Gilgit, if we could manage to get seats on one of the few planes that do the trans-Himalayan trip during winter. I heard later that an American couple, travelling to Gilgit by jeep, had stopped – in defiance of Islamabad instructions – to photograph the Chinese soldiers who are building the road and who deeply resent being photographed. As a result the Chinese insisted on all foreign travellers being banned.

From Flashman's I proceeded down the Mall to Pakistan International Airways' imposing offices. A side entrance leads to a special Northern Areas department and the staff here works in an atmosphere of permanent crisis, with which I was to become only too familiar during the weeks ahead. But I never heard one of them utter an impolite or impatient word to even the most slow-witted peasant or peremptory army officer. The passengers seen in this booking-office are very unlike the affluent Pakistanis who frequent the main part of the building. Most are fair-skinned, with a scattering of Mongolian types. Some have racking coughs, a few have huge goitres, too many have an eye missing or useless. The majority wear woollen, roll-rimmed Chitrali caps, that may be turned down to protect forehead and ears from frost, and quite a few are self-consciously proud of their high-class mountaineering garments, acquired from some expedition and not really the most appropriate garb for the plains. Others wear loose shirts and baggy trousers; an occasional youth sports a cheap lounge-suit tailored in the bazaar; a few elders from Gilgit look regal in gaily-embroidered ankle-length robes of homespun wool. And the Baltis often carry heavy goat-hair blankets neatly folded and draped over one shoulder.

While awaiting met. news one sits for hours in this large room on long back-to-back seats, upholstered in jade-green leatherette, and all around cigarette-ash accumulates on the grey tiled floor, and some men eye the lone foreign woman a little uneasily. I never saw another female in that booking-office. Women of the Northern Areas rarely come down-country and the few women who do fly – the wives or daughters of government officials or army officers – invariably send servants to attend to their tedious ticket business.

On my first visit a very tall and debonair official behind the high counter shook his head and said smilingly, 'I'm afraid you've left it too late. We can't take tourists into the Northern Areas during winter – you might not get out till April!'

'But we don't want to get out before April,' said I. 'We mean to spend the winter in Baltistan.'

The young man stared at me – a trifle apprehensively, as though he fancied I might at any moment become violent. 'Do you know where Baltistan *is*?' he asked. 'Even the Baltis wouldn't spend the winter in Baltistan if they could help it!'

'Never mind,' I said soothingly, 'we have lots of warm clothes. How soon can you get us into Gilgit?'

'You are travelling with your husband?'

'No, with my daughter. So I want one half-fare please. She'll be six next week.'

The young man shrugged, conveying that this further evidence of instability removed me from those realms in which rational discussion is possible. He glanced down at a thick ledger. 'You will be number 287 on our waiting-list. You have no chance of a seat before 10 December. And it could be 10 January, if we get the winter rains now.' I paid then for our tickets which cost only five pounds because flights to and from the Northern Areas are subsidized by the government.

Walking back towards our host's house, near the National Park, I decided to go to Saidu Sharif in two days' time. Swat stood high on the list of places I wanted to revisit, eleven-and-a-half years after my first journey through Pakistan.

We were staying with Pathan friends a few miles outside Pindi. Their village lies well west of the Indus, their luxurious, brand-new city-house stands on a hilltop, in the shadow of an old fortified dwelling. From its flat roof we looked down on level farmland, and the evergreen trees of the National Park, and a wide stretch of reddish, fissured wasteland which daily becomes more fissured as earth is removed for making bricks. At the end of a November which had provided no winter rains the land looked ominously parched, yet our friends' new garden was an exuberant, improbable dazzle of colour. Like most peoples of Central Asian stock, the Pathans are ardent gardeners: an unexpected and disarming trait in a race of warrior tribesmen. Equally unexpected is their interest in poetry, though even today the majority are illiterate. Pushtu is a rich, flexible language and over the past three or four centuries almost every tribe has produced a major poet, whose descendants or followers are still highly regarded.

In Karim Khan's household I had an uncanny sense of being at home again, rather as though I had been a Pathan in some previous incarnation. In my experience Pathan hospitality is unique. Its blending of complete informality with meticulous attention to every tiny need makes one feel simultaneously an honoured guest and a loved member of the family.

Our host had himself designed his rambling, flat-roofed mini-palace, every detail of which bespoke enormous wealth regulated by instinctive good taste. 'We don't often stay in houses like this,' observed Rachel, standing ankle-deep in an olive-green carpet and looking from the carved walnut doors of our bedroom to the gilded moulding on the ceiling. Every mod. con. was available, from a huge box of Lego on Rachel's bedside table to the latest type of Swiss electric hair-drier in the bathroom. Here, one might think, was a family that in all essentials had completed its transition from East to West; but in fact this transition affects only the inessentials. Behind the façade of Westernization, Pathan life proceeds as usual with rifles to hand, women in purdah, children married to first cousins, prayers said regularly, goats in the backyard, feuds simmering, bodyguards on the alert, and dozens of poor relations from the village being given food, shelter and affection. But 'façade' was an ill-chosen word, since one of the Pathans' most attractive characteristics is their utter lack of pretence. When they can afford the material comforts and conveniences of modern civilization they seize them with both hands, yet even the younger generation – with few exceptions – is not concerned to appear Westernized on any other level. To me, this seems both remarkable and consoling in the 1970s.

Next morning Rachel was taken to visit the family village near Nowshera and I went shopping. A riding-cum-pack saddle cost the exact equivalent of £6, plus £1.50 for a girth and crupper, all new. The leather was inferior, and the saddle's mulberry-wood frame had a few woodworm holes, but as these purchases would have cost at least £60 in Ireland I was not disposed to complain. (From England we had brought a hard riding-hat, with safety chin-strap, and irons suitable for a six-year-old). I also bought a large canvas zip-bag, which could be worn as a rucksack if necessary, five yards of strong rope, a Chitrali cap for myself, a woollen balaclava for Rachel, a kerosene-stove (£1.25), a kettle, a saucepan and two electric-blue plastic bowls out of which to eat. Only our emergency supply of tinned food was expensive: over £7 for a dozen small tins of meat, fish and cheese.

These purchases took up most of the day; bazaar shopping is an essential antidote to staying with a family whose wealth and education set them apart from 95 per cent of their countrymen. I collected much fascinating gossip – especially from the young leather-merchant, who claimed to have a cousin working on the international telephone exchange. His scandalous stories about the love-lives of Asia's leading politicians (and their wives) would undoubtedly involve me in several libel actions if repeated here. For over two hours I waited in that tiny shop, surrounded by piles of suitcases, handbags and saddlery, while finishing touches were being put to the cotton-padded girth. The smell of new leather mingled with the smell of spices and frying onions from a small, shadowy eating-house across the way, and at intervals our detailed consideration of cosmopolitan sex was interrupted by the arrival of customers. Many were tall Pathan tribesmen from the hills, with splendid hawk faces and untidy turbans. These carried perfect Afridi-made copies of Enfield rifles over their shoulders and invariably wanted to purchase holsters, bandoliers or tack. They were very hard bargainers. The merchant spoke Punjabi, Urdu and English but most of the tribesmen spoke only Pushtu, so there were occasional misunderstandings during which Pathan eyes flashed. Then the little merchant would look nervously around at me – sitting in the background between cliffs of suitcases – as though I were a remnant of the Raj and somehow capable of defending him from his unpredictable compatriots.

We left for Swat at noon next day, having spent two hours sitting in a full bus that had been supposed to start at ten-thirty. Pakistan's bus-services are less well-organized than India's. By this stage our gear formed a daunting pile: my big rucksack, Rachel's small rucksack, that large canvas bag, a cardboard carton securely roped, a heavy saddle made of wood, iron and leather and a two-gallon plastic jerry-can. For the first time in my life I was travelling with more luggage than I could carry single-handed and a great nuisance I found it. But in that battered bus, full of Swatis on their way home, everybody was extra helpful because we had been driven to the bus-stand in a friend's car – and that friend was Aurangzeb, son and heir of the recently deposed Wali of Swat.

Between Pindi and Nowshera the countryside looked like a semi-desert – grey-brown, cracked, parched. The farmer sitting beside me stated with curious precision that if no rain came within six days next year's wheat crop would be ruined. For me this journey awoke many memories. On my way to India from Ireland, I had cycled along the Grand Trunk Road in June 1963, against a scorching headwind that kept my speed down to five m.p.h. And now my daughter, undreamt of then, was sitting beside me excitedly pointing out various objects of interest along the route – which she had travelled over the day before on her way to and from our friends' village.

The attraction of the Frontier Province is quite extraordinary. As the red-brown-grey landscape became more broken and rugged and harsh, and the mountains became more distinct along the horizon, and the houses became more fort-like – their windows mere slits, the better to fire through – I felt a surge of nostalgic excitement.

At Nowshera we turned north towards the Malakand Pass and beside an octroi post stood a freshly painted notice saying – among other things – 'Foreigners are advised not to travel by night and to carry no valuables in this territory'. I had cycled over the Malakand through a deluge and seen nothing, but now we enjoyed a dramatic bronze and smoky-blue sunset as our overloaded bus chugged slowly into the hills. From Pindi to Mingora is 165 miles so it had been dark for half-an-hour when we arrived at the bus-stand, loaded everything into a covered motor-cycle rickshaw and went bouncing noisily off through the cold black night.

At the empty Waliahad – all Aurangzeb's family were in Islamabad – I was touched to find myself remembered and warmly welcomed by the senior servants. Since my last visit a lot of water had passed turbulently under Pakistan's political bridges. In 1963 Swat's legal status was that of a princely state within Pakistan: the Central Government had a right to intervene only on foreign policy and the Wali administered justice according to custom, Islamic law and his own common sense – which was abundant. I had stayed with Aurangzeb and his wife Naseem, eldest daughter of the late Field-Marshal Ayub Khan, who was then at the height of his power as Pakistan's benevolent military dictator. And I had been impressed by the efficiency of Swat's non-bureaucratic administration and by the state's comparatively high level of prosperity.

In April 1974 Ayub Khan died in Islamabad, five years after the collapse of his regime and his resignation as President of Pakistan. Meanwhile the new parliamentary government had abolished all the princely statelets: Swat, Dir, Chitral, Hunza, Nagar, and the numerous tiny chieftainships of Baltistan. Hunza, Nagar, Baltistan and the former Gilgit Agency are now known as the Northern Areas, while Swat, Dir and Chitral are administered by a District Commissioner who has his headquarters at Saidu, just across the road from the Waliahad. Aurangzeb still represents Swat in the National Assembly – as a member of the opposition, naturally – and is on the friendliest terms with Captain Jamshed Burki, the very able and charming D.C. who has been appointed by Mr Bhutto to replace the Wali. To me this seems a measure both of Aurangzeb's fair-mindedness and Captain Burki's tact.

I have no head for politics and I cannot pretend to any deep understanding of political developments in Pakistan over the past decade. But most knowledgeable commentators seem to agree with Gilbert Laithwaite's assessment that 'Ayub was concerned to establish for Pakistan a half-way house to democracy – a democracy that could be understood and worked. His eleven years as President were marked by substantial achievements in the fields of economic advance, of Pakistan's standing in world affairs, of order combined with progress . . .'

However, many Pakistanis deny the 'benevolence' of Ayub's regime and will accuse me – no doubt correctly – of being biased. I cannot deny feeling a natural sympathy for the Pathans, a deep admiration for what Ayub Khan tried to do and a great personal affection for his widow and family. He certainly made mistakes, but often these were based on military forthrightness and an impatience with the sort of humbuggery that distinguishes too many of the subcontinent's more successful politicians. A good example of this sort of 'mistake' was his uncompromising commitment to Family Planning. He even appeared on television in an attempt to counteract a widespread campaign of anti-contraceptive rumours which was being cleverly organized by unidentified groups. Probably these groups were led by Muslim equivalents of Ireland's more unsavoury bishops, whose fanaticism had been harnessed by Ayub's political opponents. The President's determination to lower Pakistan's birth-rate was a most valuable stick with which to beat him, in a country mainly populated by illiterate, gullible, hide-bound peasants. Indeed, many observers believe that it contributed even more to his downfall than the charges of corruption – much publicized but never proved – that were brought against his immediate family. At any rate, it is perhaps worth recording that one of India's most distinguished public figures – a man full of years and wisdom – said to me in March 1974, shortly before the Field-Marshal's death: 'If only India had had one leader like Ayub Khan!'

To everybody's relief, it rained heavily throughout our first night in Swat and until noon next day. After lunch Rachel and I explored under a grey sky patched with blue. As the cloud was not low we could enjoy the craggy mountain walls that enclose Saidu on three sides, but the snow-peaks to the north remained invisible. Near the Waliahad hundreds of flat-roofed stone and mud hovels cover the steep hillsides and between them run narrow alleyways or flights of steps. Purdah is strictly observed in Swat and because I looked male to local eyes our progress was marked by the scurrying indoors of numerous veiled figures, some of whom abandoned heavy water-jars in their flight. Even little giggling girls of eight or nine completely covered their faces while peeping at us around corners.

A deep, dry, stony nullah-bed wound between the slopes and was in a disgusting state; being a general dump and public latrine, it stank most abominably after the night's rain. Having spent the previous winter in India, I caught myself constantly making odious compari-sons – for instance, between the filth of many Muslim villagers and the scrupulous personal cleanliness of even the poorest caste-Hindu.

I spent that evening with the lively-minded Burkis, and as I was leaving Mrs Burki invited Rachel to play with her three children next day.

Back at the Waliahad the chowkidar in what used to be the sentry-box was still rapidly knitting, as he had been when I left five hours earlier. The men of Swat are keen knitters and at first one is slightly taken aback on seeing six-foot sentries standing with rifles over their shoulders and incessantly clicking needles in their huge hands. They turn out an endless number of sweaters, scarves, socks, caps and gloves for themselves and their families – an aspect of Pakistani life that Women's Lib would surely applaud.

We woke next morning to a cloudless sky; thick frost sparkled on the burnt yellow lawn outside our window and a glorious glisten of new snow lay on the long, jagged line of the Himalayas, now clearly visible to the north. At nine o'clock I deposited Rachel on the Burkis, where I suspect she found the forceful Pathan young rather disconcerting after her malleable South Indian playmates of the previous winter. Then I spent a happy day climbing a mini-mountain, revisiting some of Swat's Gandhara sites and gossiping around Mingora bazaar. Thirteen out of the fourteen English-speaking men with whom I discussed local politics were decisively pro-Wali and said so openly. I thought it an important point in favour of Mr Bhutto's government that they felt free to criticize it thus to a total stranger.

An innovation called the Tourist Wagon Service has recently appeared on Pakistan's roads. These fast mini-buses, each seating eleven plus the driver, operate non-stop between cities and are used by the less poor Pakistanis rather than by tourists. Our tickets for the 112-mile journey to Peshawar cost Rs.16 (eighty pence), whereas the ordinary bus fare would have been Rs.4.50. As females we were entitled to the two roomy front seats beside the driver; in all Tourist Wagons these, and the back seat if necessary, form the Ladies' Compartments.

When we left Mingora the valley looked superb in sparkling sunshine, with autumn colours still glowing on poplars, elms, birches and planes. Under a cloudless sky the Swat river was a gay ribbon of blue, tossed across the landscape, and hundreds of multi-coloured goats were grazing on the tawny mountainsides. We met three buses coming up the Malakand Pass on the wrong side, their roofs piled with a singing, waving overflow of passengers and their wheels inches from lethal drops as they swung around hairpin bends.

Our driver seemed to keep his right hand permanently out of the window, in order to squeeze his bulbous rubber horn; no doubt he reckoned that negotiating such bends without a horn would be even more dangerous than steering with one hand.

In my first book, *Full Tilt*, I described Peshawar as being 'like an English city with a few water-buffaloes and vultures and lizards thrown in'. Those words were written the day I came over the Khyber Pass, after months of cycling through the remoter regions of Persia and Afghanistan. But in 1974, having come straight from the fleshpots of Karachi, Islamabad, Pindi and Saidu, I found this 'Paris of the Pathans' – Lowell Thomas's phrase – a very special place. It seemed less a city in the modern sense than an agglomeration of medieval bazaars inhabited by attractive rough diamonds of many races. It is one of the three Pathan cities – the others are Kandahar and Jellalabad, in Afghanistan – and since my first visit it has become one of the hippies' main junctions.

In 1963 the great eastward Hippy Migration had not yet started and *Full Tilt* has frequently been accused of increasing its momentum, which suggestion troubles my conscience more than it flatters my vanity when I see groups of drugged wrecks dragging themselves around Asia. However, Peshawar's attitude to strangers has been only slightly modified by the hippy influence. Pesh Awar means 'Frontier Town' and for at least 4,000 years this city has been dealing with invaders of many types. The hippies are merely a source of local amusement – and of course profit, for the many drug-pedlars in the bazaars.

We stayed on the outskirts of Peshawar with the Khanzadas, who in 1963 had entertained me at their Abbottabad home and nursed me through a devastating attack of dysentery. But having been unable, from Saidu, to warn Begum Khanzada of our arrival, we spent our first night in a doss-house.

By five-fifteen it was dark and beneath a gold-flecked sky we set off through crisp frosty air to explore some of the ancient bazaars. Rachel was enthralled as we wandered from one narrow, dimly-lit alleyway to another. Above us loomed tall stone and wood houses, centuries old, and we passed butchers and bakers and candlestick-makers (literally: one coppersmith was at work on a candlestick). Often we paused to watch men weighing huge chunks of marble, or carving wood or mending transistors or cobbling shoes or beating brass or tailoring shirts – all by the light of lanterns hanging from the roofs of their little stalls. A flour-covered baker gave us a length of hot *nan* from his underground mud oven, and we were invited into one eating-house for juicy *kebabs*, and into another for small bowls of delicious tangy curds, and into two primitive tea-houses for little red and blue china pots of green tea – *gahura*, the Pathans' national drink – which filled me with an almost unbearable longing for Afghanistan. As we sat cross-legged on filthy matting in one tea-house a small boy came strolling up the alleyway, noticed us, hesitated a moment, and then stood on tiptoe to hand up to Rachel a glorious pink rose bud, about to unfold. Before we could thank him he had disappeared into the surrounding shadows, his impulsive gesture having completed the perfection of our evening.

A few days later we returned to Pindi to see how flights to the Northern Areas were faring. 'No hope for you until the sixteenth,' I was told. 'Weather's been terrible this past week.'

As I turned away from the counter a young Punjabi army officer, stationed in Skardu, suggested that if I were to exert a little pressure the waiting-list might be cooked. I was uncertain what sort of pressure he meant – whether moral or financial – but I did not doubt that my debonair P.I.A. friend would be genuinely insulted if offered a bribe. In any case, looking around at all the wretched men who had been stuck down-country for weeks, and were longing to get back to their families, I felt it would be unforgivable to jump this queue.

We spent the next three days in Islamabad, as guests of Begum Ayub Khan. This was only seven months after the Field-Marshal's death and his family were still mourning a beloved husband and father. Begum Ayub vividly reminded me of my own mother after my father's death. My mother, too, was a woman of exceptional fortitude; and though such people tend not to give way outwardly to grief, its effects are all the more lasting for that.

The Ayubs' spacious new house is on the extreme north-eastern edge of Islamabad. Just behind it lie green, rounded hills, on which patches of light-brown earth or grey rock make an irregular pattern, and behind them rises the high blue ridge of the Murree Hills. We found the house and garden full of sons, daughters, in-laws, grand-children, nephews, nieces and various unidentified relatives from the village. Yet Begum Ayub's motherly hospitality is so boundless that within those walls we felt not merely accepted but cherished.

Aurangzeb and Naseem live about a mile away, down a long straight road bordered on one side by the homes of diplomats or rich Pakistanis and on the other by miles of open scrubland. Over this wide expanse at the foot of the mountains are scattered the National Assembly buildings, the Prime Minister's residence-cum-government-offices, the Bank of Pakistan's headquarters, a colossal United Nations building, a colony of suburban villas for the British Embassy staff – looking as though it had strayed from Bexhill-on-Sea – and several of the larger embassies, including the Russian, Canadian, British and Chinese.

I remember cycling past Islamabad while it was being built and thinking how frightful it would soon look – another Chandigarh. But in fact Pakistan's new capital is an agreeable place of wide, bright boulevards, many trees, brilliant gardens, no high-risery and much attractive domestic architecture that is original without being 'way-out'. Despite its official status it feels like an elegant, cosmopolitan suburb of Pindi – some fifteen miles away, but very close in spirit – and one hopes it will remain so. When Ayub Khan planned it he specified 'no industrial development nearby' but his successors may have cruder ideas.

A more immediate threat than industry is basic Asian squalor; it does not take the Orient very long to impress itself on the latest in Occidental architecture and town planning. Islamabad is disfigured by too many areas from which builders' rubble was never cleared and where men squat around relieving themselves in the shadow of imposing banks, embassies and shopping arcades. Even amidst the diplomatic residences some corners are piled with rubbish and occasional houses already show symptoms of jerry-building, while throughout the less affluent quarters squalor is gaining fast. In ancient Asian cities this sort of thing seems tolerable – even picturesque – but there is something peculiarly unprepossessing about disintegrating new buildings. And inevitably Islamabad has its beggars, though far fewer than any Indian city I know. These piteous bundles lie on the ground, hidden by a thin sheet of filthy cotton or a ragged burkah, and one would never suspect their humanity but for a stick-like arm and motionless begging palm outstretched on the pavement beside the fine new buildings of a new country with very old problems.

Tourist Wagons constantly ply between Islamabad and Pindi; passengers get on and off anywhere they like at either end, or in between, and pay a fixed rate of one rupee per ride. One rarely has to wait more than a few minutes before being picked up, but if a bus is almost empty its driver may cruise around the streets for half-an-hour, filling enough seats to justify a journey. Even when one starts out from the most swinging quarter of Islamabad, most women come aboard wearing burkahs. To discover what sort of person is sitting beside you it is necessary to study the hand that will soon appear to grip the dashboard bar as the driver swings recklessly around corners. From that hand and its adornments quite a lot may be deduced about the age, physique, social status and approximate ethnic origins of the shapeless figure lurking silently within those folds of (usually black) cotton or nylon.

Despite their looking so spick and span, these buses, like most Asian vehicles, will accommodate on the roof virtually anything that is capable of somehow being hauled up there. Enormous bales of hay and bundles of firewood, pyramids of stainless steel cooking-pots, trussed-up, frantically bleating goats, a plastic kitchen table, a day-old buffalo calf, a sack of wheat, two geese in a wooden crate – up they all go, and are deftly secured to the roof-rack by the driver's mate, who is usually a good-natured adolescent anxious to help everybody. Rachel's favourite Islamabad anecdote concerns a goat belonging to one woman passenger who got at a bale of hay belonging to another woman passenger. When the goat's perfidy was revealed, on our arrival at Pindi, the two women exposed their faces, the better to tear each other's eyes out, and order was not restored until a passing mullah, outraged by this display of nudity, belaboured both with his walking-stick.

Around Islamabad, the daily life of the peasants remains unchanged by the proximity of their sophisticated new capital. I spent a day walking alone over the nearby hillsides and the villagers' astonishment on seeing me indicated that Islamabad's foreign colony does not often take to its feet. A still, grey day it was, reminiscent of late autumn in Ireland, and I reflected gloomily that in such weather there would certainly be no flights to the Northern Areas.

During the afternoon two young women shyly invited me into a stone hut – the first Aryan invader of the subcontinent would have found it familiar – and insisted on refreshing me with green tea, which took almost an hour to brew. Only a few villagers have acquired a little newfangled cement to mix with the mud normally used to pack crevices in stone walls.

From one hilltop I watched a line of ten women slowly ascending the path below me, each balancing two ochre pitchers of water on her head whilst helping to drive a communal herd of goats and kids – the goats wearing 'bras', to conserve their milk. Then I looked from the low, oblong huts nearby, over a furlong of level grazing land, to a wide, smooth ring-road along which sleek C.D. cars were swiftly purring past ingeniously-designed villas incorporating every conceivable mod. con. Between these villas, lining the distant streets of Islamabad, stood hundreds of slender poplars, their branches retaining enough orange-yellow leaves to make them seem like rows of giant candles glowing through the late afternoon greyness. I returned home across an expanse of thinly-wooded land where the sound of axes rang out from every side as branches were lopped off for evening fires. By five o'clock a long band of crimson was flaring above the western horizon – a startling sight, after the uniform dullness of the sky all day – and moments later it was dark.

From Islamabad we went up to Murree for two days. Murree is the only one of British India's hill-stations to have gone to Pakistan; it is 7,500 feet above sea-level and we found it thickly covered in snow.

We stayed in a ramshackle hotel which charged Rs.5 a night for what might be hyperbolically described as 'a double room', and on our return to Islamabad one of my young Pathan friends, who takes an unusual interest in the world beyond her own circle, asked me wistfully what it felt like to stay in a doss-house. The undertones of envy in her voice made me consciously value, as nothing else had ever done, my own freedom of movement. We European women take this completely for granted. Yet no Pakistani woman, however independent-minded or strong-willed, could possibly travel alone through her own country sharing the life of the poor. Granted, not many Pakistani women would ever want to do such a thing. But suddenly I found the fact that they *could* not strangely disturbing. Antipathetic as I am to Women's Lib, its indirect influence may yet do some good in Asia.

Early on 15 December we got back to Islamabad from Taxila, where we had spent five days exploring what was once the centre of Gandhara civilization. During the previous night the longed-for rains had at last come and we were reminded of the worst sort of cold, wet, dark, Irish winter's day, with the added disadvantage of mud hock-deep throughout the city. Obviously we were not going to get to Gilgit on 16 December. This time we were staying with the Aurangzebs and on the seventeenth I set off alone – in brilliant sunshine – for a day's scrambling through the foothills.

I followed an ancient, precipitous path not much used in this motorized age, when peasants go forty miles *around* by bus instead of ten miles *over* on foot. Until one has crossed the first ridge urban noises ascend through the still, clear air in an almost uncanny way: the blaring of horns, the high-pitched cries of street vendors, the preaching of some modified Trade Union gospel from a van with a loudspeaker. Then suddenly the city becomes invisible and inaudible. All day I saw only two people – carrying huge loads of firewood on their heads – and this rare degree of silence and solitude gave me a chance to try to sort out the impressions I had received since landing at Karachi three weeks earlier.

The previous evening I had met an elderly gentleman who, on

hearing that I had recently visited India, asked eagerly for news of Delhi. An hour and two whiskeys later he was confessing that the older he gets the more he longs to see once more the Moghul capital. For over five centuries his family had lived in Delhi and on one level he spoke of the city with nostalgia and love: but on another level it was the enemy capital. Tangled are the roots of Pakistani nationalism.

He declared that to his children's generation, too, Pakistan must always be to some extent a place of exile; and I was reminded of my West Punjabi friends in Delhi, who still speak of Lahore as 'home'. But there is one significant difference. 'Pakistani' Indians tend to regard Pakistan's creation as a massive robbery, organized by the British and the Muslims and condoned by the world. 'Indian' Pakistanis, on the other hand, tend to regard partition not angrily but sadly. They have no wish to see it undone, but some of them still deplore that spectacular deterioration in communal relations which made it essential. As Ian Stephens has more than once stressed, in his thoughtful books on Pakistan, 'something describable as a joint Hindu-Muslim or Indian culture did exist, both under the British regime, and more genuinely perhaps in the sixteenth and seventeenth centuries . . . The point needs emphasizing, to keep a correct balance. Over long periods, the two religious systems have functioned alongside one another without overt antagonism, and sometimes with mutual sympathy.'

Sitting on a level ledge of ground under a clump of pines, I found myself wondering, 'Should Pakistan exist?' A silly question, in the 1970s. Yet it continues to occur to foreigners more often than they could tactfully admit to their Pakistani friends. Does this indicate that the 'joint Hindu-Muslim or Indian culture' is stronger than anything an exclusively Muslim state can create on its own in the godless twentieth century? Or does it simply mean that no hastily improvised new nation can give a convincing impression of nationhood after less than thirty years in existence?

It is easy to forget just how hastily Pakistan was improvised: for years Jinnah was as opposed to the idea of Partition as any Hindu. In 1916 he became known as the 'Ambassador of Hindu-Muslim unity'; twenty years later he was being commended by the Governor of the

Punjab for having successfully reconciled warring factions of Sikhs and Muslims, and not until 1940 did he accept the inevitability of Pakistan. So there was no long historical gestation, no era of frustration during which the Muslims of the subcontinent dreamed impatiently of their own Islamic state. And this must be why one senses so little genuine regret, in present-day Pakistan, about the loss of Bangladesh. The ordinary man in the bazaar naturally resents the humiliation implicit in that loss and spits fire when he thinks of the part played by India. But his emotions seem not to have been seriously involved – as they are on the Kashmir issue – when half his nation was amputated. There was never much mutual sympathy, interest or wish for understanding between the ordinary peoples of East and West Pakistan. They were of different ethnic stock, they wore different clothes, ate different foods, spoke different languages, built different houses, grew different crops, kept different animals and lived against utterly different cultural and geographical backgrounds. Only religion united them, and even their interpretations of Islam – the results of quite different historical experiences – were not identical.

Many Pakistanis said outright to me – and there was no tang of sour grapes in their voices – that they feel their country is better off without Bangladesh, that now they can get down to making something worthwhile of what remains. I was surprised by this widespread willingness to admit that Pakistan, as originally conceived, had been a mistake. One young army officer said to me, 'You can't found a nation just on a great big ugly negative – the inability of Muslims, Sikhs and Hindus to live peaceably together. There has to be something more positively unifying, even if it's just geographical.'

However, the change in Pakistan's mood that struck me most on this return visit was not very positive. It has come about through the growing-up of a generation with no lingering shred of affection for the rest of the subcontinent, nor any awareness of being linked to it by countless bonds forged throughout centuries of shared history. I met many members of this first-born generation of Pakistanis – doctors, farmers, lawyers, merchants, teachers, bank-clerks, journalists, civil servants – and the majority seemed to feel for India only a contemptuous, uncomprehending hostility. Unlike their parents, they have no memories of growing up with Hindu neighbours, taking part in Hindu festivals, seeing pictures of Hindu gods and goddesses in the bazaar. I found them disquieting, for they represent a considerable increase in the world's sum of hate. They were enormously disconcerted when told that we had spent the previous winter in India and met there with nothing but kindness. They did not really want to know that beyond the border were other ordinary men and women, as generous and helpful as themselves.

One might expect embittered prejudices from those who have personal memories of murderous clashes with Hindus or Sikhs, but in fact the older generations show much less animosity towards India. They knew the Indians as human beings, capable of ferocity and compassion. Nor have they forgotten that when the chips were down there was little to choose between the ungovernable savagery of Muslim and Hindu mobs. Their children, however, know Indians only at second hand, through prejudiced media, and so merely see them as dehumanized symbols of greed, cunning, injustice and cruelty. It was this development which occasionally tempted me to wish that Pakistan had never been created, that some other way had been found out of the 1947 impasse. But of course that was over-reacting. It is understandable that while the Kashmir dispute continues Pakistani chauvinism will flourish. And perhaps the flowering of that noxious weed is an inevitable stage in Pakistan's cultivation of a national identity.

At noon, as I was walking along the crest of a ridge, the Gilgit plane passed directly overhead. Looking up, I could see its propellers revolving in whirrs of whiteness against the deep blue sky. It was the third plane to have taken off that morning for the Northern Areas, so I began to feel hopeful about our chances of getting away on the nineteenth.

1

Gilgit in the Jeep Epoch

All travelling becomes dull in exact proportion to its rapidity.
John Ruskin

GILGIT. 19 DECEMBER 1974

I can hardly believe that at last we have arrived. And it is good to be back, despite the many changes that have overtaken Gilgit town since 1963.

The fifty-minute flight from Pindi is complicated by a rule forbidding planes to take off unless they can be sure of returning at once: otherwise they might be lying idle here for weeks. So two hours of clear weather are needed, allowing twenty minutes for unloading; and on every 'possible' day one has to wait at Pindi airport because there is rarely time to telephone would-be passengers when Gilgit signals 'Take-off!'

This morning we sat for five suspenseful hours in the newly-built Northern Areas Waiting Room. It is a desolate, dusty hall, permeated by the stench of its own neglected latrine, and just outside a concrete-mixer was mixing and a pneumatic drill was drilling. Cascades of electric wires poured from holes in the walls and flowed across the floor, restricting Rachel's movements. Occasionally two worried-looking young men dashed in, fiddled vaguely with these cascades, abused each other vehemently and dashed out again. Soon our mouths seemed full of concrete dust but as there was no loudspeaker system we hesitated to go to the far-away restaurant. When at last we risked it the worst would have happened but for a young Hunzawal who pursued us across acres of builders' chaos and dragged us on to the plane seconds before the door shut. All our fellow passengers were male: soldiers, government officials, merchants and several schoolboys starting their long winter holiday.

This flight is said to be the second most dangerous in the world – after Skardu – but P.I.A. has a proud record of only two crashes in twenty years. Today, in clear winter light, I found it both more beautiful and more comfortable than on my very bumpy midsummer trip eleven years ago. But my feelings have not changed since I wrote – also here in Gilgit town, on 4 June 1963 – 'this was the wrong approach to a noble range. One should *win* the privilege of looking down on such a scene, and because I had done nothing to earn a glimpse of these remote beauties I felt that I was cheating . . .'

We picked out Murree and Abbottabad as we droned at 16,000 feet and 300 m.p.h. over a crumple of brown foothills. Then quickly the hills became higher, sharper, whiter and nearer – much nearer – until we were not over but among the mountains. Soon Nanga Parbat appeared, another 10,000 feet above us, half-hidden by her personal veil – the only cloud in the sky. And along the horizon stretched the almost unbearable beauty of the Karakoram-Himalaya, the greatest concentration of high peaks in the world.

I pointed out to Rachel the Babusar Pass, scarcely 3,000 feet below us and already snow-bound. 'You must have been dotty to cross *that* on a bicycle!' said she scornfully. Then we were over the barren Indus Valley – a fearsome sight from the air – and I gazed down at that thread-like track along which I had bicycled to Chilas, where I collapsed with heat-stroke and was tended by the locals with never-forgotten kindness. Minutes later we were descending towards a width of flat, cinnamon fields only varied by dark clumps of leafless trees and by the olive-green Gilgit River, which we had just seen joining the Indus.

About fifty men – plus countless children – were awaiting the plane and everybody stared curiously at us. The first change I noticed was a severe airport building of grey stone which seemed to have grown out of the sheer mountain behind it. As we stood on the sandy edge of the airstrip Rachel surveyed the giant surrounding rock-walls and said, 'This place is like a cage!' She was a little disappointed not to find herself at once waist-deep in snow. It rarely snows here and only a few white summits are visible above the walls of the cage. But one splendid, sharp, triangular peak shone to the north-east like a silver torch against the cold blue sky. It was catching the sunlight that already, when we landed at 2.25, had been cut off from the valley.

Most people wait to watch the plane's departure. Flying out of Gilgit is even more difficult than flying in and from the airstrip one fancies the little machine is heading straight for a towering mountain. Then suddenly it climbs, seeming to be *on* the precipice like an insect on a wall, and moments later it has turned sharply and disappeared into a narrow cleft between two other towering mountains.

A P.I.A. minibus took us into the bazaar, past a neat new signpost saying: 'Islamabad 400 miles: Chilas 90 miles.' Then we saw two petrol pumps, a gaily painted Peshawar trader's truck, a motor-van, several tractors and many jeeps being driven at criminal speeds. What a transformation! Yet the changes are not so drastic as I had feared. To travel on the embryonic Indus Highway is still precarious and so something survives – at least in winter – of Gilgit's traditional remoteness. Moreover, the many additions to the bazaar and its environs are of well-cut local stone and perfectly acceptable. For the foreseeable future transport costs seem likely to preserve this region from multi-storeyed monstrosities.

On the outskirts of the bazaar we found a 'Tourist Hotel' built in dak-bungalow style around a dusty quadrangle. At first Rs.60 were demanded by the smooth young manager who speaks passable English and is obviously dedicated to fleecing tourists. As every room was vacant he soon climbed down and for Rs.30 we have a cell with dirty bedding, no table or chair, a fifteen-watt bulb, no water for the reeking Western loo and no heating. (A few moments ago I had to stop writing to sit on my hands for long enough to thaw them.) The P.T.D.C. unwisely encourages this sort of overcharging. In their Tourist Bungalow near the airstrip a basic room with no mod. cons. costs Rs.75 a night.

On the plane we had met a doctor who knew a man who might have a pony for sale. So our first concern was to find Abdul Khan, who lives in one of Gilgit's agricultural suburbs. But alas! the pony was bartered last week for 300 litres of Punial water (a strong local wine). To console myself for this near miss I bought one litre – good value at Rs.10. Abdul, using his adolescent son as an uncertain interpreter, said that few non-polo ponies remain in the Gilgit area. Oil and petrol are government subsidized so it is cheaper to hire jeeps than to feed ponies. How quickly men abandon what has served them so well for so long!

Abdul's home was one of a group of small but substantial dwellings built of mud and stone and surrounded by seven-foot-high compound walls. Near the crudely-made wooden door in each wall stood a tall, gnarled, leafless tree packed with golden maize straw for winter feed. Not even the most enterprising animal can pilfer these 'storage trees' and no more elaborate 'barn' is needed where rain so rarely falls.

Walking along narrow alleyways, with quick-flowing irrigation channels at one side, we attracted a delighted mob of children – laughing, curious, ragged and unwashed. They were wildly excited to see Rachel and eager to touch her silky hair and examine her fur-lined boots and feel her fat rosy cheeks – so unlike their own pinched, pale little faces. She found their boisterous attentions a bit much. Clearly she is not going to mix as well with her contemporaries here as she did in South India. South Indians make gentler playmates and in any case six-year-olds are less spontaneous than five-year-olds.

As we returned to our hotel the sun was close to setting and that magnificent triangular peak swiftly changed from pale to deep gold – and then to a faint rose-pink.

We abortively discussed pony sources in the hotel manager's cramped and kerosene-impregnated office and then emerged to look for a tea-house. In an otherwise empty dusk-blue sky the crescent moon was shining above the western mountain-wall, beside a brilliant Venus. 'Look!' exclaimed Rachel. 'The Pakistani flag!' And I relished this symbolic celestial coincidence. Eleven years ago Pakistan had not quite made its mark on this region but now it most certainly has – for better or worse.

The few bazaar stalls not yet shuttered and padlocked were lit by dim kerosene lamps which cast no light on to the uneven street. At the far end of the town we found a filthy tea-house where lukewarm tea cost fifty paise a cup, as compared to thirty-five down-country. The smoke-blackened ceiling of this big, twilit room was supported by six tree-trunks and the floor was of beaten earth. Several men, wearing Chitrali caps and wrapped in blankets, were noisily using thick chapattis to mop up meagre helpings of stewed goat in chilli-hot gravy. They spat pieces of gristle on to the floor and viewed us with amused contempt. My memories of Gilgit town's particular brand of passive unfriendliness were immediately revived.

We walked back here by bright starlight through a deserted bazaar. The snow-mountains glimmered like live things above the black bulk of the valley walls and occasionally, in yard or compound, we saw a little huddle of figures around a tiny fire. All afternoon it had been no colder than a normal December day at home but once the sun sets the temperature drops dramatically and the Gilgitis get ready for bed. Fuel is a major problem in these unforested areas. Gilgit when last I saw it in midsummer seemed Paradise-on-earth. Now it is no less beautiful in quite a different way, but without our luxury clothing it would seem Hell-on-earth tonight. Yet most of the locals go about barefooted, or sockless in open leather sandals, wearing only cotton shirts and loose pantaloons under their blankets – if they are lucky enough to possess blankets. And judging by appearances the majority are also inadequately fed. No wonder the death-rate soars during winter.

I am writing this from within my astronaut's blanket, a weird object six feet square yet weighing only fourteen ounces. When first it was drawn to my attention it aroused considerable sales-resistance (the name was enough) but now I see its invention as ample justification for all that lunar lunacy. Allah only knows how it is made. Certainly its colour and texture are all wrong, psychologically, for one side is ice-blue and the other silver and it feels and sounds like tinfoil. You wrap yourself up – a joint for the oven, as it were – and Hey Presto! within moments you are oven-warm. Very odd . . . But this evening I bless the salesman who overcame my resistance.

GILGIT. 20 DECEMBER

A happy day, though I must confess I would not now come here in summer, when by my toffee-nosed standards the place swarms with tourists: at least a dozen a week, according to the P.T.D.C. Actually I do feel that travel-snobs, of which I am such a shameless example, are much less blameworthy than most other kinds of snob. If one of the objects of a journey is to observe how the other half lives, then it is essential to travel in areas where the other half remains uncontaminated by one's own half – if you follow me. (You may well not follow me very far this evening, as I am now three-quarters through my bottle of innocent-sounding Punial 'water'.)

We were up with the sun, craving bed-tea, but none was available. So we wrapped ourselves to the noses and went forth along an icy road – bustling with people at 7.10 a.m. – to find a *chi-khana*.

Instead we found the Jubilee Hotel, scarcely two furlongs away, and I soon realized that this is Gilgit's most respectable non-tourist doss-house. Its grubby restaurant is some forty feet long and the half-glazed door has a smashed pane and a broken handle which deters all but the initiated or the very hungry. Leaning against the outside wall is a large board inscribed 'Jubilee Hotel' in faded lettering. It was evidently meant to be above the door but one feels nobody will ever actually erect it and this little touch made me feel quite homesick. Around my own house are several objects in just such a state of suspended efficacy. Behind the restaurant eighteen small rooms enclose a yard on three sides, looking not unlike stables. In fact they are better furnished than the Tourist Hotel's and are heated by smelly little kerosene stoves. Moreover, they have no stinking loos attached – there is a communal latrine at the end of the yard – and the charge is only Rs.20 a night, heating included.

After a delicious breakfast of crisp paratas and fried eggs we moved our gear, despite awful flea-warnings from the smooth young Nagarwal. Here the owner-manager is a burly, unshaven Hunzawal who spends most of his time sitting at an improvised cash-desk just inside the door wearing a threadbare English-tailored tweed overcoat, two scarves, one glove and a leather cap with ear-muffs.

At ten o'clock we called on the Resident: an old friend who, as Political Agent, welcomed me to Gilgit in 1963. Tea and biscuits were served in his office – a museum of Imperial days – and he recalled Roz (my bicycle) leaning against the giant mulberry-tree on the Residency Lawn while I devoured fresh apricots as fast as they could be provided. He thinks we have very little chance of buying a pony here and advises us to go by jeep to Skardu, where horseflesh is more plentiful.

On our way downhill from the Residency we were joined by two nineteen-year-old schoolboys, sporting fine moustaches. They had several more years to do at school because they had to help herd sheep until they were ten; then younger siblings took over. One boy, Behram Khan, spoke enough English to give me this information and invited us to lunch with his married sister in a hamlet near the airstrip. His face lit up with joyous pride when I accepted.

We arrived at noon and sat on an untidy child-filled verandah basking in hot sunshine. At this season the Gilgitis tend simply to relax, enjoying free warmth, during the midday hours – and who can blame them? Today was so hot that I had to take off my heavy ex-German Army parka, yet within moments of the sun's disappearance we needed gloves.

Lunch consisted of hot chapattis, pickled green chillies and a big enamel bowl filled with lumps of tasty braised beef. It was served only to us: lavish helpings of meat do not form part of the normal diet of the locals. Behram informed us that he had eight brothers and six sisters, all of the same mother and all living. The eldest, our hostess, is twenty-two and already has a son and two daughters, the youngest of whom is three. Through Behram, his good-looking but already worn sister enquired if it was true that people in the West had medicine to stop babies coming. I confirmed this rumour, half-expecting to be asked to send some by post, but our hostess looked pitying and puzzled rather than envious. Behram said she couldn't understand how or why the rich people of the West were unable to afford all the children they wanted.

I find the insect population of this room peculiarly nauseating, though I'm not an anti-insect person, apart from spiders. These horrors come scuttling across the table, apparently attracted by the light of two tiny candles provided by the management. (Gilgit's electricity supply rarely functions for more than thirty consecutive minutes.) About an inch long, excluding a lot of antennae, they are yellowish-brown and seem, as they move, to be of a rubbery consistency. They look not unlike a cross between mini-frogs and maxi-spiders and if I hadn't observed them before opening my Punial water I might have mistaken them for a symptom of Central Asian D.T.s.

GILGIT. 21 DECEMBER

I had just turned in last night when Behram called, with two younger classmates, to offer me hash or opium – or both, if I felt like mixing smokes. It depressed me to learn that during this past summer a number of hippies had made their way here. What with Chinese-built motorways, and P.T.D.C. tuition in fleecing tourists, and opium-hunting hippies, the stage really is set for the degeneration and despoliation of this whole region. I certainly would not wish to return after another eleven years. And inevitably the knowledge of what is about to happen tinges with sadness one's present pleasure.

We went for a memorable four-hour walk this morning, up the left bank of the river. Rachel was thrilled to find herself on the longest suspension bridge in Asia, which can take only one jeep at a time and swayed perceptibly even when we crossed on foot. Half-way over we paused to watch three magnificent yaks being driven down to a butcher's slaughtering area by the edge of the water. The Muslim feast of Id, during which much meat is eaten, coincides this year with Christmas. Normally yaks are not seen here because the altitude – 4,500 feet – is far too low for them.

As though to celebrate its winter solstice the sun never once shone today and beneath a pewter sky the Gilgit Valley looked grim indeed; but it was the sort of grimness I love. Snow-powdered rock peaks rose above the jade-green river as it swirled between wide beaches of fine brown sand, from which Rachel delightedly collected a pocketful of many-coloured, water-smoothed stones. Near the path were rounded boulders, the size of cottages, sculptured into Henry Moore shapes by aeons of sandstorms and summer floods. And on our right vast slopes of grey shale – the very epitome of aridity – swept up and up to merge at last with the greyness of the sky. By the time we got back to the Jubilee it was penetratingly cold and we could see snow falling on the surrounding mountains.

Our immediate plans have acquired a fine patina of uncertainty. We may or may not set off for Skardu on the 23rd, depending on such a variety of factors involving the private lives of so many jeep-owners that I have long since given up trying to grasp the situation. But in Gilgit this vagueness about future movements worries me not at all. One can't help liking this odd little town, though today it was at its least attractive with sheets of ice, mud and diesel oil on its street, and a piercing, gusty wind raising clouds of fine dust, and the stony mountains frowning down on its barren valley.

We spotted some nice legends in the bazaar this afternoon: 'THE HAZARA BEAKER AND CANFECSHNER' and 'RE-PEARS FOR AUTO MUBOILS DONE HAST'. After some thought I concluded that 'hast' must be the illegitimate offspring of 'hastily' and 'fast'. But is it prudent to re-pear auto muboils hastily? Would it not be more effective to promise careful work? Obviously not, in a town where most drivers have a death-wish. Nowhere else have I seen such appalling driving; the avoidance of jeeps, trucks and tractors has had to become a new popular sport. The Military Police jeeps are among the worst offenders; tractors go at speeds I never conceived possible and all rules of the road are ignored.

Gilgit's is very much the bazaar of an area where no one is rich, not even the hereditary Rajas. The only shop offering what might be called 'luxury goods' is owned by a handsome young smuggler who gets all his stock from the notorious Landikotal intercontinental market. Today he was displaying several brand new Marks and Spencer sweaters for the equivalent of £1.40; and also an astonishing array of transistors, tape-recorders, cameras, watches, bottles of scent, glassware, china and Irish linen table-napkins. Fascinated, I asked who in Gilgit was likely to crave these last items. He laughed and explained that they were left over from the summer trade. It seems the more astute American tourists by-pass the Irish House in Bond Street and go to Gilgit bazaar for their table linen. Everything in that shop was being sold for about one-third the normal price in its country of origin.

At the government depot I bought two gallons of subsidized kerosene for Rs.3.50 a gallon, the down-country price, and no one can deny that such concessions are needed here. Today we saw a small boy carefully mopping up some oil that had leaked on to the road from a parked truck; his oily rag, when burned in an old tin this evening, will slightly shorten the cold hours. It amazes me that the locals can remain so cheerful in winter; and because their tough, squalid, impoverished existence doesn't seem to demoralize them, it doesn't affect the observer as Indian slums do. Yet the Gilgitis are without the Pathan's vigour, charm and intelligence; I suspect their average I.Q. is rather below normal.

I was honoured just now by a visit from a locally famous Ismaili 'saint and scholar', Haji Nasir, who comes from Hunza. He is an impressive character, in the mid-fifties with fine features, very fair skin and an aura of goodness, calm and strength. He it was who devised a script for Brusheski, the hitherto unwritten language of Hunza, and he has published several books in Urdu and Persian.

Haji Nasir was introduced by the man whom Rachel describes as 'our best friend in Gilgit'. This is – I quote from his green-printed, gold-edged visiting-card – 'Ghulam Mohammad Beg Hunzaie, Honorary Secretary, His Highness the Aga Khan Ismailia Supreme Council'. Ghulam is a tall, well-built man who always wears a Karakul cap and dark spectacles. He lives in the Jubilee for months on end (the owner is his brother-in-law) and has done a lot to help us.

GILGIT. 22 DECEMBER

We woke to a crisp, sunny morning, with powdery snow – which soon vanished – softening the harshness of the nearby mountains.

Haji Nasir had invited us to call on him after breakfast 'For more talk of religion and insignificant refreshments' – an irresistible invitation! As it is difficult to find individual houses in Gilgit I asked a youth in the bazaar where Haji Nasir lived and he promptly replied, 'Follow me! I am his son!' We were led up a narrow, winding passage, between the smooth grey mud walls of many compounds, until we came to a double-door of weathered and warped wood, leading into a neat little compound with rooms opening off a verandah on two sides. Our guide took us straight to his father's study-cum-prayer-room, where Haji Nasir was sitting on the floor, on a red velvet quilt spread over cushions, reading a superbly illustrated and illuminated seventeenth-century Persian manuscript. We sat on the edge of a charpoy and Rachel drew pictures while the Haji and I talked about Buddhism. Then I was shown his latest Karachi publication, a slim volume of religious poetry written in Persian to commemorate a double family tragedy – the death of his eldest son in an air-crash between Pindi and Gilgit, and the death of his favourite nephew, a few months later, in a jeep crash between Gilgit and Skardu.

The moment we arrived our host had produced plates of dried apricots and apricot kernels from under the charpoy. After about an hour we were joined by two quiet, serious young men, who seemed to be disciples or pupils of the Haji, and then tea and biscuits were served. Our host went to the door to take the trays from his womenfolk; very strict purdah is observed in Gilgit town, which no doubt explains the covert hostility I sometimes arouse in the bazaar.

As we sipped our tea Haji Nasir asked, 'Where in America is Ireland? Is it near New York? Is it a big city?' I found this refreshing in 1974, from a scholar so genuinely learned in his own sphere. It seemed a faint and pleasing echo of Marco Polo days, when other continents were so remote that nobody could reasonably be expected to know the first thing about them.

It is very noticeable here that even those who speak English (of sorts) are quite ignorant about the outside world, including Pakistan. Most seem grateful to Mr Bhutto's government for its subsidies, but they habitually refer to 'Pakistan' as though it were a friendly neighbouring state rather than their own country. And some people – usually articulate and educated above the average – openly resent Gilgit's recent amalgamation in that new entity, the Northern Areas. This faction points out that since the link with down-country has been strengthened Gilgit's crime rate has increased alarmingly. Previously, various petty rajas administered justice within their own tiny territories and there were no police hereabouts; nor, it seems, was there any great need for them, outside of the notorious

Chilas district. But now a police force is being built up by Pakistan and in many villages is taking over the old British Rest Houses, for lack of any other accommodation. And some down-country officers are said to be introducing bribery, as an escape from punishment, into areas where rough justice was traditionally meted out swiftly and surely according to Islamic law. Luckily not many down-country officers have been imported; most of the senior police are being recruited from the ex-rajas' families – a clever move on Pakistan's part.

It was noon when we left Haji Nasir to look for the house of another friend, who had invited us to lunch today and carefully inscribed his name and address in my notebook: 'Mir Aman Shah B. A., cotracter, House No. 700.' He, too, had come to our room last evening, with a gift of half a bottle of Punial water under his blanket, and had sat on his haunches by the reeking little oil-stove telling me the story of his life. Aged thirty-five and a native of Punial, he graduated from Lahore University but failed to get a job down-country, where he knew nobody; so now he works as a part-time building contractor in Gilgit. The rest of his time is spent farming at home. He talks of his wife with an eloquent affection rare among Muslims, has great dignity and is a most entertaining and congenial companion. His forefathers migrated from Afghanistan, but so long ago that none of the family now speaks Pushtu.

As we were doggedly looking for No. 700 Behram and his best friend came beamingly towards us. There are only two streets in Gilgit, so after a few days' residence one is bound to meet acquaintances as one perambulates. Even with Behram's assistance it was not easy to find No. 700, which is one of scores of tiny dwellings tucked away between the two bazaar areas. This is a much slummier district than the Haji's. Domestic rubbish blocks the foul open sewers, the mud compound walls are crumbling and the children look filthy and starved.

When eventually we found No. 700, with the aid of a skinny one-eyed little boy, Behram and his friend accompanied us into the compound. Aman Shah had never met them before but this worried nobody. They were entertained to home-distilled arak while I enjoyed Punial water, and then Behram was sent out to fetch our lunch from an eating-house – the usual chapattis and stewed, stringy goat. In these Muslim circles the drinking of alcohol creates the sort of daring, conspiratorial atmosphere which might have been created twenty years ago in Europe by drug-taking. Yet here the use of hash, opium or anything else smokeable is as respectable as going to the pub at home. There is even a government-licensed drug-merchant in the bazaar, so no wonder the hippies are moving in.

Aman Shah apologized for his room, a small rented bedsitter furnished with two unsteady charpoys and a wooden crate. The sky had clouded over again and we sat huddled around another tiny reeking oil-stove. Chunks of mud fell off the walls as we talked, the bedding was flea-spotted and the earth floor was littered with discarded bones, cigarette ends, pomegranate husks and broken apricot stones from which the kernels had been removed.

Last evening I was very touched by the wistful longing with which Aman Shah looked at my few precious books. So I lent him one – Ian Stephen's *Pakistan* and today his conversation revealed that he had been up half the night studying it. His is a type too often met in Asia – sad with unfulfilled potentiality.

During the afternoon we went for a walk through agricultural suburbs overlooking the river. The sun was setting when we turned back towards the town and in one dusky alley we almost collided with a web of collapsed electric wires, near a fallen pole. As we hastily stepped back a youth materialized from a doorway vaguely brandishing a length of red cloth on the end of a stick. 'No pass!' he said. 'Alive wires!' And to prove his point he indicated a dead calf . . .

At this season the local livestock are the most miserable I have ever seen, with calves hardly as big as our sheep, and cows the size of our calves. My tender-hearted daughter has more than once been reduced to tears by the plight of wandering cattle in the bazaar, who ravenously eat every scrap of paper thrown to the ground – including cigarette packet tinfoil, which must surely have dire effects. All the tea-houses use condensed milk, tinned in Germany, Holland, San Francisco or Singapore and costing Rs.3.50 for fourteen ounces.

GILGIT. 23 DECEMBER

Ghulam Mohammad had assured us it would be possible to get a jeep to Skardu today but this morning there was no sign of any such vehicle. Moreover, the young government official with whom we were supposed to be sharing costs had evaporated. At 7.45 I set off to look for him but he was not in the doss-house where he had said he would be, or in the other doss-house to which I was directed, or visiting the sentry outside the Residency, who is his first cousin and the brother of his wife-to-be. Finally I wrote him off and asked Ghulam Mohammad to help me make independent arrangements. I was then told that no jeeps will be leaving here for three days because of the Id festivities; but when Behram reappeared at my elbow, in his genie-like way, he said this was nonsense – Id had nothing to do with it – it was because bad weather had made the track through the Indus Gorge too dangerous. 'It is not a good track,' Behram explained, 'always jeeps are falling off into the Indus.' An unfortunate turn of phrase, conjuring up Doré-esque visions of black yawning chasms receiving a cascade of jeeps from which shrieking victims tumble through the air en route for the river . . .

But now I feel very glad that we did not leave this morning, today has been so blissful. At ten o'clock we set off in brilliant sunshine with pockets full of dried apricots to do a little gentle climbing, and by four-thirty we had walked twelve miles and done a little ungentle climbing organized by Rachel. She is taking to the Himalayas like a camel to sand. 'Why don't we go to the top of *that*?' was her constant refrain. At times I was terrified by her casual approach to precipitous slopes above 500-feet drops; but small children are naturally sure-footed, like animals, and I insisted on guiding or lifting her only when we were moving across ice. What really made our expedition so worthwhile, for me, was the degree of pleasure she derived from being among these mountains. We came closer today as human beings (never mind the mother–daughter bit) than ever before.

Gradually we climbed from river-level on a sunless slope where in places, along irrigation channels, vast masses of ice formed intricate and astonishingly beautiful edifices, sometimes five or six feet high. Rachel walked delightedly along those solid channels, making footprints on their thin carpet of powdery snow, and soon we reached the sunny side of the mountain, where clear glacial water leaped swift and sparkling from terrace to terrace. The tiny pale brown fields were new-ploughed and an occasional leafless tree bore its huge golden burden of maize-straw, like the nest of some fabulous bird. From here Gilgit's gigantic suspension-bridge seemed a lost Meccano toy.

On a wide, sunny terrace stood three primitive mud dwellings, amidst apricot and walnut trees. We were greeted by five women – unveiled, uninhibited and handsome, in total contrast to the hidden, tongue-tied, pallid females of Gilgit town. Unwashed within living memory, they wore elaborate but clumsily made silver ornaments on their foreheads, over heavily-embroidered brocade caps. Three were suckling fly-blown babies of indescribable filthiness, normally kept under Mamma's ragged cloak but proudly displayed for our benefit. While I made admiring noises over these infants a little girl was sent to fetch a dozen walnuts. As we walked on I reflected that this gift meant more than all the lavish hospitality of our down-country friends, who are endlessly kind but so rich their generosity could never have the significance of that fistful of nuts.

Higher up the mountain, on another, narrower ledge, an elderly woman was breaking ice to fill her water-jar. She insistently beckoned us to follow her into a compound where she put her jar down beside an ancient hand-loom that was leaning against the dry stone wall. Then she took my arm, with a smile of welcome that needed no words, and led us into the living-room. A few embers smouldered in a stone-lined depression in the centre of the earth floor under a square hole in the roof, and we sat on a mud platform built around the fire. Tea was made for us in an enormous *dechi*, which meant the squandering of several fistfuls of precious donkey-dung fuel. I then saw that our wrinkled hostess could not be as elderly as she looked; she was still feeding a two-year-old boy, the youngest of her nine living children. She indicated that four others had died. The eldest was a strikingly beautiful fifteen-year-old girl who sat beside me with her first-born at her breast, encouraging me to help myself to dried apricots and occasionally leaning forward to blow the slow-burning dung. Three boys, wearing ragged homespun jackets and Chitrali caps, sat beside Rachel staring at her with comical expressions of disbelief. They all had sore eyes – not surprisingly, for dung-smoke is very acrid and as it swirled around us it made everyone cough.

Two built-in sets of four shelves held the family's few possessions – a minimum of cooking utensils and spare clothing – while straw mats on the platform indicated that this was where everybody slept, in padded quilts stacked against the wall during the daytime. From the ceiling hung two goat-skins used, as in Tibet, to make butter in summertime. A dishevelled but obviously cherished ginger cat kept close to the flames and in the doorway stood a very small, very woolly sheep, meditatively chewing a long twig.

I noted that the tea had been imported from China, though it was what we call 'Indian' tea, and when it had been brewed, with a little fresh goat's milk, it was strained into two grimy tumblers (made in France) and a tin mug holding sugar was taken down from a shelf and offered to us. But sugar is very expensive here, despite its being subsidized, so I told Rachel to decline it. Our hostess then held up a lump of pink rock-salt and looked questioning. I nodded, so she quickly dissolved some for addition to my glass – further shades of Tibet.

As we left, the fire was being stoked with maize cobs. These burn more quickly than dung and so are reserved for the cooking on an iron griddle of maize-flour chappatis. We were of course invited to lunch but everyone looked so undernourished it would have been unfair to stay. When I explained this to Rachel she said, 'But couldn't you have paid them for the food?' So then I had to try to explain the revulsion I feel at the thought of desecrating this ancient tradition of hospitality with offers of money. Coming from the greedy West, one realizes that what such people have to give is truly beyond price. It comforts me to think that less than four miles from Gilgit town the tourist-belt has been left behind. At least half the people we met today invited us into their homes.

Still higher up that mountain, on a slope that was treeless and no longer cultivable, we crossed a desolate burial-ground. The graves were nameless and dateless, so that the difference between an adult's and a child's was apparent only by the size of the outline in stones, or of the hump of earth. Amidst such anonymous barrenness death seems much more dignified than in our own macabre, flower-bedecked cemeteries where futile monuments with verbose inscriptions perpetuate the rat-race of life.

Just beyond the burial-ground we turned the shoulder of the mountain and found ourselves looking into a hidden side-valley, some 1,000 feet below – a most spectacular drop. No wonder Rachel was overcome today by the sheer scale of the landscape. We continued up our mountain and then descended by another route to the narrow head of the side-valley. In winter this is permanently shadowed and ten-foot icicles, thick as a man's body, glinted on the towering dark walls above us – cliffs immeasurable by the eye. We followed the sunless nullah down to the level valley floor: quite a feat for Rachel, as we had repeatedly to cross from side to side by scrambling over massive boulders encased in ice. This must be a tremendous torrent when the snows are melting but now the water is so low that to have fallen in would merely have been uncomfortable.

From the warm, bright fields of the side-valley we climbed again, to rejoin the main Gilgit path, and on our way home we were facing, in the near distance, a superb trio of sharp, soaring snow-peaks, dazzling against the deep blue sky.

Ghulam Mohammad was waiting for us in the Jubilee restaurant with the news that a Pathan jeep-driver, named plain Mohammad, will take us towards Skardu at 8 a.m. tomorrow – for Rs.100 if Rachel wants a seat and Rs.75 if she goes on my lap, leaving more cargo-space. This seems very reasonable for a 146-mile journey that takes two days in winter, though it can be done during the summer in one fourteen-hour marathon. Many jeep-drivers smoke hash before a journey, to calm their nerves, and as a result are often incapable of the judgement necessary to avoid the Indus. But Ghulam Mohammad assures me that Mohammad smokes only cigarettes and is reputed to be the most cautious and skilful driver on the Skardu route.

GILGIT. 24 DECEMBER

At 7.55 a.m. Begum Sahib and Missee Sahib were standing with their gear beside the relevant jeep in the jeep-yard opposite the Jubilee. We seemed unlikely to start within five minutes, but I fondly imagined that we might be on the road by about ten o'clock.

At 8.20 a couple of grease-coated adolescents strolled into view, lifted the bonnet of our jeep, exchanged lugubrious comments, inserted a jack under the front axle and began complicated repairs which occupied the next three hours. We were repeatedly told they would be finished 'in one quarter of one hour' and though this seemed decreasingly credible we optimistically stood by. It was a dour morning, with snow falling heavily on the nearby slopes and occasional flurries here. I preferred not to leave our gear for very long but at intervals we had to retreat to the Jubilee to thaw out on tea. The local insensitivity to cold seems unnatural. Five ill-fed youths were lounging about all morning in the jeep-yard, wearing only cotton rags and open sandals made of old tyres. Twice they lit tiny fires to thaw their hands but they seemed not to feel any real discomfort. Lucky Gilgit has no litter problem; every minute scrap of everything is either devoured by wandering animals or collected for fuel.

When at last the jeep was pronounced fit to travel Mohammad could not be found. An hour later he appeared to explain that the trip was off because of heavy snow towards Juglote, but he promised that if the weather improved we would start tomorrow punctually at noon. I'll believe it when it happens.

We joined Ghulam Mohammad and Aman Shah for lunch in the Jubilee – chappatis and stewed goat, need I say. Aman Shah observed that of course Mohammad had never had any intention of leaving today, because tomorrow at 9 a.m. he has to say his Id prayers at his own local mosque. This Ghulam Mohammad indignantly denied, but I fancy Aman Shah was right. Probably Mohammad was simply manoeuvring to keep our custom lest we take off with some less pious driver.

After the meal we were introduced to Jemal Khan, a lively young Hunzawal with fair, freckled skin, light brown hair, a long, thick auburn beard and eyebrows that are one straight black line above hazel eyes. He comes from a village eight miles south of the Chinese border and is studying Political Science at Lahore University. He means to be a professional politician but seems unsure of the procedure for getting launched on this career. Like every other Hunzawal to whom I have spoken here – quite a number, the Jubilee being their Gilgit headquarters – he bitterly resents the Mir's deposition and claims that his country's whole way of life is being rapidly changed for the worse. As an example, he quoted the present fate of Hunza women. Before the introduction of soldiers and police from down-country they went about their villages unveiled, but now they are being put into purdah. A curious side-effect of 'Progress', recalling what happened in many remote Turkish villages when Ataturk the Secularist provided buses on which women could travel to the market-towns.

Jemal condemned the general Pakistani assumption that Islamabad is entitled to dictate to the Northern Areas. True, these all gladly acceded to Pakistan in 1947–8 and some fought and suffered for the right to do so. But was it fair – I was asked rhetorically – to reward their Islamic loyalty by abolishing that degree of independence which had been left to them even by the British, who were supposed to be such villainous imperialists . . .? At which point people began to stare at Jemal, whose voice had been getting louder and angrier, and Rachel made the timely suggestion that we should do some more exploring.

On our way through the bazaar we saw two groups of Chinese road-workers, getting into smart Range-Rover-type vehicles. They impinge very little on Gilgit town, despite being so numerous locally. Most of their supplies come from China, so they rarely need to shop here, and they have no other contact with Gilgitis. Yet one hears of them repeatedly doing good deeds, unasked and unrewarded, for villagers whose terrace walls or irrigation channels have collapsed; and everybody praises their energy and industry, as observed by road-users. All this is rather reminiscent of how Tibet's invaders behaved during the early 1950s, but I doubt if the same ulterior motive exists here. Yet the present unrest in these Northern Areas could easily be used by interested outside parties. Especially, perhaps, in Hunza, which has always had very close links, both cultural and political, with Sinkiang.

As we walked by the river, clouds were draping all the surrounding mountains and the air was raw and still, with bare branches black against an iron-grey sky. We passed several scenes of wayside carnage as sheep were being slaughtered for Id feasts, but these were the only symptoms of festivity. Returning at dusk through the dimly-lit bazaar, where most merchants had already closed and locked their wooden shutters, I pictured the streets of London or Dublin this evening and praised Allah for allowing me to be in Gilgit instead. But that was a selfish reaction: from poor Rachel's point of view it is extremely bad luck to have missed the thrills of two successive Christmases. Fortunately, however, she has a passion for jewellery and Rs.10 will buy unbelievable quantities of bangles, brooches, rings and necklaces.

2

Dropped in the Indus Gorge

I felt like a man feels when the motor-car at last stops and he
can get out and stretch his legs, and look at the view and . . .
really see life, instead of being at the mercy of a machine and a
mechanic, rushed through life without a chance of enjoying
the beauties on the way.

Sir Francis Younghusband

JUGLOTE, 25 DECEMBER

I doubt if Rachel will ever experience an odder Christmas Day. At
sunrise the band of the Northern Scouts (whose parade-ground was
nearby) began to play *Auld Lang Syne* very loudly and quickly and
continued to play it for half-an-hour without pausing to draw breath.
Whether this was a sentimental salute to the memory of Christian
officers, or a military way of celebrating Id, no one seemed to know.
It was a dark, cold morning, with low cloud, and at 7.30 a sudden
thundering of hooves, accompanied by blood-curdling war-whoops,
brought us rushing to the restaurant door. Twenty fast little polo-
ponies, wearing gay, tasselled saddle-cloths, were charging past like
the Light Brigade in fancy dress. Their riders – the Northern Scouts
polo team – wore mufti but carried long lances with pennants.
Nobody else took the slightest notice of the team, or knew where
they were going, or why, and quickly they disappeared into the foggy
greyness of the morning.

Not long after, the sky cleared and we enjoyed a brisk walk down
the left bank of the river while waiting for Mohammad. At four
minutes past noon he appeared, to my considerable astonishment,
but then the key to the jeep-yard could not be found; it was thought
probable that the yard-owner had taken it to his village, seven miles
away, not expecting it to be needed over the Id holiday. I volunteered

to break the lock and replace it (a new one would have cost all of Rs.2.50) but this immoral suggestion was ill-received. I then insisted that Mohammad should take action and for forty minutes we stood staring frustratedly at our vehicle through the wooden slats of the yard gate.

By the time a panting youth arrived with the key Mohammad had of course vanished. When at last he reappeared a fire had been lit under the engine to thaw it, our gear had been taken aboard and we were in our seat – but then the jeep refused to move, though the engine started willingly enough. Mohammad jumped out, looking unperturbed, and a number of hammered screws and knotted pieces of wire were 'done hast', to replace what the makers would undoubtedly describe as vital parts. These 're-pears' had the desired effect and at 2.10 we moved off, along a track I well remember following on my bicycle Roz. Despite its being now called the Karakoram Highway it remains so rough on this stretch that I had to hold Rachel very firmly on my knee and forbid her to talk lest one of the more violent bumps might cause her to bite her tongue off.

Deeply as I deplore the building of motorways through the Karakoram, I could not but admire the gangs of young Chinese soldiers, hundreds strong, whom we passed at frequent intervals. Seen toiling against the barren immensity of this landscape they seem true 'Heroes of the Revolution'. (In deference to Islamic custom, no Heroines of the Revolution work here.) Their task is one that makes the combined Labours of Hercules seem trivial and they are tackling it with the minimum of machinery. Today we saw only one electric generator on the back of a truck, to drill holes in the cliffs for dynamite, and an occasional wheelbarrow – if wheelbarrows count as machines. Most of the work is being done with shovels, picks, wicker baskets and naked hands. It is impossible to recognize foremen or gang-leaders; they wear the same denim-blue, high-collared, patched boiler suits as the rest and do the same work. This last fact enormously impresses (and sometimes disconcerts) the Pakistanis, whose own foremen would scorn to touch a shovel and wear clothes chosen to distinguish them from 'mere coolies'.

If this road-building corps has been handpicked to make a good impression on decadent capitalists, it certainly succeeds. After a week in Gilgit town these young men – all from Sinkiang – seem exceptionally healthy, well-built, well-fed and well-equipped against the cold. To us the majority look below average stature but otherwise – with their bright brown eyes, happy bronzed faces, plump, ruddy cheeks and strong white teeth – they might be older brothers of Rachel. Their formidable task is being accomplished according to schedule, yet they seem singularly unhurried and unharried. They laugh and sing as they chop up the Himalayas and often a youth may be observed relaxing on a rock with a cigarette, like road-workers the world over. They were obviously astonished to see Rachel staring out at them, yet they showed no sign of friendliness and spared us not even one of their many jolly smiles. This saddened me disproportionately; or perhaps not disproportionately, when one considers the personality-warping necessary to make these good-humoured lads freeze up when non-Communists appear.

At four o'clock we reached Juglote, a few miles beyond the confluence of the Gilgit and the Indus. Not far away are two of the huge Chinese camps and we stopped to load the jeep where a small Pakistani army camp stands on one side of the road, opposite a supply depot for Baltistan. Here down-country trucks, which have precariously got thus far on the new highway, deposit petrol, kerosene, sugar, flour, rice, dahl, cigarettes, tea, tinned milk, cloth and the few other goods that are imported into a region accessible only to small jeeps in good weather.

By this stage Mohammad was looking a little tense and one could see why. The forenoon sun had long since disappeared, clouds were curling among the harsh heights all around us and the darkness of snow lay over Baltistan. Mohammad's depot friends are pessimistic about the chances of any jeep getting to Skardu in the foreseeable future so he proposes taking his passengers and load as far as the track is clear and then dumping the lot in some unspecified hamlet – a plan I like immensely. As neither he nor any of his friends speaks a syllable of English I wonder now how we achieved all these explanations and arrangements. At times I suspect myself of understanding more Urdu than I realize, when the pressure is on.

We have both fallen for Mohammad. Tall, lean and handsome, he wears baggy Pathan pantaloons, an oil-stained anorak and a woollen scarf wrapped turban-wise around his head; yet he has that commanding and distingué air which marks so many Pathans, whatever their apparel or occupation. He is one of those taciturn but not at all unfriendly people with whom I feel a certain affinity. Even among his friends he speaks only rarely and briefly and he never needlessly addresses us. I can think of no more reassuring driver for a trip through the Indus Gorge.

Jeeps can carry a lot, if cleverly packed, and Mohammad was taking on two large barrels of kerosene, six sacks of flour, two sacks of sugar, several bales of cotton and sundry crates of tinned milk (from Germany), tinned ghee (from Holland), biscuits, soap and cigarettes from Pindi. The securing of such a load, to withstand the unimaginable jolting involved on this route, takes hours of hard work. Apart from the financial loss, should anything fall into the Indus, a loose load could cause the jeep itself to go off the track on a dangerous bend. Rachel and I therefore had plenty of time for our Christmas afternoon walk, though there was no Christmas fare to be digested. We watched a cockfight in the depot compound, where a score of men had gathered to enjoy this 'entertainment'. The army put in a brown bird and the depot civilians a speckled bird and the pair sorted it out bloodily against a background of rusty barrels marked 'White Oil. Made in the Peoples' Republic of China'. The army won and then both birds were killed for Id dinners.

As dusk fell we all squatted around a smoky little oil-stove on the verandah of the stone depot building. The manager invited us to spend the night on charpoys in a store room but for some obscure reason Mohammad insisted on driving another two miles away from the Gorge track to this doss-house in the village of Juglote. I have stayed here once before, on 15 June 1963, when I slept on a charpoy by the roadside because it was too hot to remain indoors.

Tonight it is too cold to remain outdoors for longer than it takes to pee. It was pitch dark as we bumped along the village street, where the only light came from a dim kerosene lantern hanging in the cavernous tea-house behind which we are now accommodated. The proprietor-cum-chef is a gnarled ancient wearing a greasy, gold-embroidered skull-cap, a henna-streaked grey beard and three long, protruding brown teeth in the left corner of his mouth. He genially invited us in from the freezing tea-house to the comparative warmth of the kitchen where his culinary feats are performed on a mud stove built up to waist-level and fuelled with bright yellow mulberry wood. Here the only light came from the leaping flames and our only fellow-guest was a wordless character with an Early Man brow and a rifle on the table by his tin plate. He ate squatting on his haunches on a wooden bench, wrapped in a thick brown blanket, and when he stood up to go out into the icy night I saw that his feet were bare.

Our Christmas dinner consisted of chappatis and a watery dahl gruel, followed by watery tea. Seemingly they never rise to meat in Juglote, even for Id. But as this was our first meal in twelve hours it tasted remarkably good.

Then the proprietor led Rachel and me across a narrow yard to a room in which no progressive Irish farmer would keep pigs. The stone walls are smeared with dung and mud and for ventilation we have a tiny, high-up unglazed window and a 'chimney' hole in the roof. (There are signs on the sanded floor that some guests bring their own wood and make their own fires.) One corner is occupied by a tall pile of quilts, for hire to those without bedding, and we are sharing this suite with Mohammad at a cost of Rs.3 for each sagging charpoy, which is expensive by local standards. To get to bed everyone has to clamber over everyone else's charpoy and two of my ropes collapsed as Mohammad was on his way across, just a few moments ago.

Earlier, as I was reading Rachel her bedtime story (a ritual which unfailingly takes place in the most unlikely surroundings), we heard through the gloom weird, unhuman movements and utterances close beside us in this supposedly empty room. Rachel went rigid with fright and even I was momentarily unnerved. Then I resolutely swung my torch towards the sound – and discerned a speckled hen settled for the night on that pile of quilts and engaged in a vigorous flea-hunt.

?. 26 DECEMBER

Tomorrow the question mark will be replaced by a name, when I have found out precisely where Mohammad has dropped us. So far I have been given three totally dissimilar names for this hamlet in the heart of the Indus Gorge, but none of them appears on my detailed map of Baltistan – which perhaps uses a fourth. Anyway, what's in a name? The important thing is that I can imagine no more desirable place in which to be marooned by snow for an indefinite period.

The seventy-eight miles from Juglote took eight and a half driving hours. Presumably Mohammad has little imagination and much fatalism; otherwise he could never summon up enough courage to drive an over-loaded, badly-balanced and mechanically imperfect jeep along a track where for hours on end one minor misjudgement could send the vehicle hurtling hundreds of feet into the Indus. As the river has found the only possible way through this ferociously formidable knot of mountains, there is no alternative but to follow it. Without having travelled through the Indus Gorge, one cannot conceive of its drama. The only sane way to cover such ground is on foot.

Apart from one's own nervous tension – which is not fully appreciated until the journey is safely over – there is an intrinsically intimidating quality about this landscape such as I have never encountered elsewhere. Its scale, colour and texture combine to create an impression of the most savage and total desolation. None of the adjectives usually applied to mountain scenery is adequate here – indeed, the very word 'scenery' is comically inappropriate. 'Splendour' or 'grandeur' are useless to give a feeling of this tremendous ravine that twists narrow and dark and bleak and deep for mile after mile after mile, with never a single blade of grass, or weed, or tiny bush to remind one that a vegetable kingdom exists. Only the jade-green Indus – sometimes tumbling into a dazzle of white foam – relieves the grey-brown of crags and sheer precipices and steep slopes. Many of these slopes are strewn with sharp, massive hunks of rock, often the size of a cathedral yet seeming mere boulders. Soon the river begins to have a hypnotic effect and, appalled as one is by the sight, one peers constantly down at that beautifully untouchable green serpent which is usually so far below it looks no more than a stream. We passed two of those steel rope 'bridges' across which the locals propel themselves in small wooden boxes and glimpsed one man so occupied. Rather him than me . . .

Naturally most of this area is uninhabited. But at rare intervals, where the gradient permits terracing, or a ledge of rock has allowed some soil to defy erosion, clusters of rectangular stone hovels stand amidst apricot, mulberry, plane and poplar trees. In summer these oases must look very lovely. Now, observed in the fearful sterility of mid-winter, they simply seem improbable. One wonders why and how people ever came to settle in such a violently inhospitable region, where climate and terrain are equally opposed to human survival.

This jeep-track was built less than ten years ago and based on an ancient footpath. At present the Pakistani army are trying to convert it into a conventional motor-road that will take buses, trucks and 'auto muboils', but tough as is the Chinese task theirs is incomparably tougher. One cannot see them ever succeeding, unless their methods and morale are radically changed. Yet Mr Bhutto expects them to have completed the job by the beginning of 1977. One vignette I shall never forget. A colossal boulder had been blasted to the edge of the track and was being imperceptibly shifted by a quartet of elderly privates. All four were sitting on the ground – two facing the boulder, endeavouring to push it over the edge with their bare feet while leaning against their mates' backs. How not to build roads in a hurry . . . This was a sight to gladden any motor-hater's heart.

We met only one jeep all day – near here, where the track was slippy with snow. When it backed to let us pass my stomach felt sick for I swear at one point its outside wheels were hardly four inches from the edge: and I wondered how often that day our own had been similarly placed. Inevitably on such a track drivers get into the habit of regarding four inches as an ample safety margin, despite the crumbly nature of many of these cliffs. Otherwise the traffic consisted entirely of large herds of goats being driven, I surmised, to some less barren area, for here not even an Asian goat could last without supplementary feeding. Their shepherds were among the wildest-looking men I have ever seen, wearing collections of patches rather than garments, and skull-caps decorated with pieces of coloured glass, and leather strips wound around their feet and half-way up their calves. Many looked very like Dolpo Tibetans or Ladakis – not surprisingly, since Baltistan is also known as Little Tibet. Yesterday we saw similar types, driving towards Gilgit a large herd of cross-bred cattle; each animal wore a coat of sacking despite its yak-like wool, which indicated that they had descended from a great height, sleeping out en route.

When we arrived here at 4.30 it was already dusk because of low, thick cloud and flurrying snow. At this point the Gorge widens for a few miles and the track leaves the river to cross a wilderness of grey, boulder-strewn sand, riven by narrow minor gorges. Brand-new wooden bridges, barely wide enough for a jeep, span these deep cracks which allow swift torrents to roar down to the Indus, their noise amplified by echoes from their own rock-walls.

Mohammad stopped outside a 'hotel' ingeniously built on to a huge outcrop of rock by the roadside. The boulders that were already *in situ* are used as seats, and as supports for the mud fireplace, and as a table on which the cook prepares chapattis. As the Connemara-type stone walls admit icy blasts from every angle, guests huddle close to the great glowing pile of wood over which tea is brewed in a cauldron-like *dechi* and stringy fowl are simmered in dark brown gravy tasting only of chillis. Beyond the kitchen-cum-dining-room is a dormitory containing twelve charpoys, without bedding, which are rented out at Rs.4 a night to passing travellers – who are few at this season. The locals unselfconsciously refer to this establishment as 'The Hotel' and it serves as a depot for those Skardu-destined supplies which during winter often get so far and no further. (Between here and Skardu the track is reputed to be far more dangerous than between here and Juglote – something I find impossible to imagine.)

The little group of men and youths sitting by the fire received us noncommittally. While Mohammad was unloading they made no friendly overtures but discussed our inexplicable arrival in an uncomfortably derisory way. This was my first sample of Balti; it is an archaic dialect of Tibetan and I could understand a few words. However, I don't take our cool reception too seriously. It simply means the ball is in my court and I feel relations will quickly improve once the initial shock to the social system has worn off.

When Mohammad reappeared in the doorway he beckoned us and uttered his first words of English – 'Rest House!' We had been quite resigned to sleeping in the Hotel and I stared at him, bemused. Surely, I thought, even the Raj didn't get around to building a Rest House *here*! I was right. The jeep crawled back the way we had come, through lightly falling snow, and eventually, having climbed a short, sharp hill, we found ourselves on the verandah of a small Rest House built only last year to accommodate government officials on tour. It is modelled on the Raj's dak-bungalow, though at its worst the British P.W.D. would never have put three large windows with ill-fitting frames in one smallish room at 8,500 feet.

Our room, with adjacent bathroom, is known as 'the V.I.P. suite' and sports a thick wall-to-wall carpet on its concrete floor. The other, larger room has been occupied, since October, by a down-country team of three medical workers, of whom I shall have a lot more to say tomorrow. As we dragged our gear on to the verandah I was astounded to be greeted in fluent English by their leader, Dr Mazhar Javaid, a slim and handsome twenty-four-year-old who obviously regards the arrival of fellow outsiders as a gift from Allah. We have already had a long talk, but I am too tired and cold to record it now.

THOWAR. 27 DECEMBER

I have at last established the name of this hamlet which, on the recent invention of the Northern Areas, was chosen as administrative centre for the Ronda region – more phonetically spelt 'Rongdo' by Cunningham and other nineteenth-century travellers. Ronda is about forty-five miles from east to west and thirty-two from north to south. The name means 'district of defiles' and the local Raja has always been subject to the Raja of Skardu.

Thowar's newborn importance explains our Rest House, where we have the absurd and unnecessary luxury of a foam-rubber mattress for my bed, a well-sprung couch as Rachel's bed, two easy-chairs, a table for our literary activities (Rachel is on page seven of her diary), and a handbasin and lavatory in our bathroom. Naturally there is no running water, but 'sanitary fittings' look good even if they smell otherwise. These luxuries irritate because the effort of getting them to Thowar is out of all proportion to their usefulness. Locally made furniture would have served the purpose just as well, looked a lot better and cost a lot less.

Behind the Rest House a glacial stream forms a waterfall as it jumps eight feet from the terrace above. A sheet of ice, about ten feet wide and two feet thick, has to be crossed to reach this waterfall and the first time I approached it its tremendous power knocked the kettle out of my unprepared hand. All around stand glittering pillars and mounds and giant globules of solid ice, their irrational shapes and arrangements seeming to belong to another planet.

The three windows which make it so difficult to heat our room overlook an exhilarating complexity of high peaks, many snow-covered, and the Gorge is visible far below if one knows where to seek for it amidst a shambles of dark, shattered rocks and sheer brown cliffs. This morning at eight o'clock we walked through this shambles to the Hotel, for tea and *paratas*, treading cautiously on new snow over old ice. Then we continued on for another half-mile to the Dambudass bazaar, where three Pathan hucksters between them sell flour, rock-salt, tea, sugar, tinned milk, kerosene, cigarettes, matches, cloth and soap. (Judging by the appearance of the locals this last item is not in great demand.) Another tea-house-cum-doss-house completes the 'bazaar' and is run by a charming old man with a face like an elongated walnut, under a cap of gay, glass-decorated brocade. He squats on top of his mud-stove, ready to prepare chi and chapattis on request, and he refused to accept payment for the two cups of tea we drank while waiting for a merchant to provide us with a packet of tea and a tin of milk. Now we are equipped to brew tea on our own kerosene stove.

Unfortunately the kerosene sent to the Northern Areas is often adulterated with diesel oil by unscrupulous down-country dealers and the result does nothing for either one's health or one's temper. The powerful fumes from our stove – which works perfectly and cannot be blamed – give me a small nagging headache and make my eyes sore and watery. The candles I brought from Pindi are also eccentric; they behave in a most uncandlelike fashion, hissing loudly and spitting grease all over the page as I write.

On our way back from Dambudass, as we were passing the Hotel, a scowling young man appeared at the door and beckoned us in. He wore a Chitrali cap, baggy pants and a blanket, and his long pale face was disfigured by acne. Evidently he was a person of some local importance, for he had that smattering of English which is worse than none because it can lead to so many complicated misunderstandings. For some reason he seemed to be in a foul temper and sullenly antagonistic towards us. There was an odd atmosphere in the Hotel, where we sat on the only piece of furniture – a charpoy – looking down at a firelit semi-circle of faces around the blazing logs. This time the young man was the object of covert derision and he seemed determined to take it out on us. Making no attempt to introduce himself or define his status, he asked where we came from, why we were in Baltistan, how long we were staying and where we were going. He said we had no right to stay in the Rest House, or anywhere else in Ronda, and must leave immediately. (For where? And how?) His aggressiveness became more marked as our conversation exposed more fully the limitations of his English and I soon realized that he understood almost nothing of what I was saying, despite my efforts to speak slowly and clearly. Every now and then he turned to his companions and harangued them in Balti, apparently defending himself. It was all very odd. But I could sense the rest of the assembly inexplicably veering to my side as the conversation proceeded and I began to feel quite sorry for the young man, who obviously was at some sort of disadvantage in the community.

It began to snow again, quite heavily, as we continued back to the Rest House, and we have been weather-bound since noon. Dr Mazhar Javaid called on us after lunch and we went to the medical team's room for tea. The doctor's helpers are a good-looking, but very shy young nurse from Pindi, and an elderly Skardu woman who acts as chaperone and interpreter. (There is no resemblance whatever between Balti and any of the languages spoken in Pakistan.) All three sleep on a row of charpoys; Muslims have no convention forbidding the sexes to share sleeping quarters. Their Russian-type tin stove, on which all water is heated and all cooking done, burns very expensive wood. To us the room seemed uncomfortably overheated, but Pakistanis naturally feel the cold more than we do – and the doctor comes from Multan. He is a most endearing young man and already Rachel worships him.

This 'Medical Pioneers' scheme is a gallant attempt to scratch the surface of Baltistan's health problem. It will be impossible in the foreseeable future to provide normal medical aid for the Northern Areas, so a few unselfish volunteers come to such places as this to teach elementary hygiene to carefully chosen groups of young villagers. These are selected for their natural intelligence and because they are likely to remain always in Baltistan, where it is hoped they will gradually spread the light of hygiene. They are also taught how to treat dysentery, worms, bronchitis and other common local complaints.

We had just returned to our room and lit the stove when Mazhar reappeared, followed by our spotty antagonist of the morning. Instead of his blanket he now wore a frayed olive-green sweater and a red arm-band saying P.P.P. – Pakistan's People's Police.

'This is Wazir Ghulam Nabi,' explained Mazhar. 'He is the Head Constable of Ronda and would like to see your passports.' Later Mazhar admitted that Ghulam was the only constable of Ronda but said he so appreciated the title of Head Constable it seemed unkind not to use it.

Ghulam spent the next twenty-five minutes poring perplexedly over our passports. Presuming his slow scrutiny of every page and health document to be a quest for visas, I asked Mazhar to explain in Urdu that Irish citizens need no visas. But Ghulam shook his head impatiently and continued to peer in a baffled, unhappy way at those green pages with the harp in the middle. Then suddenly he became very agitated because of stamps revealing that we had been in India earlier this year. It took Mazhar and me ten minutes to calm him

down. By this stage I had begun to feel quite fond of him; away from
the tea-house milieu, which had so put him on the defensive, he
seemed just an unsure youth terrified of slipping up in his new job.
Before leaving he smiled suddenly, shook hands warmly, thanked me
for helping him and said we must call on his brother when we got to
Khapalu. So despite our unsatisfactory passports, he has apparently
decided to accept us.

THOWAR. 28 DECEMBER

A glorious morning after the snow – all white and blue in clear gold
sunshine. I stood outside the Rest House at eight o'clock and looked
up at the nameless 20,000 foot peak directly above to the north – a
peak dazzling and sharp as a knife against the blue – and I knew no
other part of the world could so exalt me. Up the Gorge towards
Skardu cloud still hung about the tangled summits and as we set off
to find the village of Ronda the mountainside was crisp with a thin
layer of frozen snow, while the swift stream beside our path was
invisible – though audible – beneath a lid of ice. We went slowly, for
Rachel is having altitude trouble. 'I feel panted!' she exclaimed
graphically and plaintively as her mamma bounded along, feeling
as always more energetic at 8,000 feet than at sea-level. So I had to
reduce my pace.

Our path took us between brown, oblong, terraced fields with neat
stone banks, and past apricot trees hung with vines, and through a
cluster of small square stone hovels. Then we came out on a wide,
snowy ledge at the foot of a sheer dark precipice at least 1,000 feet
high: the scale of everything here is fantastic, dream-like. And there
was Ronda, the only place-name to appear between Gilgit and Skardu
on Bartholomew's map. Yet it cannot be described as even a small
town. It is simply a jumble of wood and stone dwellings, some almost
neolithic, scattered in groups over a ledge about one mile long by
three furlongs wide. Many houses have animal shelters built on their
flat roofs, to evade the snow and catch as much sunlight as possible,
and crude stone steps lead up to these. The most conspicuous building
was a large and very ancient square two-storey dwelling, standing on
its own with four unglazed upper-storey windows whose carved

wooden panels reminded me of Tamang houses along the Nepal–Tibet border. Indeed, the whole place recalled the photographs one has seen of Tibetan towns and villages.

We were soon surrounded by puny, silent children, too astounded by our appearance to speak or even smile. Many were so fair they could have been Irish; there were even two red-heads with bright blue eyes. Ginger hair and blue eyes are quite common hereabouts. Then the adults appeared, including three extraordinarily beautiful young women with delicately moulded, triangular faces, clear fair skins, rosy cheeks and bright eyes. Most women wear ornate head-dresses of silver ornaments attached to round brocade caps and all were carrying on their backs at least one filthy baby or toddler. They were no less friendly than their menfolk and trooped after us, excitedly laughing and chattering, when we were invited to the Headman's home. The Headman himself was away in Dambudass so we were entertained by his eldest son, a tall, handsome man of about thirty, whose wife and sister were two of the local beauties.

It is difficult to describe the Headman's house; here dwellings, stables and barns are virtually indistinguishable – and, I suspect, interchangeable. We were led through a conglomeration of dark little rooms unevenly built of wood, mud and stones, all huddled together anyhow and smelling strongly of livestock. Then our host ushered us into the twilit 'parlour', which had a strip of frayed matting on the earth floor, a pile of bed-rolls in one corner and no furniture apart from a small tin stove – in itself of course a considerable status symbol. As many neighbours as could squeeze in followed us and sat on the floor. They helped each other to untie children from backs while our host and I talked basic Urdu, in which language we proved to be about equally fluent. Tea took half-an-hour to prepare and was poured from a tarnished and battered silver teapot into grimy tumblers – it was very sweet but milkless. With it we were ceremoniously offered three small biscuits (imported from Pindi) on a large tin plate. Looking at the starving children all around us, I quietly told Rachel to restrain herself.

I have my own system of grading poverty and today I concluded that the local level is not 'acceptable'. I don't at once deduce poverty if

I see people studying the sun because they have no watches, or drying their hands at tea-house fires because they have no towels, or staring at themselves in jeep mirrors because they have no looking-glasses. But I *do* deduce poverty when almost everybody in a village is obviously permanently underfed. I have to admit, most reluctantly, that the opening up of this area may be a good thing. If only that process didn't always involve the destruction of local traditions, the debasement of taste and the stimulation of greed. It is tragic that living-standards in remote regions cannot be raised without drawing people into the polluted mainstream of our horrible 'consumer society'.

On the way back to Thowar we passed Ronda's tiny new police-station and were invited to drink more tea by the Head Constable and his senior officer, a gloomy native of the fertile Shigar valley who plainly resents his exile in this grim gorge. Both men were very polite but still seemed worried by our unprecedented invasion of their district. Ghulam apologetically produced a virgin ledger; across the top of one page he had painfully written in pencil – NAM AND DRES / PASPOR DETALS AGE / WORK / PARPAS OF VIST / DAT. He looked much happier when I had supplied all these 'detals', inventing our 'paspor' numbers which I can never remember. The ways of bureaucracy are wonderful. In a dozen countries I have solemnly inscribed fictitious passport numbers in the appropriate column without ever suffering any ill-effects.

This evening Mazhar told me that crime of any sort is virtually unknown here so the main function of these two officers is to settle quarrels between husbands and wives. Apparently the locals, on finding themselves with a superfluous police force, decided forthwith to transmute it into a Marriage Advisory Council. And it seems that Ghulam is at present out of favour with the Hotel patrons because last week he took the wrong (female) side in a domestic dispute involving one of their number.

Carrying a thermos of soup for lunch we rambled down the Gorge and after an hour's walking and rock-scrambling found the picnic site to end all picnic-sites – and to end all picnickers, unless they are very careful. Sitting on a colossal, rounded rock, itself the size of a

Wicklow mountain, we were overhanging the Indus some 1,000 feet below, where it has worn a narrow channel between sheer brown rock-walls that rose to 13,000 feet directly opposite us. From where I sat drinking my Batchelor's oxtail soup I could and did drop a stone straight into the green water that flowed so smooth and silent so far below. Looking up that melodramatic corridor, hewn by the river, one sees a glittering array of sharp white peaks soaring above the sombre-hued cliffs of the Gorge. I could not estimate the height of these giants but to raise one's eyes from the river to their summits gives a sense of sheer vastness such as I have never experienced before, not even in Nepal.

It was warm in the sun when we sat down at 2.15, but beginning to be chilly when we stood up half-an-hour later. Gazing around, Rachel suddenly remarked, 'This landscape looks terribly *untidy*' – an excellent description of the Indus Gorge, where it seems as if some cataclysm had occurred only yesterday, leaving everything scattered and unsettled. The mountainsides are either perpendicular walls of cracked and jagged rock, on which even goats can't venture, or smooth expanses of loose, grey-brown sand and scree littered with boulders of every size and shape that look as if about to roll down the slopes – which of course they frequently do. The fact that landslips and rockfalls are almost a daily occurrence makes the building and maintenance of irrigation channels and tracks (never mind motor-roads) a discouraging task.

We came home by another route, high above the jeep-track, following a dry irrigation channel around the contours of two mountains and then sliding down a hair-raising gradient to the Rest House.

I must admit that I am beginning to find my daughter's companionship rather trying. When one is sitting adoring the high Himalayas it is almost unendurable suddenly to be asked 'How *exactly* does radar work?'

THOWAR. 29 DECEMBER

Early this morning the weather looked unpromising, with lots of grey cloud low enough to be touched and light snow whirling

through the Gorge. But it soon improved and at ten o'clock we set off
in brilliant sunshine for what Rachel calls 'an explore'. About a mile
down the track towards Gilgit we turned away from the Indus to
follow an ice-bound tributary up a side-valley. The sun had not yet
penetrated to this ravine, yet round one corner we came on a dozen
men and boys who had broken the ice and were standing knee-deep
in the torrent washing their pantaloons and apparently aware of no
discomfort. Our intrusion was untimely; few Baltis own two
shalwars, so these unfortunates were caught with their pants not
merely down but off. In fact the decencies were being adequately
safeguarded by their long shirts, but they leaped out of the water
with yelps of dismay and sat on a slab of rock, legs stretched out
straight and knees together – the very personification of Primness. I
cannot believe that clothes dry quickly in such a shadowed valley;
they must be put on while still damp, which helps to explain why so
many of the locals are contorted by rheumatism.

The valley was a study in grey: grey dusty track, grey boulders in
the river-bed, grey slopes on either side from which twisted grey
crags jutted out of the shale like the skeletons of prehistoric monsters.
All around were signs of recent landslips and soon our track ended
abruptly, obliterated by countless tons of fallen mountain. We could
see its continuation above us and to reach this we followed a goat-
trail, sending cascades of loose pebbles and soil flowing from our
footsteps. The gradient was so severe that Rachel had to be helped
and we were both feeling 'panted' when we regained the track near
the top of the ridge. But our rewards were many. First, a trail of fresh
snow-leopard pug-marks in the fine dust; second, a majestic eagle
with a wing-span of at least four feet sailing below us over the
stream; and third a superb view of many previously unseen snow-
peaks on the far (southern) side of the Gorge.

We found another way home and were greeted by Mazhar with an
invitation to Sunday lunch. This was the first I knew of its being
Sunday. Diary-writing keeps me straight about dates but I don't even
try to remember the days, which are entirely irrelevant here.

I had fondly imagined that Rachel would relax after lunch but she
insisted on an 'explore' down the long, wide, steep slope in front of

the Rest House. This slope is covered by an extraordinary array of angular black rocks, as though an army had come along with sledgehammers and smashed up a whole mountain on that spot. Across these boulders we went leaping like goats – Mazhar tells me the locals have quite decided we're off our heads – and I got a close-up view of a magnificent fox. He was half as big again as an Irish fox, with a glowing marmalade coat and a thick white-tipped brush. Rachel missed him and was very aggrieved; I couldn't resist telling her that if she talked less she might see more.

At last we were again overlooking the Indus, from the verge of a fearsome precipice of friable, pale brown clay. The matching cliffs beyond the river had been weirdly eroded and looked like giants' rib-cages; it seems likely that quite soon – geologically speaking – the Indus will have undermined all these cliffs. In the Himalayas one becomes very conscious of the elements as creative forces.

Directly opposite was the village of Mendi. Its stone hovels merge into their background of small brown fields and would have gone unnoticed but for occasional wisps of blue smoke and the oddly toy-like movements of black cattle and brown and white sheep and goats. Above the broad ledge supporting Mendi rises another sharp, snowy mountain, and looking downstream we could see one of those 'beaches' which so tantalize Rachel – smooth crescents of fine silver sand lying untrodden and forever inaccessible beside the emerald swiftness of the Indus.

On our way home we sent several flocks of *chikor* (partridges) whirring into the sky. These are mysteriously numerous here: I cannot imagine what they eat during winter.

It is now half past ten and I have just been out to look at the full moon over Ronda. There was no movement throughout all that brilliant wilderness, and no sound but the distant song of the Indus. In a powder-blue sky few stars showed and from every side came the magic radiance of luminous snows. Towards Skardu a remote peak shone above all the rest, like a tiara suspended over the world, and the nearby mountains seemed ethereal turrets of light, almost eerie in the flawlessness of their glory. Such overwhelming experiences of beauty change one; though they may last only for moments, they permanently reinforce the spirit.

THOWAR. 30 DECEMBER

At 7 a.m. I found our waterfall frozen solid, despite its speed, and chunks of ice had to be broken off to fill the kettle. Last night the temperature fell to 38° below freezing, yet by ten o'clock this morning we were sitting in *hot* sun at 9,000 feet. We are not feeling this dry cold nearly as much as I had expected; Ireland's penetrating damp cold is far less easy to combat. But our skins are suffering from the complete lack of moisture in the air, though I frequently plaster Rachel with high-altitude lotion. (My own tough old hide is past worrying about.)

Our target for today was the mountain overlooking Ronda village and for the first hour we were climbing gradually through tiny, terraced fields bounded by glistening, frozen irrigation channels. Here were many apricot, apple, mulberry, walnut and plane trees, some with ancient vines twining around their trunks, or linking tree to tree, like fabulous serpents. Near the edge of a precipice we rested in the sun while looking down on yesterday's 'grey valley' and on the Indus still further below. Then we turned to gaze over the roofs of Ronda village at our objective. We were not aiming for the 14,000 root summit – an unclimbable buttress of fluted rock – but for a point some 2,000 feet lower, to which a goat track led from Gomu hamlet, beyond Ronda. This path could be seen running like a pencil-line straight across a vast expanse of scree, and then climbing through a jumble of broken brown rock in the midst of which it seemed to peter out.

As we approached Gomu, those inhabitants who had been sitting in the sun along the edges of their stone-walled terraces quickly stood up, shaded their eyes, and for some moments stared at us unsmilingly with mingled incredulity and alarm. But this understandable unease soon subsided and then we were made to feel most welcome. Each of us was given a sweet juicy green apple – an exotic delicacy, during mid-winter in Baltistan – and the women had no objection to being photographed. The Baltis were converted from Buddhism to

Islam some 500 years ago, but it seems the Prophet's message has not yet been clearly heard.

Gomu is a scattering of perhaps a hundred dwellings, built on different levels amidst many fruit-trees. On the outskirts is a small new mosque, constructed in the pleasing traditional style with alternate layers of granite and wood (poplar and mulberry). It differs from a dwelling only in having a carved wooden façade and fretwork eaves. The Baltis rarely bother to decorate secular buildings but some local craftsman has made a great effort for the glory of Allah.

I noticed many Tibetan-type faces and the locals also show a Tibetan-type cheerfulness, though to us it might seem they have little enough to be cheerful about. Yet Baltistan is very much an ethnic hotch-potch. Even in a small hamlet one sees fair, blue-eyed people, and others who could be of Kashmiri, Afghan, Turkish or Persian descent.

Most Gomu women wear silver head-dresses, often inset with coral, and some also wear collars of large turquoises set in silver. Men and women alike dress in dingy, sack-like, homespun gowns and during winter spend much of their time spinning wool as they sit in the sun. Between mid-November and mid-March no farm-work can be done apart from tending livestock, which means providing fodder and letting them out for a couple of midday hours to sun and water themselves.

Our taking the goat-trail onwards from Gomu caused some consternation. Nobody could understand why we were making for a cul-de-sac and a score of men, women and children good-naturedly pursued us to point out our 'mistake'. I pretended that my motive was photographic, but they remained worried and puzzled. Naturally enough, toiling up steep slopes is not their idea of fun. As we walked on, revelling in the glory all around us, I reflected that to the average Balti this splendour probably means no more than walking through my home town would mean to me.

Where the path petered out we could see, on a level with us beyond the Gorge, those immense, smooth, spotless snowfields which gather on the shadowed slopes south of the Indus. We were directly overlooking Ronda village but so far above it that the people seemed like ants. Yet as we sat on a rock enjoying tomato soup the village sounds rang out through the still, thin, clear air and I was struck by their happy note. Undoubtedly there is a collective village sound, a dominant note expressive of the nature of the people. In many regions of India it is peevish, in Eastern Turkey it is quarrelsome, in highland Ethiopia it is jovial in a subdued way – and here it is gay, gossipy and bantering, for the Baltis are much given to teasing one another.

Our Gomu friends were delighted to see us returning safely from our inexplicable peregrination. They had tea ready for us in a tall pewter jug with an ornate handle and lid. To my sentimental delight and Rachel's gastronomic horror it proved to be *Tibetan* tea, complete with rancid butter. Everyone rejoiced to find me so appreciative of their regional delicacy and we were shown the goat-skins which serve as churns and the sheet of yak-skin in which a few pounds of this precious butter, which had already been smoked for some months, was about to be buried under the snow. Several long strips of dried and salted yak-meat were hanging from the rafters above the fire. The Baltis, unlike the Tibetans, do not relish rotten meat; perhaps the local climate is not cold enough for this taste to be practical.

On the way home we met our first pure-bred yak, an already massive two-year-old. I had not previously realized how very dissimilar yak are to all other domestic cattle; they have feet like a ballerina's and forequarters like a bison's. This youngster took a great fancy to me. As I photographed him he approached to try to eat the camera and he was ecstatic when I scratched between his horns, already some eighteen inches long. But when Rachel appeared in her scarlet snow-suit he at once lowered his head, blew menacingly through his nostrils and began to paw the ground. I got out my camera to distract him and quietly told Rachel to *walk* out of sight . . . Mercifully the camera distraction worked.

We got home at 3.30 and I continued alone to the Hotel to buy chapattis for our supper. The strong wind that had risen a few hours earlier was still blowing down the Gorge, driving fine sand into everything. Yet all the few bony, shrivel-faced children I passed were wearing only cotton shifts and shalwars – the shifts open to half-way down their chests. Rachel would be dead in twenty-four hours if thus exposed to such a wind.

Outside the Hotel stood several groups of timid-looking, shaggy-haired, ragged men, many with goitres like rugger-balls. They were patiently awaiting their monthly ration of government-subsidized wheat, which they grind themselves in their village water-mills. When a man's share had been carefully weighed – with stones as weights – the precious grain was poured into sacks of sheep or goatskin, some still with the wool on. Each man then sat on the ground and when a friend had harnessed him to his heavy load, with hide thongs, he struggled to his feet, grasped his stick and set slowly off on the long trudge home to some hidden hamlet in a crevice of the mountains. Watching them go – bent under their burdens and flayed by that savage wind – I remembered Sir Francis Younghusband's summing-up: 'Baltis have a careworn, depressed look at first sight. But they are a gentle, likeable people, and whenever the care of feeding themselves is off their minds they brighten up and unloose their tongues.'

This subsidized food scheme is an act of great humanity on the part of Mr Bhutto's government; in such an area it cannot reasonably be considered a vote-catching device. Some Pakistanis argue that the Baltis don't deserve it because their poverty is largely their own fault. It is said that they are bone-lazy and that the Hunzawals, with no greater natural advantages, have always managed to achieve a modest level of prosperity. I have never been to Hunza so I cannot dispute this point. I only know that all the scientific and mountaineering expeditions with experience of Balti porters have praised them warmly for their industry, endurance, loyalty, patience, gentle-ness, cheerfulness and scrupulous honesty.

THOWAR. 31 DECEMBER

Today we went down instead of up and at last found a spot where the Indus is approachable. For five miles we followed the jeep-track towards Skardu and though the sun shone all day it never reached us because we were descending to river-level. Moreover, a knife-edged wind was cutting through the Gorge so we needed balaclavas, gloves and snow-goggles – these last to protect our eyes from the clouds of stinging dust frequently whipped up by the wind.

The grandeur, weirdness, variety and ferocity of this region cannot be exaggerated. We sometimes paused to gaze up at boulders the size of a three-storey house which were poised above the track looking as though a mouse could topple them. Rachel found these slightly intimidating and when for no reason a few pebbles came rolling down just behind us she jumped like a shot rabbit. Undeniably the potential hazards of this terrain give a special flavour to daily life. We are used to thinking of our physical surroundings as stable and long since tamed, but here the land is blatantly untamed and untameable.

The last stage of our descent, when we left the track, was down a grey, sandy slope strewn with grey stones and aromatic grey clumps of dried thyme. Between this slope and the river rose a grotesque hill of black rock with a rounded summit of golden sand; from the track it had looked like an island.

Reaching the water, we found it lapping gently on a small silver beach. It felt quite odd to be beside it, having so often during the past week gazed at it from such heights. To celebrate the occasion we solemnly drank some Indus from our thermos mug and wrote our names on the sand with my Ethiopian *dula*. But very soon the wind had erased us – which would make a good starting-point for a philosophical digression.

Near the water's edge was a tumble of toffee-coloured boulders, large and small, which had been polished, as though with wax, by the action of the wind and the sand. The effect was most striking: these rocks gleamed like pieces of well-kept furniture.

Altogether different was the 2,000-foot cliff beneath which we lunched in a cave. This grey-black wall of jagged, fissured rock (our cave was one of the fissures) extended up and up and up in diagonal layers and looked as if the mildest earth tremor could send the whole improbable mass crashing into the Indus. I felt ridiculously uneasy while drinking my pea soup – a form of nourishment that inevitably provoked several of those cloacal puns to which Rachel's age-group is so vilely addicted.

By two o'clock the wind had reached gale-force so we turned our tails to it and made for home. There was one hamlet on a ledge not far above the river about half a mile downstream from our beach, but all day we saw nobody; the ill-clad Baltis detest this wind.

It really is extraordinary how humans come to terms with such areas, showing infinite resourcefulness and determination in their efforts to sustain life. The local irrigation channels are a marvel of primitive engineering and take a lot of time and thought to keep in order. As the rainfall is practically nil, glacial streams have to be led, often for miles, along precarious mountainsides and across the faces of almost sheer cliffs to the rare oases of soil. Then, to receive this hard-won water, the soil has to be built up by hand into level terraces. If the Baltis were as lazy as some Pakistanis allege, they would long since have become extinct.

The construction of animal shelters also requires ingenuity. Even from close to, their roofs sometimes look like fields: which indicates how tiny many of the fields are. Then suddenly you realize that you are standing on a stable, and peering over the edge you see a minute wooden door in what had seemed to be the field's stone embankment. Such shelters are occupied during spring and autumn nights by goats and sheep, and are used for storing winter fodder. Cattle are almost always stabled in the villages.

Every fertile patch of ground supports a variety of trees including many young poplars, which are planted as building-material; in winter these look very frail, standing tall, slender and naked between stalwart Asian planes, with their jigsaw-puzzle barks of silver and brown, and sturdy vine-entwined mulberry or apricot trees.

It is now ten o'clock and bedtime for me; I could not possibly stay awake to see the New Year in. Nor is there anything but tea with which to greet it. I find it very odd that one completely forgets about alcohol as soon as it is not available, though at home an evening without a drink would seem intolerable.

3

Alarms and Excursions

For upwards of a hundred miles, the Indus sweeps sullen and
dark through a mighty gorge in the mountains, which for wild
sublimity is perhaps unequalled. ... The Indus raves from
side to side of the gloomy chasm, foaming and chaffing with
ungovernable fury. Yet even in these inaccessible places has
daring and ingenious man triumphed over nature. The
yawning abyss is spanned by frail rope bridges, and the
narrow ledges of rock are connected by ladders to form a
giddy pathway overhanging the seething cauldron below.

Alexander Cunningham (1854)

THOWAR. 1 JANUARY 1975

A sad start to the New Year. After breakfast we went to Dambudass
for more kerosene and there met Syed M. Abbas Kazmi, one of the
leaders of Skardu society, to whom we had been introduced in Gilgit.
He arrived here last evening, on his way home, and told us of an
appalling earthquake in the Swat area of the Indus Valley on 29
December. We are probably among the last people in the world to
have heard of it, though it took place scarcely 150 miles away. The
Aurangzebs moved up to Saidu on 21 December, but presumably are
safe: the wireless would surely have mentioned it had they been
involved. An estimated 7,500 have been killed and 14,000 left
homeless. Some forty miles of the new Indus Highway have been
demolished and repairs are likely to take a few months, during which
no supplies can come through to the Northern Areas by road;
therefore serious petrol and kerosene shortages are forecast.

Abbas Kazmi looks incongruous here. A slight, pale young man of
Kashmiri – originally Persian – extraction, he was born and bred in
Skardu but wears spotless, well-cut European-style clothes and

speaks fluent English. It would not be unfair to call him a dandy; he objected to five hens sharing the charpoy on which we were sitting outside the *chi-khana* 'because they will spoil our clothes'. Then he glanced at my grimy husky-suit and commiserated with me on the lack of *dhobi* facilities in Baltistan. I replied dryly that to us the *dhobi* situation is irrelevant as we have no change of outer garments. Despite his sartorial foibles Abbas Kazmi is a most likeable character, very knowledgeable about Baltistan and extremely kind. In Gilgit he had heard that I was planning to rent a room in Skardu for some weeks and today he assured me that this will not be necessary as we can use the empty house of a friend of his who winters down-country. In Asia it is always a good idea to broadcast one's plans.

Here no subsidized kerosene is available and two gallons, sold by weight, cost Rs.25 instead of Rs.7 – not too unreasonable, considering the transport difficulties: moreover it is unadulterated, so this evening our room is at last free of noxious fumes.

The merchant Zaffir Khan, whom we regularly patronize, today invited us into his home to meet his family. He is a Pathan, as are the owner of the *chi-khana* and the proprietor of the Hotel. The locals are as yet too unworldly to take commercial advantage of their jeep-track and Abbas Kazmi explained that all along it Pathans are to be found running stores or hotels. Often these are relatives of the jeep-drivers who in summer regularly carry loads to Skardu. Both Pathans and Punjabis are disliked throughout Baltistan, partly because of the normal antagonism felt towards meddling outsiders by isolated communities, and partly because many immigrants cheat when financially innocent villagers wish to exchange chickens, eggs or fruit for tea, sugar or cloth. However, not all immigrants exploit and despise the rough rug-headed Balti kerns. Some, including Zaffir Khan, are sympathetic, condoling with them on the recent loss of their 'Rajas', who were really petty chiefs traditionally subject to the Raja of Skardu.

We were welcomed by Zaffir Khan's elder daughter, a handsome young woman, self-possessed and charming. Like most Dambudass buildings, the Khan's house is new, but sapling poplars are already growing in the small, neatly-kept courtyard. Against the sunniest wall was a charpoy, spread with a clean quilt, and we sat beside the younger daughter, aged ten, and her little Balti friend, who wore a weighty necklace of silver ornaments. There is no girls' school within reach but this young Pathan was practising Urdu with a reed pen and charcoal ink on a mulberry-wood board. The elder girl had attended school down-country, before their father decided to become a pioneer, and she is teaching her sister the three Rs. When I asked why the Balti child was neglecting this educational opportunity I was told, 'She does not like to learn.'

After about half-an-hour our hostess carried into the courtyard a table covered with a spotless white cloth. Then a small servant-boy appeared with a pitcher of hot water, a cake of soap, a basin and a crisp, clean towel. There is never any escaping Pathan hospitality. And the meal, of predictable chapattis and goat-stew, was varied by small chunks of potato which for us transformed it into a New Year's banquet.

This has been an unusually social day. On our way back to Thowar we were waylaid outside the Hotel by Akbar, the fifteen-year-old son of a Pathan government 'contractor' who for the past year has been living with his wife and family in a hovel-cum-godown near the Hotel. It seems that in Ronda District a government contractor is the man responsible for transporting and distributing the subsidized foods. Akbar invited us to have tea with his mother and two married sisters, whose husbands assist their father-in-law. As these Peshawar women keep strict purdah they find life in Ronda excruciatingly boring. None of the local women speaks Urdu or Pushtu, so they have no one to talk to apart from Zaffir Khan's daughters and the ladies of the medical team. Akbar, however, obviously enjoys life here. He has offered to guide us to Mendi tomorrow, a trip which involves crossing the Indus by *ghrari* – a box suspended from a steel cable. I would prefer to go unaccompanied but can think of no way of politely evading him.

Mazhar has just been in for his regular evening chat. I have developed a real affection for him – something much more than the casual liking one feels for a fellow exile – and I am going to miss him greatly when we leave. He is the finest sort of orthodox Muslim, high-principled and serious-minded, yet with an effervescent sense of humour, a mature quality of compassion and an intelligent curiosity about other cultures. He is not at all looking forward to doing his post-graduate course in the permissive United States, but he admits that in Pakistan it is impossible to get a first-class medical training.

This evening he told me of his marriage plans. When he returns from America he will tell his mother that he would like to marry a particular girl from the dozen or so that his parents will have selected for his consideration. An approach will then be made to the girl's parents and if they consider Mazhar suitable it is most unlikely that she will refuse him. Mazhar does not doubt that this method of arranging marriages is best and the behaviour of young Western couples revolts him. In the tones of one who has witnessed some peculiarly depraved orgy, he described a boy and girl he had seen walking on the street in Pindi with their arms around each other's shoulders. 'This is all right behind curtains,' he said, 'but in public it offends every Muslim. It is a sight that makes us sick with disgust. How can civilized people behave like this when children and young people can see them? We do not understand.' Poor lad! He is going to need treatment for shock when he gets to his Brooklyn hospital.

THOWAR. 2 JANUARY

This morning when we met Akbar at the Hotel we were directly opposite Mendi, but the local landscape is so chaotic that to approach the *ghrari* a four-mile detour is necessary. What an approach this is! We had already partially explored it, in the course of our wanderings, and at a certain point had turned back in the honest conviction that we had come to an impasse, humanly speaking. A faint path was discernible continuing down the sheer cliff at an outrageous angle, but I had assumed that this was used only by the more youthful and agile Ronda goats. Today, however, we were led to realize that here lay the high road to Mendi.

Akbar went bounding blithely ahead, while I gripped Rachel by the hand, commended the Misses Murphy to Allah and cautiously followed him. As this path was not designed for leading people by the hand I had to proceed crabwise most of the time, thereby giving myself an excellent view of the Indus, getting gradually closer, and always ready to be fallen into if one made the slightest slip. Today, for the first time this winter, the river is carrying many large chunks of frozen snow, which give it a sinister look. It would probably have been safer to proceed in single file but the maternal instinct is not always rational and I couldn't bring myself to let Rachel go it alone, as she was perfectly willing to do. To her my quaint precautions seemed hilariously funny, but when the famous *ghrari* at last came into view she quickly sobered up.

A man was crossing from Mendi and we paused to watch that tiny figure in a swaying, shallow wooden box – the size of a small tea-chest, with one side missing – suspended on two wire ropes from a steel cable and pulley. The cable stretched 110 yards from cliff to cliff, 200 feet above the river, and on both sides solid landing-stages of cut stone have been built at the ends of the pathways.

After an 'orrible 'ush, Rachel asked in a small, unamused voice, 'Will I have to go across by myself?'

'Most certainly not,' I replied decisively. Then I began to hope there would not be room in the box for two – or even one and a half – in which case I could beat an honourable retreat from this singularly unalluring mode of transport.

We continued down, trying not to watch that box jerking and swaying in the gloomy depths of the Gorge. As we reached the landing-stage the passenger was disembarking and Akbar beamed at us and held the ghastly contraption steady for Rachel to get in. I could see now that there was just enough room for one and a half persons.

'Do you really want to go to Mendi?' asked Rachel in faint tones.

'It's the very last place on earth I want to go!' I replied frankly and fervently. Then, as I was about to suggest that we should turn tail, Rachel continued, 'But if we went back now it would be not brave.' Thus was an allegedly intrepid traveller shamed into bravery by a child.

The box rocked sickeningly as I lifted Rachel in and for one fearsome moment I thought it was going to run away on its pulley before I could join her. We were wedged tightly with our legs dangling over the river, and I gripped the two wire ropes as Akbar let go and we went swaying off at the mercy of that one little wheel running along the cable.

Oddly enough, the moment the ordeal started it ceased to be an ordeal. 'It only *looked* frightening!' exclaimed Rachel. 'Being in it is fun!' And I quite saw her point, though to describe this ride as 'fun' seemed to be going a little far. One felt surprisingly secure, however – even when the *ghrari* stopped in midstream because the chowkidar who has to haul on the rope for the second half of the trip was chatting to a crony. It was certainly a memorable experience to look up at the soaring walls of dark rock on either side and then down at the swift, snow-laden Indus. I was relieved to note that here the river is deep; if the cable did snap at least we would not be smashed to bits on boulders.

As the chowkidar pulled the box up it proceeded slowly in a series of jerks, some of which felt violent enough to make me grasp the wires even more tightly. I reminded myself that scores of men from Mendi, and several other villages, uneventfully use this *ghrari* every day of the year; but it would be idle to deny that I felt relieved when we reached the landing-stage. My relief, however, was short-lived. Akbar admitted that the upward path to Mendi is 'very dangerous'; even the Baltis go to their Maker from it with some regularity.

The Mendi side of the river is more fertile than ours, its habitable ledge extending for a few miles. But of course this is not a level ledge; traversing it involves crossing a deep, rock-filled ravine on a rickety, narrow plank bridge, climbing 300 feet up slithery grey scree slopes, climbing 500 feet down almost sheer brown cliffs, crossing acres of burnt yellow pastureland strewn with gigantic black boulders the size and shape of barns, scrambling up 200-foot embankments of friable cinnamon earth – and so on.

I found it difficult to distinguish between human and animal dwellings; some of the former are rudimentary while some of the latter are elaborate. Many stables are constructed of layered wood and stone, with an upper storey of woven willow-wands.

Akbar pointed out the two 'palaces' of the local raja. The old one is high on an impregnable mountainside and fortified; the new one was finished only a few years ago and is not far from the *ghrari*. Both are much bigger than a peasant's house but built in the same style.

Here we saw Balti ponies for the first time; these sturdy, nimble little creatures are much pampered because this is a polo-mad area. But the abolition of the rajas is affecting polo: they bred the best ponies and generally subsidized and encouraged the game, usually leading the local team on the battlefield. Today we passed two long, beautifully kept polo-grounds, the only perfectly smooth and level pieces of land I can recollect seeing since we left Gilgit. On both, teams of boys were playing ponyless polo, which closely resembles hurling. They were using appropriately-shaped branches and the ball, made of leather thongs wound around a stone, looked remarkably like a sliothar. The strength and skill of even quite tiny boys was astonishing, as they went sprinting up and down those long fields at incredible speed. Several men sat in the sun on low, surrounding stone walls, shouting advice, and I had a narrow escape when one little demon, aged perhaps twelve, deliberately sent the heavy ball whizzing past my face so that I felt the wind of its passing. No doubt he was merely showing off his accuracy, but Akbar was rightly enraged. Had that missile got me on the temple I might not now be in very good health.

We stopped for lunch high above Mendi, where Akbar knew the inhabitants of half a dozen hovels close to the snow-line. From here we had an unsurpassed view of the mountains; our whole horizon was bounded by a white fire of glittering peaks. When we sat on the ground a dirt-stiffened blanket was hastily produced to make us comfortable, but even after the regular midday wind had got up, and was stinging us with dust, we were not invited indoors. The only visible inhabitants were a few small children, ragged, filthy, under-nourished and afraid to come near us. They made no response to Rachel's overtures and the littlest ones were scared of my camera. But there were animals everywhere: yak, cows, calves, sheep, lambs, goats, kids, ponies and hens. Only man's oldest companion was missing; I haven't yet seen one dog in Baltistan, or one cat. Presumably this is because of the acute shortage of suitable food.

Akbar fetched our lunch from a hovel whose inmates were too shy to appear. The meal consisted of one round of tasty maize bread and a tin plate of watery lentil soup flavoured with garlic and wild thyme. Thyme grows abundantly on these mountains and is still aromatic if one crushes the wiry brown clumps on which some dried leaves remain. A staple diet of thyme doubtless explains why the local goat-meat is so appetizing. We stood up to go the moment we had finished our meal, for by then the wind was vicious, and as we moved away a woman's voice called Akbar. When he rejoined us he was bearing a gift for Rachel of three tiny eggs, which at this season cannot be bought at Dambudass bazaar for love or money.

Two hours later we were again on the edge of the Gorge, and now my heart sank not at the thought of the *ghrari* but at the prospect of negotiating that unspeakable path. Descents are always more difficult and Akbar had gone far ahead with a Mendi friend. Holding Rachel's right hand (the drop was on our left), I moved down slowly and steadily, trying to keep my eyes off the river – which was not easy, since its noise and movement had a hypnotic effect. All went well until we came to a point some 250 feet above the water where the path simply ceases to exist. For a distance of perhaps two yards – only two brave, carefree steps! – one has to negotiate a cliff-face on which a bird could hardly perch. The rock has been worn smooth by generations of brave, carefree Mendi feet and this bulge overhangs the river so prominently that it is impossible not to look down, and my giddiness was increased by the sight of all those lumps of icy snow swirling and whirling below us. To circumvent the bulge one has to arch one's body outwards, while keeping one's head lowered to avoid the overhang, and there is no handhold of any kind.

As I crouched there, with one foot on the slippery polished rock, trying to work out how to get by without releasing Rachel's hand, a terrible, nightmarish paralysis suddenly overcame me. I felt that I could neither go on, nor, because of Rachel, retreat up the path, which just behind us was only marginally less appalling. I realized that I had completely lost my nerve, for the first time ever, and it was an indescribably dreadful sensation – by far the most terrifying experience of a not unduly sheltered lifetime. The next stage (I was on the very verge of it) would have been pure panic and almost certain disaster. But then Rachel asked, altogether out of the blue as is her wont – 'Mummy, how are torpedoes made, exactly?' And this question may well have saved our lives by momentarily taking my mind off the Indus.

I was afraid to turn my head, lest Rachel might be infected by the fear on my face. I simply gave my standard reply to such technological questions – 'I've absolutely no idea, darling' – and the sound of my own voice uttering those familiar words at once steadied me. As Akbar stared at us from the landing-stage I shouted, 'Please take Rachel!' and he raced up the cliff. I passed Rachel to him across that horrific stretch of non-path and the moment she was safe regained my nerve. Nonchalantly manoeuvring myself around the bulge, I cheerfully imagined that if I did fall in I could probably swim out. But I shall never forget those paralysed moments. I seem to remember writing something yesterday about preferring to go to Mendi without Akbar. I take it all back. What would have become of us without him? Would the maternal instinct have restored my nerve – or had the reverse effect? I think the latter: I was pretty far gone.

After that the *ghrari* held no terrors, though with an icy gale being funnelled down the Gorge it swayed much more than this morning. Nor was there any chowkidar on the far side. Instead, a rather weedy youth, about to cross to Mendi himself, made heavy weather of pulling us up the home stretch. When we had disembarked, and were waiting for Akbar – who was pulling the youth across – I noticed that about a yard of the cable has been frayed to one-third of its original thickness. Presumably it is still safe but I am glad I did not observe this detail before we started.

The chowkidar reappeared to join Akbar on his journey and demonstrated how a *ghrari* can be operated solo, by the passenger hauling on ropes attached to iron rings which run along the cable; this is a much slower and jerkier method than being pulled. Two-thirds of the way over something stuck and the chowkidar had quite a struggle to get it unstuck. Meanwhile the little box was gyrating wildly and I felt for poor Akbar. Strangely, the *ghrari* was not designed to hold two adults comfortably and our friend was half-sitting on one side of the contraption. I judged him to be in extreme peril, yet clearly he himself was not at all apprehensive.

Ponies are sometimes roped to *ghraris* and hauled across the Indus; but not often, because the mortality rate is so high. And when the frantic creatures plunge into the river they usually take the box with them, thus seriously disrupting local communications. No boat or raft can be used within the Gorge, and no fording place contrived at any season, which proves how sensationally anti-human this terrain is.

We stopped at the Hotel for much-needed tea and there found another outsider, a neatly-dressed man of about thirty-five. He introduced himself in passable English as 'Mr Aman, Officer Incharge for road-building in Ronda District'. A slightly awkward situation at once arose, for we are occupying the V.I.P. suite that Mr Aman had expected to find ready for him. However, no one here thinks it odd for the sexes to share bedrooms so he is moving in with us. This entails my sleeping on the floor. Aman did not quite ask me to, but he moaned so much about Ronda's extraordinarily low nocturnal temperature, and the misery of having no bed, that I surrendered mine just to shut him up.

I find Aman's company singularly uninspiring. He is a Nagarwal who now lives in Skardu, from where he came today in a military jeep. Like many of his race he has brown hair, pale blue eyes, very white skin and conspicuously-developed jaw muscles – a result of having been reared on tough dried apricots and hard apricot kernels. For the past two hours he has been sitting warming his hands over our stove and watching me writing this. He has not spoken one word and his silent scrutiny is exasperating. It also underlines a basic difference between East and West. Although a man of some educa-tion, he is apparently capable of happily doing nothing for an indefinite period. I feel I am unlikely to discover any great affinity with a man who could come bookless to Ronda. But then the habit of reading books for pleasure has not yet really caught on throughout this subcontinent; even those with the necessary education and money usually read only magazines and newspapers.

THOWAR. 3 JANUARY

When we arrived here we let it be known that we wanted to buy a pony, but the jeep era has banished working-ponies from most villages within a day's walk of the track. However, this morning Mazhar told us that a pony is on offer in a hamlet high above Gomu, so our next step is to find out by trial – but not I trust by error – if he and Rachel are compatible.

As soon as one embarks on a business deal in the Orient one has to change gear. Today I resigned myself to waiting for the pony-owner's promised appearance, while not allowing myself (or the eager Rachel) to count on it. To get out of Aman's way we spent hours doing sums and reading amidst the black rocks below the Rest House, from where we could see the pony coming if he came – which of course he didn't.

Since New Year's Eve the daytime temperatures have been dropping perceptibly and our waterfall has now been frozen solid for forty-eight hours. It is quite difficult to chip off enough ice for cooking and washing – not that the latter activity occupies much of our time. The universal filthiness of Baltistan discourages attempts to keep clean; these could only lead to frustration, not to mention pneumonia. Neither of us has undressed since we left Islamabad, but we are none the worse for that, at least in our own estimation. (Admittedly my readers might think otherwise, should some magic carpet suddenly transport us to their homes.) The first few days in dirty clothes are always slightly uncomfortable; then one happily settles into one's niche among the great unwashed.

Aman is still, alas! with us, sitting opposite me as I write, flicking through Ian Stephens' *The Horned Moon*. I lent it to him in a desperate effort to render him less irritating but as he is turning the pages rapidly, with a well-wetted forefinger, my effort is having the reverse effect. He seems to half-resent our being here though we are providing him with free heating, lighting and accommodation.

THOWAR. 4 JANUARY

There has been a dramatic deterioration in the weather today, which is hardly surprising on the fourth of January in the Karakoram. We usually wake at sixish and read for an hour or so in our flea-bags, as no one in their right mind would get up here before the sun does. But this morning reading was difficult: we each had to glove the exposed hand. Several times during the night the whining of the wind woke me and by 8.0 a.m. it had become a shrieking fury that sent clouds and pillars and curtains of grey dust flying through the air – weirdly beautiful to watch, but no fun to be out in. And we were out in it, because we breakfasted at the Hotel as refugees from Aman. He has an odd way of making one feel uncomfortable without saying or doing anything positive enough to be described.

We were both impressed, between gale gusts, by the silence of a completely frozen landscape. Until they have been stilled one doesn't realize how much background noise is provided by streams, irrigation channels and waterfalls. Much of the track was covered with sheets of thick ice, and waterfalls had become towering, transparent columns, surrounded by the bizarre elegance of giant bouquets of icicles formed around clumps of thyme. Fantastically convoluted masses of ice hung from roadside rocks and Rachel was so overcome by all this loveliness that she soon forgot her discomfort. The air was so cold when we left the Rest House that she could scarcely breathe. I have been breaking her in gently and this was her first morning to be out before the sun reached Thowar – not that it ever reached us today.

When we left the Hotel at 9.30 the sky was a uniform chilly silver and the peaks were being veiled by fresh snowfalls. We had hoped to find Aman gone about his day's business (the paying of P.W.D. coolies) but he was only starting his prayers. Then he had to have his breakfast and attend to his toilet – a lengthy process, as he carefully creams his face and spends fifteen minutes grooming, oiling and setting his wavy hair in front of a hand-mirror. When Rachel asked, 'Mummy, why don't we have a mirror?' he was deeply shocked to realize that a *woman* had ventured into Darkest Central Asia without this essential piece of equipment. He is good-looking in an effeminate way but has a mean, petulant little mouth and evasive eyes.

Our potential pony lives at 12,500 feet and his owner appeared without him at noon, explaining that the way was too icy this morning to risk taking him down. Nor could Aman get much work done; most of the men he was to have paid were unable to leave their high hamlets. All day everybody huddled around whatever heat was available and the wind howled and moaned like a creature in agony; everything in our room was permeated by fine dust and the mountains disappeared as the sky sank lower and darker over the Gorge. At three o'clock I went to the Hotel to fetch *paratas* for our supper and found the door closed for the first time. About thirty men were crouching around the fire in the flame-lit darkness (there is no window) and a chorus of friendly welcomes greeted me. It seems a long time since the evening of our arrival, when we were regarded with such grim hostility. As usual I had a long wait while our paratas were being kneaded, rolled, shaped and fried by a cheerful ragged youth with a running nose who I'm sure hasn't washed since birth; he is the fourteen-year-old Balti apprentice of the Pathan proprietor. I wouldn't dare take Rachel to such a filthy region during summer: now it is too cold for bacteria to survive.

Going home I overtook an old man with a bushy beard and a big grin who was wearing a long scarlet lady's overcoat that might have been fashionable in Europe fifteen years ago; one wonders by what unlikely series of journeys it arrived here. Behind him three very small boys were struggling with a threadbare blanket, trying to make it long enough to protect them all from the searing wind; they looked like an illustration in some tear-jerking Victorian novel, yet when I passed I saw that they were giggling happily.

On every rock ice gleamed dully, under that sunless, pale grey sky, and the sandy dust whirled in sudden choking spirals, and the bleak walls of the Gorge towered blackly over a snow-flecked Indus. Ronda today seemed a place desolate and tortured and torturing, without mercy or hope. Yet in three months' time its oases will have come to life again and in five months they will be Paradise Regained.

Mazhar brought news this evening of a jeep-drivers' strike. The idea of striking seems very alien to this part of the world but I suppose it goes with modern machines. The drivers' grievance is that the Pakistani Army road-construction gangs working in the Gorge never forewarn them about blasting operations. Therefore jeeps are often held up for hours and these delays can necessitate travelling in the dark on a track which not even the most reckless driver will voluntarily tackle at night. The jeep-wallahs are demanding that the Pakistanis should imitate the Chinese, who give a forty-eight hour warning before every closure. But obviously this is asking too much; life's not like that in Pakistan.

I am happy to report that this evening Aman found our room too cold: it is heated only by our own little oil stove. So he has taken himself off to the chowkidar's wood-stove. There is a wood-stove here, too; but firewood costs Rs.40 per maund and Aman is fanatically parsimonious.

THOWAR. 5 JANUARY

Today's weather was only slightly less ferocious than yesterday's. Blizzards were visibly active on the high peaks and though the sun appeared occasionally it was unable to thaw anything. The high-altitude pony therefore remained inaccessible, but at noon another animal was brought from Ronda village for our consideration. This retired polo-pony is aged ten according to his owner and fourteen according to Head Constable Ghulam, who is determined we shall not be cheated. His long winter coat is what I call ginger, though no doubt horse-wallahs have another word for it. (I seem to remember being told once that white horses should be called greys – or is it the other way round?) He has a most endearing disposition and accepted our saddle, and Rachel in it, without demur. But clearly he has been half-starved for months. When Rachel rode him up and down the level space in front of the Rest House he went well enough, but on my leading him up a steep stretch of track he slowed ominously. His owner is asking one thousand rupees, which is absurd. A first-class polo-pony in good condition will fetch four or five thousand locally, but this poor creature is not worth more than a few hundred. If we do buy him he will have to be put in good condition when we get to Skardu – a considerable expense, at this season – before being required to transport Rachel and our kit across the length and breadth of Baltistan. I have offered five hundred and at present his owner is feigning horror at the insult implicit in such a figure.

The above is a drastically condensed account of negotiations which took up most of the day. I spent hours drinking tea in the Hotel while discussing everything except ponies with the pony-owner, a group of his henchmen, Mazhar, Ghulam and an assortment of ragged Ronda villagers who for some reason – probably connected with village politics – are obviously on my side in the bargaining. This evening Ghulam tells me that by playing it cool I am likely to get the pony for six or seven hundred. He advises me to go to the high hamlet tomorrow, weather permitting, and enter into negotiations about the other pony – but on no account to buy it, as it is not accustomed to jeep traffic.

Aman is still with us and has been trying to sabotage my good opinion of Mazhar, whom he calls 'that Punjabi'. I have discovered that this 'Incharge' is not popular locally. It seems he should reside in Ronda District, according to the terms of his appointment, but he sybaritically refuses to do so and comes only once a quarter to pay coolies who are entitled to a monthly wage.

A triangular feud is in progress between Mazhar, Aman and Zakir, our shiftless young chowkidar. It came to a head today when Mazhar told Aman, whose department is responsible for the staffing of this Rest House, that Zakir should be sacked – a conversation on which Zakir was eavesdropping from our bathroom. It then transpired that in fact Zakir was sacked a month ago for incorrigible inefficiency and laziness, but he refused to accept dismissal since a new two-roomed hut goes with his job. So he was reinstated by Aman the other day, presumably because our room-mate couldn't think what else to do, or whom else to appoint without starting a serious feud between Zakir and the new employee. As Aman plaintively pointed out, it is almost impossible to find normal chowkidar material in a region with no dak-bungalow tradition. He then withdrew from the fray to warm himself at Zakir's stove and the chowkidar turned to Mazhar and passionately denounced the Incharge's meanness, accusing him of not paying for his food and expecting free warmth. He certainly uses up a lot of our kerosene to heat water for his frequent pre-prayer ablutions, so on this issue I can sympathize with Zakir.

THOWAR. 6 JANUARY

This morning was windless, though a good deal of cloud still hung about the peaks. After breakfast we started out for the pony hamlet beyond Gomu – a 4,500 foot climb which proved almost too much for Rachel. Had the gradient been less severe she could easily have coped with both distance and altitude, but the last 1,000 feet were up an almost vertical stairway of boulders, made treacherous, and sometimes completely obscured, by new snow. Mercifully, however, there were no precipices to fall over. (Or at least not what count as such hereabouts; after a fortnight in Ronda one simply doesn't notice a few drops of fifty feet or so.) Just below this stairway was a brutally steep pathless slope of soft, loose, sandy soil – at 11,000 feet as exhausting as anything I have ever ploughed through. Leaning on my *dula* with one hand I helped Rachel up with the other and we could almost hear each other's hearts hammering.

We tackled the snowy stairway separately, Rachel following in my footsteps, and about half-way up I heard an unhappy sound and realized that my gallant companion had had enough. She looked at me with brimming eyes and said, 'I'm panted out. I can't go up any more.' So we sat on dry cushions of thyme, all the rocks being snow-covered.

I considered the summit of stark, grey-brown cliffs and felt irresolute. To force a wilting six-year-old up that last demanding stretch would be sheer cruelty, yet the idea of retreating when almost there went totally against the Murphy grain.

Then Rachel said, 'I wonder what we could see from the top?'

Inwardly, I rejoiced at this manifestation of classic travellers' curiosity, but I replied casually, 'Nothing much in this weather.' About half-an-hour earlier it had begun to snow lightly and we were surveying the world through a haze of tiny flakes.

'But I'd *like* to see over the top,' continued Rachel. 'I wish I didn't feel so tired! It's not really tiredness – I just feel too panted.'

'No wonder,' said I, listening to that distinctive silence which rests like a blessing on high places. Far below us was spread a sublime panorama of gorges, cliffs, valleys, escarpments, ledges, ravines and minor mountains, a view made all the more awesome by the thin drifting snowfall.

'I'd *like* to get to the top,' persisted Rachel. 'Could you help me?'

I stood up and took her hand and we struggled on together; because of the new snow it was becoming increasingly difficult to discern the path and twice we went astray. 'This is *worse* than a nightmare!' wailed Rachel, when we had another hundred feet to go; and I didn't disagree. She is a solid chunk of humanity and she really was too 'panted out' to be more than one-third self-propelling. Moreover, at that height the snow was freezing as it fell.

Then at last we were on level ground and I saw that we had conquered a gigantic escarpment rather than a mountain. Above us on our right rose another fifty feet of rocky rampart – the true 'summit'. It would have been possible to climb it, but I did not propose so doing.

Rachel was wildly elated, though there was little to be seen through a curtain of thickening snow. Looking both ways, she said, 'I've really got quite high up for someone who isn't even six *and one month*!'

'You have indeed,' I agreed.

The blurred bulk of several snow-giants loomed directly ahead to the north and we could just see, about half a mile away, a group of fruit trees marking the pony hamlet – a dozen hovels in the shadow of another mighty escarpment. I had doubted the place's existence on the way up, so improbable did it seem that anyone should have chosen to live at the end of such a path. Now I reluctantly decided that we must not risk continuing to our final goal, with a full-scale blizzard possible at any moment. If our tracks were completely obliterated we might never find the path down, and if we spent the night at the hamlet all Ronda would be in a frenzy of anxiety about us. So we sat cosily in an empty stone animal shelter behind the rocky rampart, drinking our kidney soup while gazing over a glittering expanse of new snow, eighteen inches deep and flawed only by our own trail. Within the past quarter of an hour the temperature had risen abruptly as the snow thickened, and now the air felt almost mild. Outside the shelter was one stunted, wind-deformed poplar on

which a tit perched and sang for a moment – to us as astonishing a
sight as the dove's branch must have been to Noah. This is the only
bird song we have heard here, though Ronda has a colony of
squalling, squeaky choughs and many crows and magpies.

We started down at two o'clock and had to go very cautiously on
the slippery boulder stairway. Then came that long slope of loose soil,
which from Rachel's point of view was enormous fun to descend. To
her delight I repeatedly skidded and either sat with a bump or went
rolling uncontrollably for ten or twenty yards. When we had regained a reasonable path she proved that she had not really been tired
by leaping around me like an ibex while conversing enthusiastically
about such diverse subjects as erosion and haemophilia. She has
entered this dauntingly scientific phase at just the wrong time, when
there is no library within reach.

On the Rest House verandah we were greeted by a tense-looking
Aman. 'You must take your baggage now,' he said, 'and move to the
kitchen quarters. I have news our Chief Engineer is coming on the
ninth for four days.'

I stared at him in astonishment and then edged past him into our
room, which I hardly recognized. It had been cleaned for the first
time since we came on 26 December, though Zakir is supposed to
clean it daily.

Aman followed us, waved a hand eloquently and said, 'It has all
been cleaned, you see, so it is better you take your baggage and stay
out of here tonight.'

I was in no mood to appreciate this superb *non sequitur*, being tired
and hungry and thirsty and able to think only of brewing a *dechi* of
tea and enjoying it in peace. All my suppressed irritation of the past
four days erupted and I furiously told Aman that we would move
neither ourselves nor our baggage until tomorrow morning when we
leave for Skardu. As I spoke he nervously backed away from me on to
the verandah, whereupon I shut the door firmly and lit our stove. I
could see how his mind was working. He also plans to leave for
Skardu tomorrow and he doesn't trust an unsupervised Zakir to make
the V.I.P. suite as it should be for their boss, who may then punish
Aman for not having replaced Zakir by some more industrious

individual. But I fail to see why we should be the victims of this situation.

Some time later Aman reappeared, followed by Zakir with the register. I had Rs.120 on the table, ready to pay for our twelve nights, but as I opened the book Aman leant forward in his chair and half-whispered, 'You must not pay so much! Zakir cannot read – put '1 January' as your arrival date – then you can save Rs.60.'

This adding of insult to injury was of course meant to placate me. Aman looked genuinely bewildered when I replied frigidly that it is not my habit to sign false statements and that if he wished to ease my financial burden he could pay Rs.5 for each of the nights he had been sleeping on the bed. He then claimed that government officers are not expected to pay for accommodation in Rest Houses, though a notice in English on the verandah declares that government officers must pay Rs.5 per night and other travellers Rs.10. I'm glad I didn't know, before we used the *ghrari*, that this bone-headed creature is responsible for its maintenance.

Mazhar and Ghulam have just been in to give me pony advice. The Ronda pony-owner has already been told by Ghulam that I have no interest in his expensive bag of bones and he is now repenting his cupidity. A dramatic fall in the price of horseflesh may therefore be expected tomorrow morning. Mazhar says I must go early to the Hotel and ask for a seat in the next Skardu-bound jeep that stops there, and Ghulam says I must at the same time announce that I have decided to buy an animal in Khapalu, where ponies are very cheap.

Poor Rachel – a naturally truthful child – was scandalized to observe her mother becoming enmeshed in such a web of lies. 'They're not really lies,' I explained disingenuously. 'This is what's known as wheeling and dealing.'

4

Enter Hallam

Part of the way we rode the forlorn-looking ponies of the district, all dirty and covered with long shaggy hair, but plucky and willing like their masters. The primitive saddles were so uncomfortable that we usually preferred to walk . . . between these impossible saddles and the pony's back goes the thick folded *namdah* (a species of soft felt manufactured in Kashgar and used throughout both sides of the Karakoram region), which has a tendency to slip out and drag saddle and rider with it. Anyone intending to take a long journey through Baltistan should provide himself with a good leather saddle.

Fillipo de Fillipi (1909)

BYICHA. 7 JANUARY

The wheeling and dealing worked: by ten o'clock this morning Rachel was in possession of a fourteen-hand, Rs.700 pony, at once named Hallam after her favourite man friend. He came complete with bit, bridle and *namdah*. The *namdah* has a sewn-on covering of what must once have been pretty flowered cotton, and the disintegrating but still serviceable reins are made of soft plaited leather with a filling of cloth.

As we concluded the deal it began to snow lightly and there was some doubt about whether or not we should leave. Finally it was decided that whatever the weather did we could make this tiny hamlet, which is only eight miles from Thowar. Mazhar also left for Skardu this morning, in a merchant's jeep.

Zakir carried Hallam's load to Dambudass; with the advent of tipping-time he had become a model of zealous endeavour and solicitude for our welfare. In the bazaar I bought a worn old sack for Rs.8; absurd prices are put on all objects that come from down-country. I then divided Hallam's load between the sack and our canvas bag, keeping the bag lighter because to it was tied our kerosene supply. A local expert judiciously adjusted the load and showed me how to tie it across the saddle, which has special iron accessories for the purpose. My own load consisted of our bedding and emergency high-altitude tent, while in her mini-rucksack Rachel was carrying a first-aid kit and Squirrel Nutkin. The capacious pockets of my parka held map, compass-pedometer, diary, pen, handkerchief, thermos of tea and the sustaining dried apricots without which no one travels in these areas.

It was noon when Rachel mounted again, to the cheers of the populace, which had assembled, seemingly in its entirety, to see us off. Already, without any load up, Hallam had proved incapable of more than 2 m.p.h. – half my own normal walking speed – and I had reckoned, correctly, that it would be about 4.30 p.m. when we arrived here.

A mile or so from Dambudass we came on three coolies 'tidying' the track; because of frequent landslips and rockfalls this is a daily task. They were Hotel friends who greeted us warmly and downed shovels to escort us across a long stretch of ice just ahead. One man lifted Rachel down while another took Hallam's bridle and the third firmly held my arm. We could easily have managed on our own but I appreciated this farewell gesture from people among whom we had been so happy.

We saw no further trace of humanity for over two hours. Then we came on an improbable youth sitting wrapped in a blanket by the edge of the track. He looked so like a large clump of thyme that I noticed him only as we drew level and his astonishment on seeing us rendered him incapable of returning our greeting. The weather did not deteriorate as expected – the sky even cleared a little for a time – but the afternoon wind blew sharp-edged and remorseless and one could sense snow in the air.

Hallam goes slightly less slowly if left in Rachel's control. Unfortunately, however, he has been trained (or prefers) to walk on the extreme outside edge of the track and this did the maternal nerves no good at all, with the Indus racing along anything from 100 to 1,000 feet below his neat little hooves. So I led him, taking care that the inner half of the load was not damaged by protruding hunks of cliff.

[Here I had to pause to thaw my hands over our oil-stove, though while writing I am wearing ski-gloves. The cold is so intense in this shack I can scarcely think through it.]

For much of the time we could see the mountain-wall at the foot of which we have come to rest. A tremendous wall it is, of pointed, oddly symmetrical peaks well over 20,000 feet but so sheer they have only a light covering of snow – just enough to enhance their austere, cruel beauty. For miles the brown cliffs on the far side of the Gorge run towards this wall at right angles, rising straight up from the water and looking as though hewn by man, so regularly are they formed. Despite their steepness, two isolated and quite tall pine-trees have somehow found root-holds, hundreds of feet above the river, on ledges that were invisible to us. These were the first green things we had seen since leaving the plains and they looked like mistakes – as if Nature had absent-mindedly put something down in the wrong place.

On our side of the Gorge numerous buzzards and eagles strutted and squabbled among colossal boulders and shattered rock-slabs on the slope above us. Their colouring blends so well with the grey-brown-black of this landscape that often one doesn't notice them until they move. Some were splendidly unafraid and perched twenty yards away to watch our passing. They seem to commute frequently to the far side of the Gorge, which is doubtless stocked with all sorts of unsuspected delicacies, and Rachel was thrilled to see their majestic wing-span as they planed close overhead, with great trousered talons spread for the descent.

It suddenly gets very cold at about 3 p.m., even on a day when the noon sun has been warm, and at 3.15 I suggested to Rachel that she should walk the rest of the way. Being obsessed with the joy of riding her own pony she vigorously denied feeling cold, yet when I insisted on her dismounting she was so numb she could scarcely stand up.

We saw Byicha from some way off, as a brown smudge of leafless trees relieving the desolation. Here trees always mean people. At Byicha the Indus swings west and on its right bank, where it curves, the Gorge widens for about a mile, allowing some cultivation; enough, apparently, to sustain life for the inhabitants of a score or so of stone hovels that seem to have grown out of the mountain and are almost invisible from the track. As one draws near, tiny fields and frozen irrigation channels and wildly writhing vines appear amidst the trees. A few goats, sheep and dzo, and one magnificent yak, were diligently searching for dead leaves; in Ronda they would all have been stabled by three o'clock but the poorer a settlement the more self-sufficient its animals have to be.

We were now at the foot of that symmetrical mountain-wall and could no longer see its peaks. The track climbed steeply for quarter of a mile before slightly swinging away from the river to cross a nullah full of icy boulders and leaping, foaming water. We were approaching the new wooden bridge when we saw on our left, a little above track-level, two incongruous jeeps parked outside a shack in the shade of several tall trees. But for this evidence of its status, we would certainly have bypassed our hotel without recognizing it. It consists of an eating-house and this store-room-cum-bedroom where we are sleeping.

When Hallam had been stabled and fed – for this I had to lead him back to the main part of the settlement – we had a surprisingly good supper in the eating-house: chappatis, curried dahl soup and outsize omelettes. The standard was much higher than in Ronda's Hotel and having eaten nothing but dried apricots since 8 a.m. I relished every mouthful. The proprietor has not yet recovered from the shock of our arrival. A gaunt, elderly Pathan with a straggling beard, he wears a purple skull-cap that slightly gives him the air of a down-at-heel bishop. It was dark by the time we ate but the little room was adequately lit by the flames of the fire – lovely tongues of scarlet and orange leaping high around the giant *dechis*. The only other guests are the two Pathan jeep-drivers, on their way back from Skardu. I had expected them to share the store-room with us but they are sleeping in the eating-house where the embers will remain aglow all night. They and the proprietor can huddle together under quilts on the square mud platform in front of the fire where customers sit cross-legged to eat their food. One jeep has broken down and a huge bonfire is now blazing outside to warm the driver as he lies under it, struggling with its infirmity. The other jeep is its mate and won't continue to Gilgit without it. Many drivers prefer to do the Gorge trip in convoy.

Our room is another of those depots where jeeps can unload, before turning back to Gilgit, when the weather suddenly worsens on the route to Skardu. It is about ten feet by fifteen and piled almost to the low roof with sacks full of something hard, sharp and lumpy, and tea-chests so heavy they can't possibly contain tea, and large cartons of condensed milk from Holland. A central tree-trunk supports the mud roof and the stone walls have been ineffectually mud-plastered by way of making them draught-proof. The floor *non est*: as in all local hovels it is untreated ground – i.e., sandy earth and pebbles. Nor is there any window at present, though an aperture blocked with loose stones obviously serves as such in summer and now admits draughts of icy air which conflict around my person with similar draughts entering from sundry other unplanned ventilation holes. When we were shown into our suite three charpoys were standing on end against the piles of sacks and the two put down for us took up most of the vacant floor space. Filthy but warm bedding is provided and as we ourselves are already so filthy there seems little point in being fussy and unpacking flea-bags.

Tonight the song of the Indus is loud. We are quite close to it here though we were climbing steadily on the way from Ronda. Between Skardu and Ronda the fall of the river is twenty feet per mile.

I am dithering now about keeping our stove going all night. The temperature certainly justifies such extravagance but not knowing what situations may arise before we get to Skardu, where kerosene will next be available, I think I had better stick to my Spartan principles.

On her way to bed by the light of a guttering candle Rachel tripped over the corner of a sack and remarked mildly, 'I don't think this room is very convenient, do you?' But all that really concerns me about our accommodation is whether or not one can write fairly comfortably and I have no complaints this evening – apart from the cold, which does diminish concentration. When Rachel was in bed I got myself organized by pulling a tea-chest into the middle of the floor for use as a table, and heaving a sack into position for use as a chair – with a folded quilt on top, to give that little touch of luxury required by ageing bones. Then I placed the stove between my feet, stuck a candle on to our tin of Nivea, took my diary from my pocket and off I went . . .

BYICHA. 8 JANUARY

We had a very good night, enlivened only by a little grey rat who made several heroic but unsuccessful attempts to get at Rachel's precious cheese supply. Our crudely-made door has a wide crack down the middle and when I woke I could see that the dawn light was uncommonly bright; there had been such a heavy snowfall that no one could go anywhere this morning. The drivers were disconsolate, having worked so hard to mend that engine, but we were entirely happy to spend another twenty-four hours here. Also the delay suited Hallam. We left him all day in his snug stable – a good deal snugger than our own – and saw that he had generous feeds of hay. He really needs grain, but none is available.

After breakfast we explored the very steep nullah and glimpsed fearsome peaks with needle-sharp summits standing in skirts of vapour at the head of the valley; the map tells us that we are close to the massive Chogo Lungma glacier. At noon the tributary began to thaw; I wonder how many degrees of frost are needed to freeze a river of its volume and power. When our tiny goat-path died amidst an upheaval of rock and soft sandy cliffs, overhanging the nullah, we returned to base and enjoyed two more king-sized omelettes.

After lunch we descended to the Indus, crossing half-a-mile of pale grey sand decorated with patches of snow and strewn with smooth, light brown boulders, some so vast we felt like beetles beside them. The scale of this landscape can be very deceptive; yesterday I would have said the Indus was about fifty yards from the track, not half a mile. And it is only on standing beside the river that one appreciates its width and its speed and force, as it churns whitely down a perceptible slope between boulders the size of cottages. All those boulders were covered with canopies of ice, delicately snow-powdered, and Rachel noticed that *between* these solid canopies and the rocks there was room for water to flow. This observation reduced her to an agony of scientific curiosity which I was, as usual, unable to satisfy. While we were collecting bright pebbles close to the ice-fringed bank we saw two minor rock-falls, one just across the river, another on our side a little way downstream. Somehow the sound of a rockfall – the thudding and bounding and slithering – is much more alarming than the sight. Again, because of the Himalayan scale, several tons of falling rock and earth look like a trickle of pebbles down the side of a sand-pit.

Altogether it was a memorable scene there by the turbulent water, enveloped in the grandeur of the Gorge. The dark rock walls showed great zig-zag scars of white – one could fancy lightning had been painted on them – and their strangely square tops, as though dressed by giant stonemasons, were in extreme contrast to the tangle of jagged summits just visible beyond. Then on all sides there was ice in unimaginable shapes and forms. The infinite variety of ice, and the exquisite grotesqueness of its formations, delights Rachel more than almost anything else here; but not more than the prodigious chenar tree near our 'hotel', which is *twenty-nine* of my long paces in circumference and reputed to be 600 years old. It still flourishes, though it has had its centre burnt out to make a large room, floored with dry leaves, which serves as the hotel latrine; and very welcome that shelter was early this morning, especially as our present limited diet has reduced me to an unprecedented state of constipation.

A HAMLET ABOVE THE INDUS (NAME UNKNOWN). 9 JANUARY

We left Byicha at 9 a.m., as early as is practical in this climate, and had covered eighteen miles by 4.30 p.m. Hallam was much more sprightly today, after his few good feeds, and we brought a picnic lunch for him. The truss of aromatic hay strapped to the top of my rucksack was not planned to act as a spur but it had that effect: whenever I slowed down or paused for a moment he broke into a trot to snatch a snack. Then we discovered that he is hooked on wild thyme, however hard and dry the clumps may be, so we let him have a few mouthfuls whenever the opportunity arose. After two miles it arose quite often for at last the Gorge widened. On our side the mountains withdrew, so that we were crossing a long, wide ledge at their base, and for much of the time the river was out of sight though never out of hearing. As we climbed gradually the snow and ice became thicker underfoot and the dramatically broken landscape became whiter. A few tiny hamlets lay on our way but all morning we saw nobody.

We stopped for lunch where thyme was plentiful, so that Hallam could have a two-course meal while Rachel ate her cheese and I ate my apricots. Now the sky was a deep blue and towards the north-west a dazzling peak – one of the true giants – was visible. To Rachel's great annoyance I could not identify it from the map; when actually in the middle of all these legendary mountains it is impossible to recognize them individually. Nor is it always wise to listen to the locals: in Ronda many people insist that K2 may be seen from Gomu.

As I chewed my apricots and looked at that proud pure peak, rising solitary and brilliant above the nearer mountains, I despaired of ever being able to convey in words any adequate picture of this region. Everything is so *extreme* here that language loses its power. Today each furlong offered a variation on the Karakoram theme; I could walk forever on such a path without any risk of boredom. Every feature contributes to the wonder and the glory of these mountains – their scale, texture, colouring, shapes, arrangements – and the clarity of the light is itself unique. Then when clouds come it seems that all the gloom of the world has been concentrated in this one profound chasm.

By three o'clock the wind had risen and new snow lay a foot deep all around us. Hallam now proved how sure-footed and sensible he is and I let him show me the least treacherous route. (For most of today it was unnecessary for me to lead him as we were not overhanging the Indus.) Our level ledge was about two miles wide at this point, from the edge of the Gorge to the precipitous slopes on our left.

Here the Indus displays adolescent moodiness, turning and twist-ing unexpectedly between the mountains, and when it again came into view we saw a long, new suspension footbridge leading to a comparatively large village. By that time the wind was blowing cruelly against us and Rachel, who needed to restore her circulation, was unable to keep her footing on a track that had become like a skating-rink. I, too, was feeling cold, despite my exertions: this was the sort of searching wind that conquers all. Yet I was afraid to take Hallam across a long, swaying bridge over a noisy stretch of Indus. He might have accepted it, but he seems not too happy while crossing the many short bridges over nullahs on this track. So we pressed on, hoping our U.S. Army map was correct (it often isn't) when it showed a hamlet some three miles further upstream on the right bank.

After a fortnight in the narrowest part of the Gorge the world here seemed very wide and bright, with the sun shining until four o'clock. The mountains on either side were about 16,000 feet and between us and them the snowy waste was scattered with huge dark boulders in white cloaks. Underfoot conditions slowed our progress and we became colder by the minute. Then we got the incense-like smell of a burning thyme-bush and came in sight of four men warming their hands: to ignite a bush gives instant though short-lived heat and is a popular device among shepherds and coolie-gangs. These coolies had been half-heartedly throwing shovelfuls of sand across the track; they live in this hamlet and accompanied us over the last few gruelling miles.

Every moment the cold became more intense but here the Gorge is so dramatic that discomfort seemed unimportant. Where the river again curves abruptly we had to ascend steeply and descend slightly before climbing at a sensational angle around a towering complex of dark, rocky precipices overhanging a boisterous Indus – roaring, raving and churning. These manoeuvrings of the track also brought into view the opening out of the Gorge into the Skardu Valley, some eight or ten miles away. Then suddenly the late afternoon light acquired a strange blue tinge such as I have never seen before, and over all that desolation of mountain, river, rock and snow lay this unearthly radiance. It may not have been magic but to us it seemed so.

One could easily pass this hamlet without noticing its few hovels high above the track. Unusually, the minute terraced fields go down almost to river-level, forming an amphitheatre which is wonderfully beautiful under thick snow as it leads up and up and up, for thousands of feet, to the vertical black crags of this summit – or rather, series of summits, each bejewelled by immensely long icicles hanging from ledges and glittering in the setting sun. (Earlier today we saw cliffs festooned with gold and green icicles as thick and long as telegraph poles – quite fantastic. I am so sleepy now that I can't remember details in the right order.)

Our kindly companions were so bewildered by the mere fact of our existence that it was impossible even to attempt a conversation with them. However, when we were about half-way across the amphitheatre they suddenly gestured towards the crags and indicated that Rachel should dismount. The youngest man gave her a pick-a-back while I led Hallam up from terrace to terrace, on paths that only a native pony would consider tackling. The load was repeatedly threatened as we passed between trees or jagged rocks and eventually our friends removed it and divided it between themselves. Then at last we were directly beneath the crags of the summit – coal-black in the brief twilight, against a faintly green sky – and some way ahead I saw Rachel's red snow-suit disappearing into a stone rectangle a good deal smaller than most of the boulders around it. She had arrived at the headman's home.

A dark, narrow hallway runs through this dwelling and on one side is a kitchen, unfurnished apart from the central fireplace, and two stables for goats and cattle. On the other side is the large living/ sleeping room, where we are being entertained, and three small store-rooms, for firewood, food and fodder, and another stable for sheep and hens. The inner walls are of woven willow-wands and the outer of thick stone neatly plastered with mud.

On first entering this room I could see nothing – the two tiny unglazed windows are blocked against the cold – but soon my eyes got used to the gloom, and to the swirling smoke from the wood-stove's leaking pipe, and I saw Rachel sitting on the floor facing an astounded semi-circle of family on whom she was fruitlessly practising her Urdu. I also saw that half the floor-space, furthest from the stove, is occupied by several wickerwork coops covered with bits of blanket and containing delicate new-born kids and lambs who frequently emit plaintive cries and, as I write, are being fed maize gruel off spoons by two children. At the humans' end of the room the floor is covered with goat-hair matting which seems not to have been cleaned since the place was built. On this we have spread our flea-bags, beside an apparently old couple (who may be no older than myself), their son and daughter-in-law, two unmarried daughters, and a filth-encrusted baby with an ominous cough. The whole family is coughing dreadfully and I fear our host is dying. He lies propped against a sheepskin full of straw and is horribly emaciated, with enormous bright eyes and hot dry hands. In Balti he begged for some medicine, but nodded understandingly when I unhappily explained that I had none. Then he asked his daughter-in-law to take one large white pill from a little wall cupboard and showed it to me, anxiously enquiring if it was any good; I could only say I didn't know, while feeling hopeless and helpless. Our hostess is not in much better condition. She seems to have bronchial asthma and is now moaning and gasping on the floor beside me, after an exhausting bout of coughing.

Yet this wretched family welcomed us most warmly, though naturally a little timidly. Food was offered, but everybody seemed relieved to see that we have our own; for supper they had only one thin chappati each with a sauce of weak dahl gruel. They watched, fascinated, while I opened a tin of tuna fish for Rachel and made myself a mug of Complan and glucose with mouth-numbing glacial water. No meal has ever tasted better to me, I felt so ravenous.

The loo arrangements are as in Tibet: a flat mud roof just outside the 'hall-door' has four holes in it and when one squats the result falls into a little house from which it is taken in the spring – having been mixed with wood ash – and spread on the fields.

On arrival here Hallam was at once undressed, except for his *namdah*, and led off to a cosy stable. But he took agin it, though his sweet-smelling supper was already within, and refused to ascend the three rounded boulders that serve as steps. It seemed unlikely that he would heed me, when he was ignoring the sort of Balti urging he is used to, but I felt bound to make an effort. At the scene of the deadlock I found him with ears laid back and eyes rolling, yet the moment he heard my voice his ears came forward. I took the halter and waved all the cursing, kicking men away and he followed me up those boulders like a lamb. He has been with us only three days but a little love goes a long way.

KATCHURA. 10 JANUARY

We had a disturbed night, there was so much coughing and groaning, and for hours on end the baby was crying weakly. Luckily Rachel slept soundly through everything while I read by torchlight from 4 a.m. until the family rose at 6.30. Then we breakfasted: tinned corned beef for Rachel, more Complan and glucose for me, futile guilt for both of us because we are being so well-fed.

At nine o'clock we ventured out into a world that seemed to have been throttled overnight by the violence of the cold. It took thirty minutes to slither and scramble down to the jeep-track on precipitous pathlets of solid ice. A boy went first to show us the least hazardous route, I followed with Hallam, two men carried Hallam's load and Rachel brought up the rear, helped by our host's son. I shall always remember that hamlet with a mixture of gratitude and despair – the welcome so warm and the destitution so extreme.

It was an intoxicating morning – the sun dazzling on new snow, the sky half-veiled by milky, wispy clouds, the Indus sparkling like a cascade of emeralds. The track was so icy that it took us over three hours to cover six miles and Rachel grew rather impatient. I could see her point: it's not much fun riding at less than 2 m.p.h. For much of the way we were on another sheer rock-wall directly above the river, and as Hallam gingerly picked his way along Rachel caused me to reflect on the perversity of human nature. When I was six I used to lie in bed secretly dreaming about galloping across unspecified steppes on fiery steeds, or riding undaunted through lonely, frowning mountains infested with cougars. And now my daughter, aged six, while riding along perilous paths hundreds of feet above a roaring torrent, through the most spectacular mountain gorge in the world, says – 'Let's have a pretend game! Let's pretend I'm grown up and married to a doctor in Lismore and we have two children and now we're moving to a new bungalow and I'm going shopping to choose all the colours for wallpapers and carpets . . .'

This village is near the beginning of the Gorge and below it we crossed the Indus by a 300-foot-long suspension bridge built twenty-four years ago, in three months, by the Pakistani Army. At first it felt quite odd to have the river on our left instead of on our right. And it was even odder to look ahead and see a flat, snow-covered plain, some five miles wide, with a solid wall of soaring mountains rising abruptly from the far side. This is the western end of the Skardu valley and after a slow journey through the Gorge it creates an impression of endless spaciousness.

From the bridge the track climbs steeply, leaving the river, and because it was already noon we had to cope with fast-melting slush on sticky, red-brown mud. This new handicap, combined with the fearsome gradient, made me sweat as though in the tropics. Neither of us could make out what route the track was about to take – whether it was going over the next mountain or around the one we were on or down to the valley floor. Eventually we saw that it was going to the top of the one we were on – a sunny, dazzling world covered in two feet of new snow. From this point we could see both the length of Gorge we had just travelled and the Skardu plain, very far below. The broad Indus looked lazy and tame as it meandered slowly across that plain towards the narrow mouth of the Gorge, so directly below us that we could not see it. Here we were at last beyond earshot of the river's powerful roar and that silence made us lonely.

Katchura straggles over a low mountain-top, riven by deep clefts and overlooked by snowy, rock-tipped higher mountains. Two 'hotels', two hucksters' shops and a police-station line the jeep-track; so perhaps, being equipped with police, it is technically a town. At the more awake-looking hotel we asked the way to the Rest House; but it is closed, we were told, and the chowkidar has gone to Skardu for the *Muharram* ceremonies. Constable Hamad Hussain then took charge of us, saying we must on no account stay in a hotel run by thieving Pathans. He installed us in an annexe to the police-station and Hallam was stabled nearby. Hamad has a hectoring manner and I don't care for him. Nor, understandably, does the friendly Pathan from whose establishment we were 'rescued'. This windowless cell, eight feet by eight, has the usual tin wood-stove in the centre of the earth floor and two broken-legged charpoys.

After a lunch of tea and chappatis we set off to explore an inviting side-valley above the village. The snow was a miracle of pure brilliance, stretching softly away on every side in unflawed billows, and at one stage Rachel had to be given a pick-a-back lest she disappear into a drift. Often we turned to marvel at the immense height of the mountains along whose ankles we had been crawling in the Gorge. We also noticed a wonderful cloud-formation: one slender length of diaphanous vapour coiling unbroken from the mouth of the Gorge for as far as one could see towards Ronda. It was at eye-level, so the blue-brown-black mountain mass against which we viewed it seemed to be wearing a silver belt.

Back in our room, we had a meal of chappatis and harsh dahl curry. I have long since realized that during winter in Baltistan privacy is unattainable; the Baltis are attracted by heat as wasps by jam. Seven men, cloaked in blankets, are now sitting on our charpoys, stretching their hands towards the heat, coughing incessantly and frequently spitting or blowing their noses on to the floor. ('People have different customs here,' commented Rachel.) They watch my pen as though hypnotized and are, I must confess, irritating me slightly. Yet to turn them out, in this temperature and with fuel so dear, would be unforgivable.

One of our visitors was a Skardu youth who introduced himself as 'a government officer' and spoke a version of English. He had a neat, almost pretty little face, and wore a cheap–smart leather jacket with a London label which he proudly showed me. 'My bust friend is smuggler,' he explained. 'He know Europe well. He have many friends of Europe. He work London–Karachi–London. Drugs to London, Scotch to Karachi. He is very rich man and my bust friend. Can I be of service to you?'

'No thank you,' I said firmly, just as the door opened to admit

Hamad Hussain's senior colleague. This tall, slim, unsmiling character had long, oiled, ebony moustaches, a livid scar on his left temple and a general air of having strayed from the cast of some *opera bouffe* dealing in handsome villains. He did not greet us but squeezed himself on to a charpoy as the Skardu youth asked me, 'Do you like chess?'

Feeling vaguely surprised that the conversation should have taken such an elevated turn, I replied regretfully, 'I'm afraid not; it's too highbrow for me.'

'You think it is bad habit?' pursued the youth.

'Of course not!' I said. 'I'm told it's very good for the brain – it's just that I've never been able to cope with it myself.'

'But here you can try!' exclaimed the youth. Then he leant across the stove and said something in Balti to the policeman, who at once produced what looked like a pellet of cow-dung. Holding this up between thumb and forefinger, and addressing me for the first time, the Head Constable said, 'I give you, you give me Rs.50.'

I took the pellet to examine it, and Rachel and I felt it and smelt it: it was odourless. 'What is it?' I asked.

'Chess,' replied the youth. 'My bust friend sell this much for Rs.500 in London, but here it is cheap.'

I handed his property back to the Head Constable and caused a gale of incredulous laughter by informing the company that in my country people are gaoled for selling 'chess'. Then, having failed to do business, the policeman sombrely rolled a joint which he shared impartially with all his friends.

NEAR SKARDU AIRSTRIP. 11 JANUARY

We were charged an outrageous Rs.25 for our cell in the police-station and the atmosphere generated this morning by the jostle of men around me indicated that argument would be ill-received.

It was snowing lightly as we left Katchura and we were the only moving objects on a landscape innocent of even a bird's footprint. Overnight every angle had been rounded and every sharpness blunted, and now every tiny sound of nature was muffled. Clouds full of the radiance of unfallen snow hid the high peaks and one could stare at the sun through veils of gently drifting flakes, while a curiously diffused light glinted hesitantly on the sweep of the Indus, far below.

Our track, having descended to the base of the mountains, ran just above the valley floor – an unbroken expanse of glittering crystals. When we paused to rest on clumps of thyme, two slowly moving dots appeared, far away on the track towards Skardu. The first jeep to draw level with us stopped and the moment the driver unmuffled his face we recognized our taciturn friend, Mohammad, on his way back (he hoped) to Gilgit. Then the second vehicle stopped and Rachel squealed with joy on recognizing Mazhar, on his way back (he hoped) to Thowar. He was accompanied by his senior medical officer, who also got out of the jeep and, as we shook hands, asked smilingly, 'Do you remember?'

I studied his cheerful, slightly plump face, but had to say, 'No.'

His smile widened. 'Chilas!' he exclaimed. Incredibly, this was the man who, as a just-qualified army doctor, tended me so effectively in June 1963, after my heat-stroke collapse in the furnace-like depths of the lower Indus Gorge. When Mazhar had told him about the Irishwoman with the child and the horse he had immediately declared, 'It can only be the same one – unless all Irishwomen are mad!'

Soon after, the track left the base of the mountains to run between a succession of little hamlets and neat apricot and apple orchards where the trees had been carefully pruned – a sure sign of government agricultural advisers in the background. At one point we were joined by two fellow-travellers. The man wore a threadbare beige blanket and had a type of face often seen here – blunt-featured, kindly, not very bright. He was leading a frisky, woolly young dzo who plainly did not approve of the rope tied round her long, sharp horns. His small son followed, tramping through ice, snow and slush in pale blue broken plastic sandals on otherwise bare feet. Our first Balti dog brought up the rear – a black, heavily built, shaggy creature, with a square head. When a third jeep noisily approached us the dzo knocked her owner flat and went careering off over the snowy waste at a speed altogether inconsistent with her bulk. The dog promptly gave chase, followed by his humans, and as far as we were concerned the entire party was lost to sight forever.

By this time a windsock was visible, hanging motionless and unlikely against the valley's eastern rampart of blue, cloud to enmeshed mountains. Then we saw Skardu's squalid 'airport', a landing-strip nine miles from the town, surrounded by broken-down bits of road-building machinery, rusty jeep skeletons, barbed wire enclosures containing petrol-barrels, an army camp and supply depot, and sundry other disagreeable phenomena recalling travellers to the 1970s. (Oddly, between Gilgit and here one comes to accept jeeps – not to regard them as vile mechanical intrusions on the landscape. I suppose this is because of their daring feats in the Gorge, which earn one's grudging respect.)

The eleven miles from Katchura had taken us over six hours and both Hallam and I were flagging for lack of adequate food, while Rachel was stiff with cold, having been in the saddle all day because of conditions underfoot.

Our hotel is new, like most buildings around the airstrip, but not offensive because constructed of local materials in the local style. It is opposite the enormous Military Supply Depot for Baltistan, so our arrival at once attracted the attention of several junior army officers who have proved most helpful, though the Pakistani Army is strictly forbidden, throughout the Northern Areas, to fraternize with foreigners. One Pathan lieutenant produced a bucket of pulse for Hallam and another told me not to order an evening meal because at six o'clock he would bring us mutton stew from the Mess. Hearing the words 'mutton stew' Rachel and I could scarcely control our salivary glands and sure enough at five minutes past six our friend reappeared, followed by his batman bearing a laden tray. We could now *smell* the mutton stew – but alas! the proprietor barred the doorway and began a tirade of abuse in Urdu, with Balti asides to his cronies who were sitting near us by the stove. I could gather approximately what was being said: that the military were a lot of idle, interfering intruders, that his *khana* was as good as anything produced in their rotten Officers' Mess, that when he had a chance to make money on a foreigner they had no business to queer his pitch, that he and his friends would beat up the lieutenant and his servant if they didn't go away fast, taking their tray with them. (The proprietor would need a lot of help to beat up anybody; he is a mere wisp of a man, with a leathery face lined more by ill-temper than by age.) I felt very sorry for our friend, who had been put in a most humiliating position, especially for a Pathan. To help him save face I pretended to notice nothing and sat with head industriously bowed over notebook. Rachel of course was *aching* for mutton stew but when I fiercely whispered 'Tact!' she remained silent. This is a codeword meaning 'Be quiet now and I'll explain later'. It is invaluable on the many occasions when if she said anything it would be the wrong thing. I must say I admired her stoicism this evening. The poor child hasn't had a decent meal for weeks and had been looking forward to her mutton stew with pathetic eagerness. Yet when it was removed from under her very nose, and I had explained why, she accepted the inevitable – in this case yet another fistful of dried apricots – and went to bed without a word of complaint.

I was relieved that our young friend had not forced the issue, as he must have been tempted to do. This incident was a symptom of how bad relations are between down-country regiments and the locals. There is as little in common between these northern mountain peoples and the Pakistanis as there was between the East and West Pakistanis.

Apart from the kitchen, this hotel has only one room, and I now see that we are to have the pleasure of the proprietor's company all night. Half-an-hour ago our four fellow-guests put down their charpoys, which had been leaning against the wall, and lay two on each wrapped in their own blankets. They, too, have hacking coughs; and one of them, whose charpoy stands six inches from mine, is snoring like a defective bath-pipe. Normally I detest sharing a bedroom but in these parts one somehow doesn't mind. Probably this is because each person wraps himself up so thoroughly that he is effectively isolated within his own private cocoon, from which he is unlikely even to peep before dawn.

My own bedding-down ritual is quite complicated. First I spread my astronaut's blanket on the charpoy (or bed or floor). Then I unroll my silk-lined, Japanese high-altitude sleeping-bag and insert it into my bulkier, quilted sleeping-bag, before spreading both on the blanket. Then I remove my long, very heavy, lined Parka jacket, which I have been wearing all day, and spread that over the flea-bags, before folding the top half of the astronaut's blanket over the lot. Finally I remove my boots, but not my woollen socks, and put on my husky bootees; these match my husky jacket and pants, which are never removed. (By now I have quite forgotten which sweaters and slacks I am wearing beneath them.) Then I gently wriggle into bed, with book and torch, taking great care not to dislocate the various layers of the structure. Having zipped up one flea-bag and buttoned the other only a small ventilation hole remains open and the temperature can – and does – drop to 40° below freezing without my noticing.

5

Urban Life in Baltistan

The misery of the Baltis has often been described. But one was
even more struck by it seeing them in winter, going about
numb with cold, barely covered by their wretched home-spun
shawls, and certainly undernourished. For three months of the
year they live almost entirely on fresh fruit, for the other nine
on dried – the famous apricots of Baltistan.

Fillipo de Fillipi (1913)

Hark to the hurried question of Despair: 'Where is my child?'
-- an echo answers, 'Where?'

Byron, *The Bride of Abydos*

SKARDU. 12 JANUARY

Were all capitals like this, I might not have such an aversion to urban
life. Yet we are seeing a Skardu that has been much 'developed' over
the past few years.

The Skardu Valley is some 7,500 feet above sea-level, twenty
miles long from north-west to south-east and two to five miles wide.
Through it the Indus has carved a bed fifty to seventy feet deep and in
places the stream is 500 feet wide. Below its confluence with the
Shigar it divides into several branches, creating many sandy islets.
The encircling mountains rise abruptly from the valley floor to
heights of 18,000 feet, and this morning all these craggy, glistening
peaks gradually became visible as the dispersing clouds eddied
vaguely around their shoulders, leaving the summits free.

We approached Skardu over a fissured plain criss-crossed with
frozen irrigation channels and planted with fruit-trees. From afar we
could see a long line of low wooden buildings on a ledge dominated
by the strange Rock of Skardu – 'like a ship out of the water turned

upside down,' to quote Rachel. But it would have to be a very big ship, for the Rock is more than two miles long and 1,300 feet high. On its far side the Shigar joins the Indus, which from most parts of the town is invisible and, at this season, inaudible.

We took a short cut away from the jeep-track and climbed steeply into the Old Bazaar, where people stared at us as though we had stepped out of a space-craft. This is Skardu's main bazaar but in mid-winter many traders hibernate; half the little stalls were closed and the rest carried very meagre stocks. Abbas Kazmi's name is known to everyone here, so despite a predictable dearth of English-speakers and a certain surliness in the atmosphere – possibly owing to this being the start of *Muharram* – it was easy to find him. But even Hallam's surefootedness was tested on the thick ice and packed snow of the town's often-used paths.

Abbas Kazmi's rambling bungalow was built by his father in 1949 when the family left Srinagar. From the edge of a steep bluff it overlooks the new cantonment area, a new mosque and the Chasma Bazaar, beyond which the eastern end of the Rock half hides the mouth of the Shigar valley. Behind the house is a secluded garden where Hallam was fed while we were being entertained in a large bed-sitter, furnished only with a charpoy, a small table and a goat-hair carpet on the floor near the stove.

When we arrived Abbas Kazmi happened to be entertaining Kalbay Abbas, the friend in whose house we are now installed. Kalbay does not in fact own it but is renting it from a local farmer named Sadiq Ali, and it is vacant merely because he found it intolerably primitive during winter. Some weeks ago he moved out to the Rest House but he is retaining this hovel for use next summer. A tall, handsome, assured young man, he has a quick brain and a nice sense of humour. His family came originally from Shigar but has now settled in Pindi; Kalbay works in his father's engineering contractor business, spending much of his time in Baltistan. A past pupil of the Irish nuns at Murree, he speaks English more fluently and colloquially than anyone else we have met since leaving Islamabad and I found it a great relief to be able to talk to another adult at my normal pace in my normal idiom.

For lunch we had unleavened wheat-flour bread and curried spinach, our first green vegetable (or indeed vegetable of any hue) for over three weeks. Spinach grows abundantly here during summer and is dried for winter use. Then came cups of salted butter tea, poured from an antique engraved silver pot, eighteen inches high, into which two red-hot wood embers had been dropped just before the brew was served. When Rachel's expression unwittingly betrayed her opinion of this concoction a pot of 'normal' was at once prepared for the *bungo* – a delightful word, meaning girl-child.

After lunch Abbas Kazmi took Rachel to our new home, at the southern edge of Skardu, by a short cut impassable to horses, while Kalbay Abbas guided Hallam and me. The track was so difficult that I could scarcely spare a glance for my surroundings: I only know they were snow-covered, and that this 'capital' seems to be a collection of scattered groups of farmhouses rather than a town.

Where we rejoined the jeep track a long, level expanse of snow lay on our left, at the foot of a boulder-strewn hill, behind a Connemara-type wall. On our right half a dozen dwellings stood at right angles to the track and then we came to a new bazaar stall, not yet in use. Beyond this, an eight-foot wall ran beside the track for fifty yards, with a rickety wooden door up two steps half-way down its length. Kalbay Abbas gestured towards the door. 'Home sweet home,' he explained. 'You needn't *say* it's OK if it isn't.'

Hallam had to be unloaded on the track; as usual he made a formal protest about the steps but then went up and through the narrow door most meekly. Just inside one turns left for the latrine – a roofless, three-sided stone cubicle with a hole in the ground – and right for the 'hall-door'. Off the dark hallway are an unfurnished kitchen and a living-room-cum-bedroom with two tape charpoys and two huge wooden chests belonging to Kalbay Abbas. These have now been converted into our table, although their raised edges and lack of height make them less than ideal for my main purpose. This room is about ten feet by twelve, with an untended mud floor which sends up clouds of dust however gently one walks. A low ceiling of mulberry beams and planks supports a flat mud roof covered in brushwood to break the weight of the snow. A large hole has been left in the middle of the ceiling for a stove-pipe and two panes of the glazed window are missing. The mud walls were once thinly white-washed but now are filthy and defaced. There is a large empty wall-cupboard and when we arrived a niche near the window was also empty but for an Everyman edition of Charlotte Yonge's *The Dove in the Eagle's Nest*. Eng. Lit. gets around . . . This niche makes an ideal bookshelf and when I had given Miss Yonge some company (but would she approve of Simone de Beauvoir?) I felt that I had marked out our own bit of Skardu territory.

As we were debating where to stable Hallam, our landlord Sadiq Ali arrived and suggested the kitchen. So I coaxed our *ghora* in, tethered him to a rafter and here we all are, very cosy and snug, our oil-stove boiling a kettle for *chai*, the window blocked with an old exercise book lent by Rachel and the chimney-hole also papered over. Outside the window is a snow-filled orchard of apricot saplings and beyond that a mighty display of mountains, less than two miles away. I fetch water from a stream near our neighbours' houses: it is unfrozen at only one point, where housewives repeatedly break the ice. We shall continue to use candles. In theory Skardu is electrified but in practice the current flows only rarely and weakly despite – or because of – the many wires that drape the town. These run from tree to tree like tropical creepers, at just the level to strangle or otherwise dispose of unwary riders. Indisputably this is an endearing capital.

The mod. con. I miss most is newsprint – as a household aid, rather than as an intellectual stimulant. Newspapers are neither demanded nor supplied here and only when without them does one realize how varied are their domestic uses. An equally conspicuous but more convenient lack is insect life. In summer this room must vibrate under the tread of its flea and bed-bug population, but mercifully all such creatures have been atrophied by the intense nocturnal cold and will reappear only towards the end of March.

In Skardu one remembers that Baltistan has a history, something easily forgotten while wandering through the isolation of the Indus Gorge. There it is hard to relate this land to the rest of the world, either in the past or the present but approaching Skardu the traveller notices if he looks hard enough – it blends very well with its surroundings – a fortress which vividly recalls distant wars. At the eastern end of the Rock, some 300 feet above the valley floor, a natural shelf supports this unexpected building, described by de Fillipi as 'so imposing as to be out of all proportion to the wretched little town at its feet which it was intended to defend'. It was designed by Ali Sher Khan, a famous king of Skardu who between 1590 and 1610 conquered Ladak, forcing the king to marry his daughter, and also Khapalu, in the Shyok Valley. From that date until 1947 the histories of Baltistan and Ladak are interwoven. During the post-Partition troubles, and the 1966 conflict, the people of Skardu continued to take refuge in their fortress, disregarding the fact that not even Ali Sher Kan's cunning could outwit Indian Air Force bombers. But luckily those bombers devoted all their attention to putting the airstrip out of action.

Balti is a language without a script, nor do the people have many reliable oral traditions about their own past. In Thowar our Head Constable friend assured me that 'before the conversion to Islam, 1200 years ago [sic], all Baltis were Hindus or Sikhs'. There is a hazy racial recollection of the language once having had a script and presumably this dates from Buddhist times. Then the Tibetan script would have been used, at least by the lamas and probably by all educated lay-folk.

The first known mention of Baltistan occurs in the Chinese annals, which refer to a Chinese military expedition aiding Ladak against Tibet in AD 747. Ladak and Baltistan are called Big and Little Poliu. At about this time Baltistan is believed to have come under Tibetan rule and cultural influence; and so far as we know the Baltis remained subject to the Tibetans until their conversion to Islam in the early fifteenth century. Fosco Maraini is interesting on the linguistic link: 'Balti as spoken today is an archaic form of Tibetan, the words being still pronounced as, in Tibet itself, they are nowadays only written. Rice, for instance, is in Balti *bras*, and in the Tibetan script it is written as *bras*. But . . . today Lhasa knows rice as *dren*! . . . Hundreds of such examples come to mind. Balti grammar and syntax too reveal archaic features.'

The next specific mention of Baltistan in the history books records the marvellous travels of Sultan Said, a Mongol Khan of Kashgar, who achieved the almost impossible by taking an army of 5,000 men across the 19,000-foot Karakoram Pass in the spring of 1531. For over two years the Sultan and his merry men roamed through Ladak and Baltistan, living on what they could pillage. Then Sultan Said died, while his son Iskander was attempting the conquest of Lhasa. During this attempt the Kashgar army was reduced, by altitude, cold and hunger, to twenty-seven men.

Research can do little to illumine Baltistan's past because those few records which once existed were destroyed comparatively recently. When the Sikhs took Skardu in 1840 they burned an ancient chronicle of the Makhpons, or Buddhist kings, and Vigne mentions hearing of the destruction of another famous manuscript during the burning of Skardu castle in the reign of Zufar Khan.

The Englishman G. T. Vigne spent long periods in Skardu during the 1830s and wrote the first description of the valley. His host, Ahmet Shah, was a direct descendant of Ali Sher Khan and the last independent Raja of Skardu. At one time each Balti oasis had its own hereditary chief whose family usually intermarried with that of the Rajah of Skardu and who normally allied himself with his overlord against a common enemy, though on domestic issues he might oppose the Skardu line. Most such dynasties were of non-Balti extraction, being the descendants of soldiers of fortune or conquerors' right-hand-men. Many came from Hunza or Nagar, where the people are much more enterprising and less docile than the Baltis, who seem never to have produced a leader of their own.

De Fillipi succinctly describes the final destruction of Balti independence, if one can call it that. 'In a succession of campaigns between 1834 and 1840 Zorowar Singh and his Sikh army had conquered Ladak for his liege lord Gulab Singh, first Maharajah of Kashmir; a pretext for attacking Baltistan was not hard to find. It was furnished by the quarrel between Ahmed Shah and his first-born son Mohammed Shah, whom he had cut off from the succession. Zorowar Singh espoused the cause of the deposed heir, and invaded Baltistan towards the end of 1840 with an army of 15,000 men.

Some of the Ladakis fought on his side, others who had remained faithful to the old regime joined Ahmed Shah. But the climate itself was the best ally of the king of Skardu; the Indus, too, was unfordable, and its bridges broken; altogether the expedition came near to ending in disaster. An early winter found the Sikh army still on the right bank; hunger and cold soon made their position critical. Many of them lost hands or feet through frost-bite. A column of men sent up towards Shigar from Khapalu in the Shayok valley fell into an ambush, and of 5,000 men it is said that only 400 survived. But at last the army succeeded in crossing the Indus on the ice. They surprised and routed the Balti defenders. Ahmed Shah took refuge in the fortress of Skardu, but was soon obliged to surrender. His son Mohammed was set upon his father's throne; but of course the little country lost its independence for ever. Ahmed Shah and his favourite second son, at the head of a contingent of Balti soldiers, had to follow Zorowar Singh when he set out to conquer Tibet – an expedition which ended disastrously with the slaughter of the leader and the destruction of his army. Ahmed with his son was captured by the Tibetans and ended his days at Lhasa, where he was treated with respect and kindness. With the accession of Gulab Singh as Maharajah of Jammu and Kashmir, Skardu became the official capital of Baltistan, which, with Ladak, was added to the new kingdom (1846).'

His ruler's identity might seem of little consequence to the ordinary Balti, but in fact the cruel avarice of the Dogras made itself felt even in these impoverished valleys. Moreover, the Dogras were Hindus and altogether out of sympathy with their Muslim subjects. They are still hated and their barbarities and injustices are repeated from father to son. During this period the Baltis were strictly forbidden to kill cattle and though not many of them could ever afford to do so they bitterly resented this imposition of Hindu taboos. The British influence helped only a little to curb Dogra tyranny. Baltistan and Ladak were both administered by a high Kashmiri functionary, the Wazir-i-Wazarat. (And usually 'e waz, too.) Under him were two Tahsildars, one stationed at Kargil and the other at Skardu. The British government was represented in the two districts by an English official stationed at Leh and subordinate to the Resident of Kashmir. But in such a region one Englishman could do little to defend the Baltis from numerous petty Dogra officials who knew that their superiors cared nothing for the rights of inarticulate peasants. When the Dogra Maharajah of Kashmir acceded to the Indian Union in 1947 the entire Muslim population of these Northern Areas revolted spontaneously and insisted on being considered part of Pakistan. They won their point and by international convention Baltistan is now regarded as Pakistani territory.

SKARDU, 13 JANUARY

Today we went to the Post Office with three instalments of diary for registration but on entering the building my nerve failed me and I took them home again. I have dealt with some bizarre P.O.s in my time, but Skardu's has an air of not believing in itself which is demoralizing because so logical. The last mail came in ten days ago and the next may go out in two or three or five weeks' time, so naturally there is an aura of unreality about the place. One moronic young clerk – perhaps merely stupefied by boredom – squatted in a corner wrapped in a red-brown blanket and morosely cracking walnuts. He looked just like a squirrel. I couldn't send off my postcards, which I would have entrusted to the System as a test case, because there were no stamps available, pending the arrival of the next plane at some remote future date. This institution was established by the British and seems physically unchanged, in every particular, since its opening a century ago. But now the reliable Mail Runners have been largely superseded by capricious aeroplanes so it has given up the struggle to be efficient.

From the Post Office we continued west into the New Bazaar; it struggles for half a mile with the only stretch of tarred road in Baltistan. We stood transfixed with astonishment on coming to it. 'This is like London!' exclaimed Rachel, a trifle hyperbolically. Most of the new stalls that line the road (a dual-carriageway) are either closed for the winter or as yet unoccupied, and a few have already collapsed under the weight of recent snow. Half-way up the street is a stone column surmounted by a bronze eagle looking down on his prey; it commemorates the many Baltis who died fighting for the right to join Pakistan.

To new arrivals from Thowar, Skardu seems truly metropolitan, yet its range of merchandise is limited. There are some totally unexpected items – Imperial Leather soap, Parker pens, Rothmans cigarettes – but these have either been sold off by expeditions or imported from Landicotal. In the Old Bazaar, where most of the trading is done, the many small stalls carry virtually identical stocks – bales of cheap cotton, a sack of rice, a few sacks of pulse, a sack of sugar, tinned milk from various countries, tinned ghee from Denmark, tea, possibly a few onions, cigarettes, matches, trinkets, bars of soap, tin kitchen utensils, 'Tibet' cold cream, mouldy biscuits at Rs.5 for six ounces, rock salt, plastic footwear, exercise books and ink so inferior as to be unusable (I speak this evening from experience). Almost everything is of the worst possible quality but nothing is cheap. I sought in vain for meat and eggs, and even the ubiquitous tea-houses are rare here because a cash economy is new to Baltistan. Moreover, the few we did locate are closed at present: no Balti Shiah would do anything so frivolous as drinking tea in public during these *Muharram* days of deep mourning. Food-wise Hallam came off best with a seer of pulses, which he greatly relishes, and a bale of good sweet hay. It seems odd to be feeding high-quality red lentils to a *ghora* but no grain is to be had at any price. His treat is a lump of beautifully glittering pink rock-salt, which he crunches with a look of ecstasy.

One cannot fairly judge the collective personality of the Skardu citizenry during *Muharram*. This annual season of mourning may be likened to a medieval Lent taken very, very seriously. The majority of Baltis are Shiah Muslims, who venerate the descendants of the Prophet by his daughter Fatima and regard Sunni Muslims as phoney. (Most Pakistanis are Sunni.) *Muharram* is celebrated by Shiahs all over the Islamic world to mourn the deaths of their revered martyr Hussain of his small son and his relative Hassan. Hussain was the second son of Ali, the son-in-law of Mohammed, who was killed at Kerbela on 10 October 680 while fighting the army of the Sunni Caliph Iasid.

During the ten days preceding the *Muharram* procession no merriment – or even relaxation – is considered proper. No smoking, no gambling, no sex, no listening to a transistor (should you happen to have one), no eating big meals even if such could be conjured up in Skardu in January, no frivolous chatting in tea-houses, no foot-polo for the children, no laughter for anybody. As a result the whole silent town has at present a brooding, tense, rather sullen atmosphere. The comparatively few citizens to be seen in the bazaars look grim and often unfriendly. They are always male; Skardu women rarely leave their domestic territory, which explains why I get some hostile sideways looks from those who have correctly diagnosed my sex. To them a bare-faced woman wandering through their town during the season of austerity and abstinence must seem devil-sent.

The population of Baltistan (about 200,000) is very mixed. Fearsome as these valleys are, they have for millennia been important channels of communication – for lack of anything better – between different empires and cultures. Their present cut-offness is new, brought about by the exigencies of modern politics and the development of air transport, and walking through the bazaars today we saw faces that could have been Irish, Tibetan, Arab, Russian, Afghan, German, Kashmiri, Punjabi, Italian: there is no type one instantly picks on as 'typically Balti'. Yet most Baltis obviously belong to that far-flung anthropological category known as the 'Eurapoid group', which includes most West Asians and a number of North African peoples. In 1880 Roero di Cortanze was the first to note that the Baltis are on the whole 'of the Caucasian or white race, in contradiction to the Ladakhis, who are Mongols and copper-coloured'. But naturally there is a pronounced Mongoloid strain and as far as our observations went today the Tibetan-type Baltis are the poorest of all. A persisting tradition in the Skardu and Ronda areas says that the aboriginal Baltis were Aryan Dards who gradually became fused with various groups of Mongol invaders. But what astonishes me is the number of distinct *unfused* types to be seen here, despite the fact that there has been little recent migration into these valleys.

Today I have again been assured, for about the sixth time, that all Baltis are not as poor as they seem. While living in hovels and wearing rags some may have a fortune buried under the floor, and the old British Rs.400 note quite often turns up in Skardu, though it has not been legal tender for years past. But I still find it hard to believe that there are many rich Baltis.

SKARDU. 14 JANUARY

This morning we set off with Hallam to explore the far side of the Rock, going first through the Chasma and New Bazaars and then out along the Gilgit track for half a mile. To skirt the western end of this extraordinary mountain we followed a broad sandy path across a snowfield with the grey slope of the 'liner's' bows towering above us. We met many little groups of bent men wearing tattered homespun gowns and carrying eighty-pound loads of firewood (mainly mulberry) tied to their shoulders with yak-hide thongs. The majority had conspicuous goitres and several were dwarfs – scarcely bigger than their load – and/or cretins. Ahead was a jumble of rugged, lowish peaks (about 12 or 13,000 feet) and when we topped a slight rise we saw the Indus, broad and slow, between us and those mountains. On their lower slopes are a few hamlets from which the wood-carriers had been punted on *zhak* – rafts of inflated goat- or yak-skins, to which planks are tied.

Where our path descended, to curve around the Rock, Rachel dismounted and I led Hallam while we were investigating the equestrian possibilities of the route. Then we turned a shoulder of the mountain and before us lay the mile-wide confluence of the Shigar and the Indus – seemingly a turquoise lake, from which the snowy northern face of the Rock rises sheer. And beyond the rivers, to north and east, were giant peaks like great white scars on the intensely blue arc of the sky. We walked on until the path became unhorseworthy, and the silence, beauty and peace on that 'forgotten' side of the Rock reduced even Rachel to wordlessness for about three minutes.

Before turning back we rested on a boulder where we could look straight down a sparkling white slope into the Indus and watch it being augmented by snow melting off the foot of the mountain. I remember that was one of those 'special' moments which unfailingly bring out the animist in me. Sitting there beside one of the greatest rivers of the earth, at the foot of some of the greatest peaks, it seemed entirely natural to worship the power and the glory of water and rock.

When we got back to the sandy track Rachel remounted: and that was the last I saw of my daughter for an hour and a half. Watching Hallam disappear over a rise at a reasonable trot I thought nothing of it, expecting them to wait for me nearby, but when I topped that rise they were already far away. I immediately assumed that Hallam had bolted. Then, focusing better across the undulating snow, I saw that far from his being out of control Rachel was using her switch on his rump like a jockey coming up to the finish. As they disappeared over another rise I yelled ridiculously, 'Rachel! Stop! Rachel!' And besides me the great grey wall of the Rock echoed – 'Achel!'

I walked on at my normal speed, seething with rage and sick with anxiety. This sort of caper is all very well on a soft sandy track where there is no traffic, but how was Rachel going to cope if she met a military jeep being driven by some lunatic young conscript at sixty m.p.h.? Hallam is intelligent and responsible, but also quite highly-strung: and no Balti animal is at ease with motor-traffic. I noted from the depth and setting of his hoof-prints that he had galloped all the way. Approaching the jeep-track I looked desperately for the black riding-hat and scarlet snow-suit – and then came my worst moment, when I saw what appeared to be a *riderless* Hallam. Almost at once I realized that it was in fact a cow of the same colour, but the bad moment had lasted long enough to make me tremble. During the long walk into and through the New Bazaar I saw scarcely anybody and began to feel reassured; had she been thrown and injured someone would have been searching for me. Then at last I saw the pair of them in the distance, waiting near the Old Bazaar, surrounded by a puzzled crowd. Even from a distance I could tell that Rachel was feeling inordinately pleased with herself. 'Hello, Mummy!' she called over the heads of her bewildered entourage. 'You took a long time to catch up – we've been waiting *ages*! I hope you weren't worried?' 'Of course I was,' I said sourly, repressing all the other things I wanted to say. 'I was afraid you might be,' said she, showing the belated beginnings of remorse. 'But I've discovered galloping is much easier than trotting! And Hallam was very good when two jeeps passed, so you were silly to worry, weren't you?'

'No,' I replied crisply. 'He might not have been very good – or the jeep-drivers might not. *You* were silly, not me.' But despite this snub she continued to expatiate on the delectable sensation of galloping as we proceeded homeward.

SKARDU. 15 JANUARY

Last evening I opened our one remaining tin of Pindi Complan and found it very mouldy; but with my usual parsimony, reinforced by hunger, I attempted a mugful against Rachel's advice. It tasted so repulsive that I was forced to give up, though not before drinking enough to cause havoc within. This morning, having fed Rachel and imbibed tea, I only wanted to crawl back into my bedding. I felt poisoned, and no doubt to some mild extent I was.

However, I had recovered sufficiently by eleven o'clock to accompany Rachel on Hallam six miles up the valley towards Khapalu. Here the landscape is wilder and more broken. At the base of the mountains, grey and black boulders stand gauntly in deep snow, interspersed with occasional large thyme-clumps or juniper bushes. Then come level white stretches – probably fields – often surrounded by Connemara walls and with orchards nearby; and there are unexpected 200-feet deep cleavages in the soft earth, which necessitate long detours. Some of these cracks must be recent since the old track runs to the edges on both sides. For much of the way the Indus is again visible, far below. As it wanders mildly in its deep, wide, gravelly bed it seems quite unrelated to that rollicking torrent which forces its way through the Gorge. At river-level lines of poplars and willows look like toys and make one newly conscious of the scale of the landscape. Beyond the Indus stretch miles of pale brown sand-dunes, beautifully wind-moulded, and from these rise two more isolated, oblong rock mountains, not quite as high or long as *the* Rock but scarcely less dramatic.

We passed through two hamlets where an appalling number of the visible inhabitants had goitre; and many of the inhabitants were visible, sitting on their roofs enjoying the midday warmth while they pounded apricot kernels, or spun wool, or wove lengths of blanket. Both men and women greeted us cheerfully and seemed either temperamentally more amiable than the folk of Skardu town or less oppressed by *Muharram* privations.

On the outskirts of the town a little building stands on its own in the snow not far from the hospital, with 'Goiter Clinic' writ large over the door. It was built a few years ago but has not yet been opened. This is typical of Skardu, where those with worthy ambitions to improve things for the locals repeatedly find themselves thwarted by inter-related staff/communications/transport problems.

We managed our equestrian affairs more rationally today, arranging that Rachel could go ahead of me for half a mile or so, but must pull up and wait. Tedious for her and Hallam, but one can't have one's young permanently out of sight.

On the way home I suddenly felt very weak, thirsty and hungry; but the two tiny tea-houses we passed had neither tea nor food. Then, when I went to put the kettle on, our dratted stove played us up and had to be dismantled. When I had broken two fingernails, while trying to adjust the intractable wicks, Rachel observed maliciously, 'You're using a lot of new words today.' And after all that the small kettle took forty minutes to boil. New wicks are indicated.

SKARDU. 16 JANUARY

This has been the sort of day that would drive one to screaming point at home; but here, because everyone is completely indifferent to time, it was positively relaxing.

We were told that kerosene would be available at the Government Supplies Depot in the New Bazaar at eleven o'clock, so off we went at ten-thirty to join a patient throng bearing every imaginable sort of container – including a chipped enamel chamber-pot the origins of which I studiously investigated. I should have been able to guess that it once belonged to a touring British Official.

As we sat in the sun near a tethered Hallam, we were approached yet again by a harassed-looking young policeman who has been haunting us for days. Abbas Kazmi has repeatedly assured him that our passports are in order, our characters unblemished and our motives of the purest, but he still seems to feel it his duty to throw doubts (most politely) on the legality of our presence in Baltistan. To allay the poor man's anxiety I offered this morning to show our passports to the Chief Superintendent for Baltistan and the relieved young P.C. arranged to meet us at 3 p.m. outside Police Headquarters.

At 12.40 the Depot opened and we were informed that tomorrow we must go to the Office of Government Supplies and fill in an application form in triplicate for a ration of subsidized kerosene. So on the way home we borrowed a gallon from Abbas Kazmi, who always seems able to solve our problems. There is no unsubsidized kerosene left in the bazaar and without our stove we could scarcely survive: these are the very coldest weeks of the year.

At 2.55 I was tethering Hallam to a verandah-post outside Police H.Q. and at 3.45 our young P.C. friend appeared to explain that the Chief had not returned to his office after lunch – so would we please come back at 11 a.m. tomorrow.

We then went for an hour's walk/canter and got home just before the night cold took the valley in its vice-like grip. On the way I tried unsuccessfully to buy some form of bread; food was much more plentiful in remote Thowar. Here the population has recently been artificially increased by an influx of Pakistani government officials and their staffs and sometimes their families – not to mention the military, who cannot have *all* their food airlifted in, though they try to be as self-sufficient as possible. However, Skardu is best for Hallam's fodder and he is responding well to a good diet. He doesn't look any fatter, but there is little in common between the wreck who dragged himself out of Thowar and the spirited steed who now goes streaking towards the horizon at a touch of Rachel's switch.

SKARDU. 17 JANUARY

Sadiq Ali visits us regularly every morning, often accompanied by one or more friends, relatives and neighbours. The locals say we are the first foreigners to have wintered here for over forty years, which may or may not be true. Certainly we are a novelty, the more so as we do not live aloofly in our own camp or in the Rest House, but are available for inspection at all times. Our door can be bolted from inside as well as padlocked from outside, but I have never yet used the bolt, even at night. (What greater tribute could be paid to the essential friendliness and goodness of the Balti atmosphere? One feels completely safe going to sleep at night in an open house.) In such places as this the foreigner must choose an extreme: either to live in the sort of isolation traditionally associated with Western travellers or to integrate and forget about privacy. In Hindu communities the latter course is difficult because of caste taboos, as I found in both Nepal and South India, but in Muslim lands there are no such barriers. The prolonged and often silent scrutiny of unknown chance callers can be very trying, yet it would be churlish to begrudge these wide-eyed visitors the pleasure they get from watching me washing-up, or brushing my teeth, or polishing the tack, or reading to Rachel, or peeling onions to give some air of reality to our packet soups.

De Fillipi remarked that 'By nature the Balti is . . . of a timid disposition with a mixture of respect and fear but without servility towards the European'. He is so without servility that when I go off to fetch my morning bucket of water it occurs to none of my breakfast-time callers – sitting warming their hands at the stove – to offer to fetch it for me. But in fact I like this attitude of leaving me to fend for myself; there is no unkindness implicit in it and that is how I want to live here.

Sadiq Ali is full of good advice which he somehow manages to get across in Balti. For complicated explanations he enlists a nephew, Mohammad Ali, who speaks a little English with an effort painful to watch. Mohammad Ali is nineteen, spotty and ambitious; he has light brown hair, hazel eyes, a too-pale face and crooked teeth. Having had some contact with mountaineering expeditions he wants to migrate down-country where he believes he can get 'best-paid job in office'. I have been trying to dissuade him from quitting his job here – he works in some recently-imported government department – because with a Skardu education he could not possibly get any job down-country. His ambition, however, is not uncommon. While the Pakistanis pine to escape to England or America, an increasing number of young Baltis pine to escape to Pakistan.

Sadiq Ali – with his crinkly, tanned face, blue eyes and concern lest Hallam feel cold at night – reminds me of an undersized, bow-legged, horsey Irishman. He has insisted on lending us a ragged but still useful horse-blanket and he frequently brings us gifts of dried apricots and mulberries, mingled with a few tiny raisins and walnuts. He also buys Hallam's fodder – undoubtedly a profitable occupation – and has even managed to locate a source of precious barley. His morning visits normally last about an hour; then he wanders off to his winter job, which is in the Government Supplies Office near the Police Bazaar, where we too were going this morning in quest of our kerosene chit.

The office is part of the old British administrative headquarters and everything is falling to bits – doorways, windows, floorboards. All is twilit, crowded and confusing, with staff and visitors wrapped in blankets and huddled around wood-stoves and files hanging out of disintegrating cupboards. But Sadiq Ali soon found the man we needed, a charming Gilgiti who conjured efficiency out of chaos, handed us our chit within five minutes and then entertained us to lukewarm tea, decaying biscuits and intelligent conversation.

So far so good – but would the kerosene depot be open again today? Nobody was sure: peons were sent running to other offices to enquire: finally the Gilgiti said he thought not, this being Friday. Therefore we went next to the Police H.Q. – another old and shaky structure – and were greeted in the Chief Superintendent's office by a most delightful elderly character with a courtly manner who proved to be a brother of the deposed Mir of Nagar. He and I had more lukewarm tea, while Rachel flirted with delighted recruits on the parade-ground, and he explained in startling Cambridge English why the local police are so worried by our visaless passports and eccentric insistence on touring alone in mid-winter on foot. A few government departments in Islamabad have got their lines badly crossed. On the one hand the Northern Areas police have been ordered to treat all foreigners with suspicion and double-check their visas and permits. On the other hand the Ministry of Tourism has decided that foreigners are not to be discouraged from visiting Pakistan's chief tourist attraction by the necessity of obtaining permits. Moreover no one has bothered to tell these misfortunate unlettered young constables, most of whom have never even been to Gilgit, which nationals do *not* require visas to enter Pakistan. No wonder they fret about us settling near their sensitive borders for the winter. The remarkable thing is that they have been so consistently polite and co-operative, when in their eyes I practically qualify for handcuffs. They have been put in a most invidious position, from which they should be quickly extricated. This can easily be done by requiring tourists to obtain permits – a standard procedure nowadays, to which no reasonable traveller could object unless frustrating delays were involved.

From the Police H.Q. we proceeded to the P.W.D. H.Q., about two miles away towards the southern mountains. Because of imported bureaucracy we need a chit from the Chief Civil Engineer, authorizing the chowkidar of Satpara Rest House to admit us for three nights. As the Chief Engineer has gone to Gilgit (his native place), we were sent a furlong up the track to the office of the Assistant Engineer, who had just left to say his Friday prayers. We are to return at 10.30 a.m. tomorrow, since the five-day-week has not yet arrived in Skardu. But this means postponing our departure for Satpara.

A bazaar hunt for new stove-wicks occupied the next hour. Then I was unable to insert them, so we went to call on Abbas Kazmi, our all-purpose saviour, only to find that he too had gone to the mosque. However, we were invited in by his next-door neighbours, the Sadiqs, an endlessly hospitable family who have already several times entertained us and now seem like old friends. Mr Sadiq is stout, jovial and very busy, being President of the local Pakistan People's Party (Mr Bhutto's party). His nine handsome, healthy, charming children dote on Rachel; they range from a grown-up daughter to a cherubic four-year-old nicknamed Apollo. Mrs Sadiq is President of the women's branch of the P.P.P. and works hard to arouse feminine interest in regional developments and improvements. But I find it hard to believe that she is achieving much, or that the average Balti male would wish her to. She looks like the more fine-boned type of Spanish beauty and is warm-hearted and competent, with a dry sense of humour that quickly becomes apparent though she speaks no English.

There was a newcomer in the family circle today, a strikingly handsome woman who looks about twenty but has five children including an elegant son as tall as herself. She it was who volunteered to put in my new wicks and when Abbas Kazmi returned from the mosque he introduced her as Mrs Sadiq's niece and the wife of the newly-appointed Assistant Commissioner for Baltistan.

In a warm, sparsely-furnished room, crowded with people of all ages but dominated by Apollo, we had tea and slices of homemade cake – which rare delicacy aroused our uncontrollable enthusiasm, though normally neither of us eats cake. By then the Assistant Commissioner had joined us; he is a youngish man, from the Kharmang valley and no less congenial than his wife. It was 3 p.m. when we left and anywhere else these people would certainly have invited us to lunch. But here not even the most prosperous householder can easily feed unexpected guests.

I make a habit of fetching water at sunset and as I set out with my bucket this evening the snow-laden valley was already full of pale dusk. Beside the stream a few poplars and willows stood blackly against a cold greenish sky and in the near distance the Rock loomed huge and dark and strangely purposeful. Then unexpectedly to north and east the highest summits briefly reflected a pink-orange-copper glow; and for a few unforgettable moments those peaks seemed detached from their own massive shadowy bulks – islands of radiance, floating far above the twilit world.

6

Pain and Grief

> . . . we are not ourselves
> When nature, being opprest, commands the mind
> To suffer with the body.
>
> William Shakespeare

> The Balti is very gentle, never quarrelsome . . . Even so, I have
> seen this people completely transformed by religious fervour,
> displaying an immoderacy of passion unbelievable in a folk so
> paganly indifferent in their daily lives.
>
> Fillipo de Fillipi (1913)

SKARDU, 18 JANUARY

At last the inevitable has happened: an almost unendurable toothache
beyond reach of skilled care. When it started five days ago I
pretended it wasn't there – my usual formula for treating bearable
pain, the theory being that minor pains go away more quickly if
ignored. By last night, however, it had become abundantly clear that
in the present case stoicism is not the answer. This is my first ever
real toothache, as distinct from vague twinges, but today is Saturday
so I must wait until Monday for treatment. The hospital, which
includes the dental clinic, closes down from noon on Fridays to 9 a.m.
on Mondays. Odd behaviour for a hospital, but we *are* in Skardu . . .
However, I tell myself that things could be much worse – an infected
appendix for instance, or a broken spine.

After breakfast we went in search of our Satpara chit and for two
hours sat awaiting the Assistant Engineer in a tiny room where a
friendly group of P.W.D. officials were crowded around a stove.
Those who had studied engineering in Peshawar University spoke
adequate English and one young man – with shoulder-length wavy

brown hair, a mustard-coloured suede jacket and sky-blue knife-creased trousers – introduced himself as 'an electrical and telephonic engineer'. He volunteered the riveting information that Skardu's telephone system, which was installed by the British and still occasionally works, is the 1864 model. One wonders if any equipment installed anywhere in 1964 will still be working in 2075. He also told us that it costs four million rupees to import into Baltistan a generator worth three million. Even today the mountains are mighty. Of course we didn't get our chit. The Assistant Engineer had gone to – who knows where?

The minutiae of domestic life take up quite a lot of time here. Rock salt is well named and one buys it in large lumps: I spent thirty minutes this afternoon hammering half a seer into practical bits. Then I devoted an hour to carefully cracking our large collection of apricot stones, so that the nourishing kernels remained intact. My harvest was about half a pound, which the ravenous Rachel ate for supper. It was a choice between kernels and dahl, which she had already had for both breakfast and lunch. We finished our supply of imported food yesterday and because of the earthquake cannot now hope for those supplementary rations which Naseem was to have sent up by jeep.

This morning in the Old Bazaar we made what seemed at first sight a heartening discovery – four small toasted buns selling at twenty-five paise (two and a half pence) each. Unfortunately, however, they are too hard for Rachel's teeth and jaws to make the slightest impression on them: nor could I cope, in my present delicate dental condition. But as they are obviously several months old already they should keep for another few weeks. In the next tiny stall I found a curious yellowish-grey greasy substance which was full of hairs and grit but looked as though it might be edible. I cautiously tasted some and it is either goats' cheese or goats' butter – too strong for Rachel but I like it and bought half a pound for Rs.3. Now all I need is something to spread it on.

SKARDU. 19 JANUARY

Rachel spent today with the Sadiq children while Abbas Kazmi took me to visit Shakir Shamin, who has published a book of poems in

Urdu and was introduced as 'Baltistan's only author'. Shakir is engaged to the eldest Sadiq girl, which means that despite his being a close friend of the family he cannot at present visit their home unless his betrothed is away. He lives in a not-yet-completed bungalow about half a mile beyond the town where the land rises towards the high Satpara valley. There are several inoffensive new buildings on that slope, mostly government offices and the residences of senior army officers and civil servants.

Shakir is Director of Development Schemes for Baltistan, a comparatively well-paid, if frustrating, post. But neither money nor influence can procure more than the minimum of food at this season and lunch consisted of one small fried egg each, a dish of curried spinach between the three of us and six rounds of *roti*. Shakir repeatedly apologized for the meal though I was being perfectly sincere when I assured him that by current Murphy standards it seemed a banquet.

I have felt slightly ashamed of myself today. At times the nerve pain became so unbearable that I could not fully conceal it from my companions, who obviously thought me exceedingly effete to be so put out by such a commonplace and trivial affliction. I was reminded of the last lines of my favourite travel-book, when Eric Newby and his companion, after their short walk in the Hindu Kush, meet Thesiger and are dismissed by him as a couple of pansies. There was I, rather fancying myself as the hardy traveller roving through remote Baltistan – but the first touch of real pain has revealed me in my true colours as a degenerate product of twentieth-century over-civilization, accustomed to having the best possible medical treatment the moment anything goes wrong. Now I am in such hellish agony that I cannot write any more.

SKARDU. 20 JANUARY

Last evening Sadiq Ali told me that Skardu's Punjabi dentist, being averse to Balti winters, has long since gone home to Lahore; and I was not glad to hear that his understudy is a young Balti. This morning my ache was a few degrees less hellish and I considered leaving it to nature. But then I decided that that would be rash, when we are soon going into the wilds.

The Government Hospital – new but already grubby – is a rambling one-storey building staffed by the army, for lack of qualified civilians willing to live up-country. In the large, gloomy, empty hallway we were greeted by a handsome Punjabi sepoy, from the Corps of Engineers, who supervises the electricity supply when there is any. He said the dental surgeon would soon come and pointed down a long, silent, shadowy corridor to a protruding notice marked 'Dental'. When I rather tactlessly asked if the dental surgeon really was one he assured me that he had graduated last year from Lahore University and has documents to prove it. I then asked if there were any patients in the hospital – the stillness was uncanny – and the sepoy twirled his fine moustaches and said that mostly they had gone home for *Muharram* but would probably return afterwards.

Twenty minutes later we were summoned out of the waiting-room by an unkempt young man wearing several days' beard and a grubby *shalwar-kamiz*. Some underling, I assumed – and was considerably disquieted when he waved me into a streamlined but dusty dentist's chair, picked up an unshiny instrument with unclean hands and began to poke hesitantly around my mouth. As I indicated the seat of the pain I realized that he spoke no more English than a schoolboy in the bazaar, though English is the language of instruction in Pakistan's dental schools. I made a violent gesture signifying 'Yank it out!' but the 'dental surgeon' (he really must have inverted commas) shook his head while a fleeting expression of alarm crossed his face. At that moment five laughing young men erupted into the room and everybody exclaimed joyously, shook hands, embraced closely, kissed warmly and began an animated conversation while I sat forgotten, surveying the room and again recognizing Skardu's characteristic aura of unreality. The sleek German equipment seemed very up-to-date but there was no source of running – or even standing – water and I doubt if such equipment could ever be operated effectively on the available electricity supply. After a few moments, and without a glance in my direction, the dentist and his friends disappeared for a quarter of an hour. Rachel advised an immediate retreat, having not unreasonably concluded that our oafish friend had failed his examinations. But by then the whole scene had begun to have a certain macabre fascination for me and I longed to see how the situation would develop.

When Oaf returned he ignored my mouth and began to fumble uncertainly through cupboards. Eventually I saw that he was assembling the makings of a filling, and though I do not normally object to being drilled without an injection I now found the prospect unpleasing. But I need not have worried. Oaf said, 'Mouth big open!' and then clumsily stuffed something into a completely irrelevant crevice between the aching tooth and its neighbour. Much of the filling promptly disintegrated on to my tongue, causing a new kind of pain. When I yelped indignantly Oaf betook himself to a drawer and after much rummaging found a bottle of oily liquid which tasted vile as he applied it vigorously in an unsuccessful effort to remove the metallic deposit. This evening I have a very sore tongue, as well as a toothache. The rest of the filling fell out during the afternoon – naturally enough, as no cavity had been prepared to receive it.

Before we left, our well-meaning Oaf produced from some far recess six yellowed codeine tablets, a dozen oval brown pills and six capsules which, judging by their blotched complexions, have been grossly over-exposed to damp and/or heat. Another young man came in to tell me when to take these medicaments: obviously Oaf was loath to reveal the limitations of his English. As he was wrapping the pills in grimy pages from a schoolchild's discarded exercise-book two fell to the floor and he and I watched them roll away. But neither of us referred to the loss, thereby tacitly agreeing that it was of no great significance. When we got home I scrutinized the remainder and felt it might be wise to preserve them as antiques. Mercifully the slight improvement noted this morning is being maintained; probably some dying nerve has almost expired.

At noon we unearthed the Assistant Engineer in the Forestry Department H.Q. and got our Satpara chit. But we have been advised not to go to Satpara with less than two gallons of kerosene as fuel of any sort is very scarce there, and the present oil shortage is acute. Yesterday, in Shakir's house, we all sat in overcoats and mufflers since firewood is too dear now to be used before sundown. It would cost at least £14 a week to keep a small wood-stove burning moderately well all day and nobody here has that kind of money. Our own way of life – taking exercise from nine-ish until four-ish – is the most economical and effective heating-system.

Last night's snow fall was the heaviest of the winter and today the valley is laden with brightness. Yesterday I was struck by the fact that after *eight* days Skardu's previous snowfall was still pure and glittering, except along the very edge of the jeep-track. Where else in this polluted world would week-old snow in a town centre look newly fallen!

SKARDU. 21 JANUARY

Normal life in Skardu is now in abeyance, for these are the last days of *Muharram*. The feeling in the air reminds me of an Irish Good Friday.

This morning we got two gallons of kerosene from a sly Kashmiri hoarder for an outrageous Rs.34. He argued that since wood has gone up to Rs.50 a maund this was not excessive. But as we want to see the *Muharram* processions on the 23rd Satpara has been postponed to the 24th.

All day it was snowing lightly and when we went for a ride/walk towards the valley's southern wall ours were the only sounds and movements to disturb the stillness. From high above the town we gazed upon the whole length of Skardu's valley, through a silver curtain of pirouetting flakes – and then suddenly the deep silence of that white world of mourning was shattered by a passionate, semi-hysterical declamation from a mosque. This eerie sound seemed to tear at the peace of the valley, harshly vibrating across the bright snow and being caught and thrown back by the dark precipices behind us. It was a local version of the Shiahs' 'Passion Play', during which mullahs remind the faithful of what took place at Karbala, when Hussain was trampled to death under the hooves of horses, and his little son killed by a flying arrow, and his nephew mutilated and slain by the sword. To the Shiahs Hussain is a Christ-like figure, who atoned by his death for the sins of mankind. Shiahs also stress the pre-existence of Mohammed; the Prophet is said to have appointed Ali (his son-in-law and Hussain's father) as his successor a few days before he went *back* to heaven.

The Baltis are almost all Shiahs (except in the Shyok Valley), which seems odd when they are completely surrounded by Sunnis – in Kashmir, Pakistan, Gilgit and Chinese Turkestan. An ancient tradition attributes their conversion to four missionary brothers from Khorassan, whom one would expect to have been Shiahs. But it seems these brothers in fact converted them to the Nurbashi sect, which still flourishes in Khapalu and survives throughout the Shyok Valley. Then, it is said, the local rajas, noticing that the oldest and most aristocratic families of Kashmir were Shiahs (of Persian descent), themselves became Shiahs for snobbish reasons and were imitated by their people.

Today's dental development was the replacement of that indescribable nerve-pain by an extreme soreness which seems almost pleasant in contrast.

SKARDU. 22 JANUARY

Yesterday in the bazaar we met a handsome young army officer who introduced himself as Captain Doctor Haroon, a Kashmiri seconded to the Government Hospital. When we had chatted briefly about Balti problems he invited us to breakfast with him today in his living-quarters at the hospital, promising me some data on the new Rural Health Scheme – which I fear is but another humanitarian castle in the thin air of Baltistan.

At 9.30 a.m. we found the hospital as deserted as the town. A notice explained in several languages – none of which the average Balti could read – that the whole establishment closes down at week-ends and for public holidays and religious feasts; in other words, it is at present a statistic rather than a reality. However, Captain Haroon was awaiting us and I settled down to get as much information as possible from him. But within moments I had been made uneasy by his pawing of Rachel. One is accustomed to men and women alike affectionately kissing and cuddling her, but his fondling was different. And soon Rachel of her own accord took refuge from him on the far side of the room, though normally she likes nothing better than sitting on men's knees. He next tried to undress me on the pretext of examining my husky outfit: and when forced to desist he fetched a photograph album from his suitcase – portraying himself at every stage of development – and sat beside me on the charpoy with an arm around my shoulders and his face close to mine. Plainly he was at an advanced stage of sexual frustration and because of Rachel's presence I felt rather alarmed. When he began to kiss me frantically she was looking out of the window but, as I tried to stand up she turned to see me being pushed back on to the charpoy and rekissed even more frantically – an activity from which our host desisted only when I gave him a crack on the head with my *dula*. Rachel has described the incident much more succinctly in her own diary – 'A man kissed Mummy and she was very angry and I felt embarrassed'.

This incident would not have been worth mentioning had I been alone, but to behave thus in a child's presence was reprehensible – and utterly untypical of a Muslim. 'Damned impertinence!' I fumed aloud as we returned home. Rachel had by then recovered from her embarrassment and thought the whole thing a huge joke. 'But *why* did he kiss you?' she asked. 'Did he like you very much? Has he no wife to kiss? Why don't you get angry when men like Aurangzeb and Uncle Jock kiss you? Is it because they don't take so long? Would you hit them too if they did? I didn't like him either – *why* do you think he liked us so much?'

Then I, too, saw the funny side. A more unlikely sex object than myself at the moment it would be impossible to imagine. Unwashed for five weeks; in filthy shapeless garments; greying hair stiff with dust, sweat and grease; nails black and broken; hands like emery paper and cracked and bleeding; face so weather-beaten that I must look closer to seventy-three than forty-three – enough, one would have thought, to turn any man's mind towards celibacy as the lesser of two evils. It was not hard to forgive Captain Haroon. He has been posted to Skardu for two years and cannot bring his wife and young family to this fringe of civilization, and Skardu as yet has no red-light district. It is often assumed that in such situations Muslim men find their own sex amply consoling, but I doubt this. Although homosexuality is perhaps commoner and certainly more 'respectable' in Islamic societies than in our own, it does not follow that a man accustomed to a normal sex-life can become happily homosexual overnight. And I am told that any man who attempted to contact a Balti woman, married or unmarried, would soon get a knife between his ribs – despite the Baltis' reputation for gentleness. If this is so, times must have changed since de Fillipi reported sixty years ago – 'Balti girls marry at ten or twelve, and become mothers before they reach their full growth. There appears to exist also a sort of temporary marriage which may last from a week to several months, and is really a legalized prostitution. For the rest, adultery is common, by the connivance or at least the indifference of the husband.' Undoubtedly the marriage age has risen slightly, to fourteen or fifteen, and it may be that the husbands have become less permissive in reaction to the great numbers of unattached non-Balti males now loose in their land.

SKARDU. 23 JANUARY

When I woke last night to use our 'commode' (that same bucket in which water is fetched during the day: of such unsavoury details is domestic life in Baltistan compounded) – when I woke at midnight I heard in the distance sounds so uncanny that my skin prickled. Then I realized that this was merely the wailing and lamenting of Skardu's population, which stays up all night on the eve of *Muharram* preparing thus for the culminating ceremonies. In other parts of the Shiah world *Muharram* processions are often magnificent affairs, involving gorgeous pageants and elaborate rituals. But impoverished Baltistan knows no such pomp and splendour and, as a result, the central – mourning – purpose of the occasion is emphasized to an alarming extent. The only 'props' are multicoloured ragged silken standards, tied to long poles and borne in the centre of the procession, and a horse shrouded in a white cloth who carries on his saddle two turbans, symbolizing Hussain and Hassan. These must be of white material, interwoven with red to represent blood, and they are repeatedly touched by weeping mourners who then reverently pass their hands over their faces and heads.

Skardu's main procession starts soon after sunrise from the large village of Hussainabad, four miles east of the town, which we have twice visited in the course of our rambles. By 8.30 we were on our way to meet the mourners, walking through thin clouds of icy vapour as the sun lifted them from the Indus; the river's course was just visible, far below, marked by its own pearly mist. (Later on the weather was perfection: long hours of warm golden sunshine, a deep blue sky overhead, gauzy white veils draped around the summits and sparkling miles of snow in every direction.)

We approached Hussainabad across a flat, glittering snow-field broken by occasional gigantic black boulders. Then far away we heard rhythmic shoutings – 'O Hassan! O Hussain!' – accompanied by what sounded like muffled drums, their regular beat amplified by a sheer mountain-wall that rose from the plain nearby. When the procession at last appeared there was something unexpectedly touching about that minute patch of darkness on the snow. Man and his griefs seemed so puny and ephemeral, set between the colossal backdrop of those indifferent mountains and the timeless flow of the Indus. Yet only man has the power to keep alive the memory of fellow-beings who died 1300 years ago. Seen thus, today's procession of simple peasants, moving slowly across the valley's vastness, was a triumphant assertion of spiritual strength.

It was Rachel who first realized that the muffled, rhythmic thudding was being produced – incredibly – by the breast-beating of some fifty men at the centre of the procession. These were thumping their chests with all their strength, like angry gorillas, while gazing fixedly at the tattered banners and lamenting their murdered heroes. Many were naked from the waist up, though the temperature was still below freezing point, and already their chests were bruised and reddened. (The average Balti torso is as white as a northern European's, without even the Latin swarthiness.) Frequently the leading mullah halted the procession to declaim passionately and then the entire crowd – some 200 men, the majority quite young – breast-beat zealously, as though each were trying to prove that he could thump harder than his neighbour. We were standing on a rock-slab some ten yards from the edge of the track, where we could see all without getting in the way, and as the procession passed at a funeral pace no one even glanced in our direction though normally every Balti we meet stares at us intently.

We followed at a discreet distance, as the procession rapidly gathered strength. It must have numbered at least 500 when it left the track to cross a field three feet deep in snow. It was converging, with two other similar but larger processions from different parts of the valley, on a little mosque called 'The House of Wailing'. At every pause the mourners' grim refrain grew more frenzied. Now thousands of men were frantically drumming on their chests while chanting, 'O Hassan! O Hussain!' in voices hoarse and choking with grief. And faintly the mountains threw back those sacred names, seeming to fill the valley with muted, ghostly echoes.

As we were about to turn off the track towards The House of Wailing a scowling young policeman appeared and curtly ordered us home. I had already been assured by our good friend the Chief Superintendent that foreigners are allowed both to follow and to photograph these processions, so I firmly declined to be bullied. But in the tense atmosphere that has been built up by the last day of *Muharram* it seemed wisest to compromise, especially as the P.C. was fingering his *lathi* as though he longed to use it on the impious foreign females. Therefore we made a detour which took us out of sight of the irate P.C. but allowed us to keep The House of Wailing under observation. Throughout the day the many police on duty repeatedly tried to shift us from our chosen vantage points. Perhaps some were being protective towards us – *Muharram* crowds are notorious for turning nasty at the slightest provocation – but without doubt the majority personally resented our presence, whatever their Chief Superintendent may think.

We paused about 100 yards from The House of Wailing, into which each procession briefly took its banner and its horse, though most of its followers could not squeeze into the small building. They stood outside, some leaning exhausted against the wall, others continuing to chant and chest-bash with undiminished vigour. As we were waiting I decided to photograph Rachel on Hallam and at once, misunderstanding my target, six small boys, wearing curiously adult expressions of rage, began to pelt us with pebbles and to try to throw snow at the camera. So I quickly put it away.

We next made for the Police Bazaar to watch the united

processions passing towards their final destination – a mosque near the New Bazaar. But this was a point at which for some reason trouble was expected, either between rival factions of mourners or between the mourners and the down-country security forces. We therefore found ourselves amidst a concentration of senior army officers, armed troops, senior police officers and P.C.s with *lathis*. The Chief Superintendent was sitting on a shooting-stick trying not to look flustered; he is a sensitive, gracious, bookish gentleman, not at all suited to controlling riots. He advised us to go ahead of the procession for another mile or so, past the Chasma Bazaar, and there to climb a low hill from which we could observe it in safety.

Having tethered Hallam to a tree in the sun, well away from all the excitement, we sat on the hilltop to await developments. When the procession reappeared an hour later, in four groups, it must have consisted of about 3,000 men. The expected trouble had not broken out but even from our hilltop the sight of that distraught mob seemed slightly ominous. We descended to track level and saw that now many men had stripped to the waist. Their battered chests were the colour of mashed raspberries – but still their arms were being flung up and brought down with all possible force on heaving rib-cages, to produce that unforgettable drum-like effect. Other mourners were scourging their own naked backs – literally tearing off strips of flesh – or were cutting their scalps, necks and chests with knives or razor-blades, so that blood poured down their torsos. As the joint procession slowly moved forwards, halting frequently, the whole valley reverberated with the chanting, moaning, roaring, shrieking and groaning of these demented creatures who had worked themselves into a state of insensate grief. And much as I admire many aspects of Islam I found myself being switched off by this display.

At the foot of the hill a few score veiled women were standing some yards away from the track and others were hurrying to join them – groups of four or five stumbling over the whiteness on one of their few outings of the year, holding brown shawls across their faces with one hand and with the other trying to keep gaily-coloured pantaloons out of the snow. (The burkah is not worn by Balti women.) To watch the procession's ultimate stage we joined a gathering of women on part of a disused aqueduct that bridges the track. It felt odd to be amongst so many women in a region where they so rarely appear. In their extremity of grief most soon dropped their veils from ravaged, tear-swollen faces, and as they gazed at their frenzied menfolk they struck their temples with clenched fists and sobbed uncontrollably. Had their own children just been murdered they could not have displayed more heartfelt and devastating anguish.

One Hussainabad youth, whom I had first observed at 9 a.m., looked on the point of collapse as his section of the procession passed below us. It was now 2.15 p.m. and he had almost scalped himself. The skin hung in strips from his shaven head and his back was criss-crossed with ugly red welts, oozing new blood, while his chest was covered with darker dried blood. His eyes were glazed but still he kept on breast-beating like an automaton and shrieking hoarsely. There were several others in as bad a state or worse; two unconscious figures had been dumped at the side of the track. None of these 'extremists' had Mongolian features, which may not be a coincidence.

A perilous degree of mass-tension had been generated by this stage and when I photographed one of the horses a woman beside me tried to seize my camera, struck me hard across the face and screamed abusively at me. Luckily Rachel did not notice this incident. She happened to be talking just then to three young government clerks from Lahore – Sunnis, who were watching the proceedings with the smugly appalled expressions that some Irish Catholics wear while watching an Orangemen's parade on the Twelfth.

I now decided that we had observed enough. During the last lap many men whip themselves to the limit of their endurance, and sometimes beyond, but I felt no eagerness to witness that crescendo. And Rachel would have been badly frightened had some section of the maddened crowd suddenly turned against the bare-faced female heathen.

On 11 December 1913 de Fillipi saw that year's *Muharram* procession in Skardu – it is a movable feast – and since then there seem to have been three major changes. He mentions a group of women preceding, or leading, the procession, whereas today the women merely watched and lamented on the side-lines. He also mentions two mock-biers – wooden frames covered with red material – being carried by bearers, one of whom was the Raja of Skardu 'arrayed in pure white wool'. But today there were no biers, and I have been told that the multi-coloured silk standards now serve not only as the focal points for each village's procession but as symbolic biers. Finally, de Fillipi observed no bloody flagellations, which he could scarcely have missed had the custom then been fashionable in Baltistan. Yet he noted that 'The spectacle of a whole population displaying such violent and immoderate despair is truly extraordinary. This grief and piety are so real and moving one forgets that it is all a play.'

I must admit that my own reactions were not so sympathetic. A decade ago they might have been, but in Ireland during the past several years we have had our fill of unbalanced religious fervour. And we have seen too many tragic results of emotionally dwelling on the past and keeping old grievances alive. I am not imputing to these innocent Baltis any of the viciousness of the extremist Catholic and Protestant thugs of my own country. But I cannot help thinking of the frightful consequences if such primitive, powerful religious feelings were harnessed by political agitators – as they so easily could be, among simple people.

On our way home I struggled to understand the 'truly extraordinary spectacle' we had just seen. Some critics, including many Sunni Muslims, assert that *Muharram* processions are simply a public indulgence in a sexual perversion; and they add that it is not safe for any woman to be out alone when the excited mobs disperse. But now, having seen a procession close to, I simply do not believe this. No doubt a few men are adversely affected, yet baffling as it is to us, and distasteful as we may find it, none can dispute the authenticity of the grief manifested today. Probably in Europe's Ages of Faith Christians felt similarly about Christ's sufferings and death.

SKARDU. 24 JANUARY

There seems to be some jinx on our getting to Satpara. This morning, when we were all packed up and ready to go, Hallam began to limp slightly on his near hind leg. Sadiq Ali thinks he knocked himself against a corner while entering or leaving his 'stable' and if this is so he should have recovered by tomorrow. After yesterday's unusually heavy foot-traffic the town's tracks and paths were like skating-rinks today. Bereft of her steed, Rachel was house-bound most of the time, thus wrecking my carefully calculated kerosene supply for Satpara. Entertaining her became something of a problem as she already knows by heart the four books in the junior section of our mobile library. When I went shopping there were many anxious enquiries about my *bungo* and *ghora*; some people feared that the latter had run away with the former. I got home to find that the said *bungo*, crazed by boredom, had embarked on *War and Peace* and grimly battled her way to the top of page six, understanding perhaps half the words en route.

Although no more kerosene was available I have decided that if Hallam is fit we really must leave for Satpara tomorrow and chance freezing to death on the lakeside. I bought a seer of rice to vary our present ration of dahl and onions three times a day, followed by tea and apricots – a sensationally wind-making diet. Dahl is far more nourishing than rice but I thought we had better dilute it before Sadiq Ali's little house is blown to bits.

7

A Veterinary Interlude

The springs of enchantment lie within ourselves: they arise
from our sense of wonder, that most precious of gifts, the
birthright of every child.

Eric Shipton

Animals are such agreeable friends – they ask no questions,
they pass no criticisms.

George Eliot

SATPARA. 25 JANUARY

When I walked Hallam to the stream at sunrise he appeared to be
moving normally and by 9.30 we were on our way. The track was two
feet deep in crunchy, squeaky snow, and the thin, dry, cold air had that
exhilarating quality which makes one rejoice simply to be alive and
footloose. A violent glare made tinted goggles necessary until we
reached the narrow Satpara Gorge. From the edge of the Skardu Valley
the track descends abruptly to river-level between sheer, jagged
mountains, and then climbs towards the high moraine that closes the
mouth of the Satpara Valley. In the sun we felt almost warm but out of it
the air seemed to freeze our very lungs. The Satpara River falls 1,300
feet in less than six miles and is noisy out of all proportion to its winter
volume; the only sound we could hear was its roar – and sometimes an
echo of that roar, weirdly resounding where cliffs overhang the track.
The riverbed boulders were beautifully encased in glittering ice and
wore ermine capes of snow, and when we lifted our eyes to the heights
we saw peaks like giant white swords, or colossal squared battlements,
filling the sky in every direction. We met nobody and observed no trace
of human or animal life; within that hidden gorge one feels totally
isolated from the rest of the world, despite Skardu's nearness.

The gradient was so severe, the path so icy and the terrain so fascinating that we took two hours to cover four miles. I thought of Fillipo de Fillipi, whose *Karakoram and Western Himalaya* I finished last night. He wrote: 'Walking is really the only kind of locomotion that puts us on equal terms with the world about us. Our modern mechanical methods of transportation tend to make us lose sight of our relative importance.' Thus, travelling on foot in 1975 is not the pointless eccentricity it may appear to be; when we 'lose sight of our relative importance' everything else in life becomes to some extent distorted. And 'mechanical methods of transportation' prevent one from forming a relationship with the landscape. The motorist can admire it, in a restricted and detached way, but a steep hill is merely an occasion for changing gears, a storm merely an occasion for shutting the window, a village merely an occasion for reducing speed. And yet with what alacrity do people like the Baltis avail themselves of motor transport, once it comes within reach! Soon there will be few people left, anywhere, who have not lost sight of their 'relative importance'.

On foot in Baltistan, one becomes increasingly aware of its landscape as a 'temporary arrangement'. This morning, walking up that short, steep, narrow valley, we were surrounded by the marks of recent violence and drama: everything seemed to have been born out of some cataclysm. Our whole visible world was a mad jumble of crags, cliffs, rocks, boulders, stones, pebbles and sand. In the river-bed detritus of all shapes and sizes had been flung down by avalanches to mix with enormous accumulations of alluvial deposits, and avalanche scars were plain to be seen on the awesome slopes beyond the river. From these slopes occasional stones broke loose even today, despite the intense frost, and bounded thousands of feet to the valley floor; and directly above the track were precipitous broken cliffs whose fractured façades promised further disintegration in the near future. Below the track some boulders were smooth and shiny – ancient works of Nature's art – while beside them lay gigantic sharp-edged chunks of rock, newly riven from their parent crags. The scene we looked on this morning has changed a great deal since de Fillipi looked on it in 1909, yet in geological terms sixty-five years are but an instant. As he himself wrote: 'Geological evolution is proceeding [in the Karakoram] . . . with such activity and on such a scale that nothing elsewhere can be compared with it.'

Just before Satpara Lake comes into view the steep climb ends and a few stunted willows and fruit-trees appear on the far side of the river, and then one small stone dwelling. By stages the lake was revealed: first a corner of dark shadowy water at the foot of a snowy slope – then a wider sheet of jade, with a low islet near the eastern shore – and finally the whole expanse, half a mile wide and a mile long, with not a ripple stirring its sheen of clear green as it reflected the snowy flanks of its guardian mountains. There was enchantment there, in the brilliance and silence of that noon hour, with golden light pouring from a dark blue mountain sky and the lake a steady mirror full of the beauty of glittering peaks. Rachel stood up in the stirrups, her face transformed with joy, and her delight helped to compensate for the hours of tedious chatter one has to endure in the company of a small child.

Evidently Satpara Lake was formed when a high moraine closed the valley's mouth. Its shape is unusual – almost rectangular, apart from two slight indentations on the east shore, in one of which is the new Rest House. Before continuing, we examined the remains of an ancient dyke on the north shore, some thirty yards from the track. The buttress is about sixteen feet high and there are many traces of what presumably were locks and floodgates. One local tradition says the dyke was built by the last Buddhist ruler of Skardu, who was slain by Mongol invaders. If this is true, the remains must be almost six centuries old. But a conflicting tradition attributes them to the last independent Raja of Skardu. However, it is known that until about 1885 the lock gates were decorated with Buddhist carvings on stone, which were carried off to Nepal by Buddhist troops serving in Skardu. The remains certainly look more than 130 years old and I gazed at them with some awe. In a land where Nature dominates so inexorably and Man seems incidental, existing only on sufferance, the traveller rarely comes on any enduring monument of human endeavour.

As we continued around the lake, some 100 feet above the water,

Hallam began to limp again. I knew the Rest House was close so we kept going and soon could see it below the track on a ledge overlooking the islet, which is only about 100 yards in diameter and boulder-strewn, with low shrubbery growing around its shore-line. Having unloaded and unsaddled Hallam I turned him loose. Normally he would have made straight for the few accessible clumps of thyme but today he began to wander around in circles, moving as though he had lost control of his hindquarters and repeatedly shaking his head. Tears sprang to Rachel's eyes and she hurried up the slope to fetch him nourishment. I wasn't feeling too happy myself, though it cheered me to see him eating what little thyme Rachel's small hands could wrench from the frozen earth. As I was tethering him to a mulberry tree, two young men emerged from a ruined dwelling that stood close to the Rest House and was the only other building in sight. I assumed one of them to be the chowkidar, but as they scrambled up a steep embankment I saw that both were barefooted and clad in loosely-associated patches of homespun cloth reaching to their bony knees. One was a semi-idiot and the other almost totally blind: definitely not chowkidar material, even in Baltistan. When they had been given time to digest our arrival the blind young man agreed to fetch the chowkidar and went off – guided by the semi-idiot – towards the solitary house we had passed near the mouth of the valley.

Half-an-hour later the chowkidar arrived and said Hallam would be dead by morning. He may well be right – I know too little about equine ailments to dispute the point – but the satisfaction he appeared to derive from making this announcement annoyed me intensely. In other ways, too, he is tiresome. He tried to persuade me to return to Skardu at once because of Hallam's imminent demise (an odd reason for making a horse walk another six miles), and he insisted that there was no stabling within reach, though I could see a roofed shelter attached to the broken-down shack. He also said there was no firewood available, and no water. When I replied that we have our own kerosene, and a whole lakeful of water on the doorstep, he was visibly put out. His reluctance to admit us to the Rest House made me suspicious: and sure enough, this new bungalow has no charpoys.

Clearly these have been appropriated for his own use during the winter season, when visitors of any kind are unheard of in Satpara, and I cannot say I blame him for this peccadillo; it was his evasiveness that irritated me. With luck our astronaut's blanket will preserve us from pneumonia.

I was about to demonstrate the adequacy of the next-door stable when the chowkidar's likeable brother arrived (probably a step-brother, since he looks at least twenty-five years older) and invited Hallam to a cosier stable down the road. So off we went, leaving the chowkidar sulkily fetching a tin of water from the lake. He is a young man much given to being put out and he had not approved of his brother's intervention, possibly because it has deprived him of a chance to overcharge us for hay.

To get to his lodgings Hallam had to ford the Satpara River, at this point a shallow, very fast stream scarcely ten yards wide. I crossed on a home-made 'bridge' of two thin, ice-coated tree-trunks, vaguely tied together, and as Rachel sensibly showed no desire to use this contraption I left her playing with king-sized icicles by the water's edge.

Our friend's dwelling, at the foot of an 18,000-foot mountain, had looked minute from the track, but seen close to it proved quite substantial in its primitive way. A few summer tourists must now visit Satpara annually, yet my advent sent the women and children fleeing indoors and a red-brown mastiff had to be intercepted on his way to my jugular vein – which is so wrapped up these days that his arrival would not have mattered very much. Coaxing Hallam into an unfamiliar stable was a more difficult task than usual, no doubt because of his indisposition, but once through the low, narrow entrance he enthusiastically made for his lunch. There is now a perceptible swelling on his near flank, but I feel that as long as he continues to eat well he is unlikely to expire as forecast.

Rejoining Rachel, I found that she had slipped into the glacial torrent and was soaked to the waist – a major disaster, when we have no clothes to change into and no means of drying anything, apart from our kerosene stove. She was suitably penitent – I had empha-tically warned her about this risk – but to my annoyance seemed to feel no retributive cold or discomfort on the way home. Small children are almost unbelievably durable. It was only 3 p.m. when we got back but we had to waste both kerosene and sunny hours drying her padded snow-suit trousers, flannel slacks, woollen tights, woollen stockings and fur-lined boots. The chowkidar, the semi-idiot and the blind man were all delighted to find our stove going and came to squat in a row against the wall while Rachel sat wrapped in our united bedding, morbidly drawing pictures of jeeps falling over precipices.

SATPARA. 26 JANUARY

Last night I was wakened by cold for the first time on this trip – not surprisingly, at 9,000 feet in mid-winter, lying on a concrete floor in a room with very ill-fitting doors and windows and a temperature 35° below freezing outside. An astronaut's blanket has its limitations. However, it did save me from being *kept* awake; I merely surfaced occasionally for long enough to register that I was not warm. Although the stove was burning all night a small lump of snow, deposited on our floor at 4 p.m. yesterday, had not even tried to melt by 7 a.m. today. Yet Rachel reported having slept soundly and snugly.

At 8 a.m. I set out to visit Hallam, leaving my daughter sitting up in her fleabag happily doing sums: by some genetic freak she *enjoys* arithmetic. Last night there was a heavy snowfall, and then it froze hard. The savagely cold early air hurt my face and the sky was completely clouded over – a pewter lid on the valley.

I found Hallam eating a hearty breakfast, though his swelling is larger. We would not in any case have worked him today as the track beyond the Rest House is no longer *ghora*-worthy. Nor is it *bungo*-worthy, the chowkidar informed me when I got back here. So I felt justified in setting off alone for Satpara hamlet, in search of kerosene. I had not reckoned with drying clothes and keeping the stove going all night.

By ten o'clock clouds were enclosing the whole valley in opaque walls of silver vapour. Then snow began to fall swiftly in minute, dry crystals and every moment the air grew warmer. The lake today was bottle green and the reflections of its guardian peaks were not the sharp 'photographs' of yesterday but pale smudges on the surface, like the ghosts of snowy mountains.

For two miles the icy track switchbacked along precipitous slopes; then it descended to a wide snowfield stretching from the shore of the lake to the head of the valley. Here the stones used to mark the track were not tall enough for present conditions and I was soon floundering about in three feet of fine, dry, sugary snow, which concealed many streams and the Satpara River (it flows through the lake). All these streams were frozen over and I used my *dula* to test the strength of the ice before committing myself to it. When I came on the unfrozen Satpara – hardly five yards wide – I crossed by an exquisitely beautiful but not very reliable-looking bridge of solid ice. Then I saw two small dark figures coming towards me across the whiteness, bent in a familiar posture that meant they were carrying firewood – the chief product of Satpara hamlet. I altered course to meet them, intending to use their tracks, and as we approached each other they looked so startled I thought for a moment they were going to drop their loads and run away.

Satpara is marked by the usual lines and groups of pale brown, leafless fruit-trees, sheltering grey stone hovels on a steep mountainside. As I struggled up an ice-covered path no sign of life was visible and one could imagine the place had long since been abandoned. Then three small boys came tentatively around a corner, clad in coarse homespun brown *shalwars* and ragged bits of blanket. They had pinched, lined, filthy faces and were poised for flight should I seem menacing. When I appealed for help they recovered their nerve and led me through a shadowed labyrinth under tall trees between huddled dwellings. Like all these settlements, Satpara is much bigger than it seems from a distance. The Baltis, accustomed for centuries to conserving their meagre arable soil, can squeeze an astonishing number of hovels on to a small rocky ledge, or build them on to almost vertical slopes in apparent defiance of the law of gravity.

We paused at the foot of a long, crudely-made step-ladder and one boy led me up to a five-foot-high doorway. Bending to enter, I stumbled over the raised stone threshold and fell on to the horns of a ruminating dzo. She made indignant noises as she scrambled to her feet and my guide gave an alarmed squeal; but she hadn't really taken umbrage and was in any case tethered to a roof-support. Half this room was filled with neatly stacked firewood and sweet-smelling hay. My guide beckoned me on through an even lower door into a dark, smoky living-room, very hot and crowded, where my head just touched the roof-beams when I stood erect. In the centre was a wood-stove and sitting cross-legged on the floor beside it was an elderly man, with a small face under a big turban, running up a *kamiz* on a sewing-machine. I peered around as the womenfolk shrank back against the wall, modestly drawing their cloaks over their faces and protectively clutching their whimpering small children. The tailor stared at me, unsmilingly, while continuing to operate his machine. When I held out my container and asked for kerosene he stood up, still without any change of expression, and led me through the lowest door of all into an adjacent cubby-hole – his 'shop'. It was stocked with two jerrycans of kerosene, half a sack of *ata*, four bars of soap, a cardboard carton of tea-dust, a bag of rock-salt and a small cluster of nylon socks hanging from a nail. (I fail to see the point of nylon socks in the Karakoram, but they have probably become a status symbol.) This, I felt, was as far from Harrods as one could get.

By now the news of my arrival had spread and as I held my container steady the room beyond filled with excited, curious youths. They jammed the tiny doorway, fighting to see me and talking rapidly in Shina, the Gilgit language. At some unknown date this settlement was either founded or conquered by Gilgitis and their descendants still speak Shina. The linguistic barrier has caused them to lead an exceptionally isolated life, even by local standards, and the consequent in-breeding has produced a type regarded by 'true' Baltis as undesirable.

When I left Satpara's Supermarket I was followed by the youths – a wild, tough-looking lot, all in brown homespun and disposed to jeer at the foreigner rather than to attempt conversation. They deliber-ately led me astray and laughed raucously when I found myself on the edge of an impassable chasm. Then they ran away, leaving me to rediscover the right path as best I could – an exasperating delay, for the snowfall had become much heavier and there is a limit to even Rachel's self-sufficiency. Back on the valley floor I searched for my own footsteps, but already these had been obliterated. However, I could more or less remember the route and I thoroughly enjoyed the return journey. There is nothing more solitary and soothing than a walk across a deserted landscape of undefiled whiteness, where the only movement is the silent dance of the snowflakes.

Near the Rest House I overtook the two firewood carriers, sitting on a rock, and with friendly grins they applauded my speed. But then I am not permanently undernourished (only temporarily), nor was I carrying sixty pounds on my back. When I had passed them it struck me that the only three people out in the valley today were all concerned with the basic Balti problem of keeping warm.

I got back at two o'clock to find that Rachel had just cut the thumb and forefinger of her left hand with a razor-blade, while trying to sharpen colouring-pencils. The place looked like a slaughter-house and I – typically – had left our First-Aid box (unopened since leaving London) in Skardu. Luckily the chowkidar arrived then and re-deemed himself by tearing a strip off his shirt-tail, burning it over the stove and rubbing the charred cloth into the cuts, which he then wrapped in tinfoil from his cigarette-packet. The St John's Ambu-lance Brigade might not approve but the patient is now comfortable. And so is Hallam, whom I visited after a late luncheon of dahl and salt. (The onion supply has petered out.)

SKARDU. 27 JANUARY

It snowed all yesterday afternoon and all through the night, and it was still snowing when I visited Hallam this morning. The western half of the lake was covered in ice which was covered in snow, and when I found that Hallam could move without limping I decided on an immediate return to Skardu lest we might find ourselves snow-bound with neither food nor fuel. Loading was extraordinarily difficult, standing thigh-deep in snow with numb fingers, and either through stupidity or ill-will nobody made the slightest attempt to help. But at last all the vital knots had been tied, Rachel was in the saddle and we were off.

I felt a strange sort of exhilaration as we moved slowly along the lakeside through that world of snow triumphant. All the angular, dark rocks were now curved mounds of pure white, all the few leafless trees were fairy-tale illustrations, all the slopes of grey shale were sheets of unflawed brilliance. And still it was snowing – the sort of gentle, subtle, casual fall that seems very slight yet blots out footprints within moments.

When we left the lakeside the track became almost impassable and every step of the way was difficult for Hallam and me. But we were in no hurry. I felt I never wanted to leave this magic valley where today all harshness was disguised and even the torrent was hidden by weird arcs and canopies and viaducts of snow – like the works of some demented sculptor – while the dazzle of sunless light made it seem as though the earth were illuminated from within.

We got home at 2.30 and as I was unsaddling Hallam Rachel gave a gasp of horror and pointed to his near flank: an abscess the size of a tea-plate had just burst and pus was oozing hideously through his thick winter coat. I pointed out to the stricken Rachel that the worst was now over, from Hallam's point of view, and while she gave him love and apricots I got the stove going and cooked a hot barley mash. Then Sadiq arrived and assured me that there is a good horse-doctor here, which information I received with some scepticism, remembering the quality of the human hospital. I'm not sure that a *ghora-hakim* can do much good at this stage – presumably one simply waits for nature to heal the wound – but I would like to have an expert's opinion on what caused it.

SKARDU. 28 JANUARY

Mercifully Nazir, the local 'animal dispenser', is some improvement on the local dentist. Having diagnosed an infected mongoose bite he said that Hallam must have a course of seven injections and advised a tonic to go in his barley mash. By the end of the course he should be fit for work. I observed that the expiry date printed on the injection box was November 1973 but as it cost only Rs.5 this is not surprising.

Apparently mongooses are plentiful here; they live in the roofs during winter and when they become frantic with hunger quite often attack animals, and even sleeping humans. Vampire-like, they suck blood from horses and cattle and these bites can quickly go septic, especially if the victim is below par. One night about a week ago Hallam made such a fuss during the small hours that I went out to see what was wrong but could find no cause for his alarm. I hope that mongoose was a visitor, not a resident.

Nazir is a Skardu man who was trained for six months in Lahore. He left school at fifteen, having passed no examinations, but he speaks adequate though halting English and is full of horse-sense and natural intelligence. Aged about thirty-five and powerfully built, he has a strong, square, honest face and no pretensions. Like most Baltis he is endearingly vague about the rest of the world and finds it hard to believe that not all countries are Muslim. He was astounded to hear that there are no Irish Muslims and that Irishwomen never veil their faces when they go into public places.

Both Nazir and Abbas Kazmi were distressed today about the news from Gilgit. The town is in a state of emergency, with telephone wires cut and a curfew imposed. At the end of the *Muharram* procession a gang of Sunnis attacked the Shiahs – there are many of both sects in Gilgit – and the police and army had all they could do to separate the mobs. According to Abbas Kazmi, the Gilgitis' latent sectarian animosity is being used by political agitators. Home Sweet Home!

One becomes increasingly food-obsessed here and I regard the disappearance of dahl from the bazaar as a major news item. We have now embarked on a life of rice-pudding thrice daily. I cook the rice in water and then add sugar and condensed milk – this last being one of the few plentiful commodities in Skardu, though it is very dear at Rs.4.50 for a fourteen-ounce tin. Sugar is also dear and not plentiful; it has gone up during this past week to Rs.7 a seer and today I spent an hour tracking down half a seer.

SKARDU. 29 JANUARY

This morning Sadiq announced that the Civil Supply Officer has taken pity on us and decided to issue us with rations of subsidized sugar, kerosene and *ata* (wheat flour). When it was suggested to me a fortnight ago that I should apply for this concession I had scruples about taking from the mouths (or oil stoves) of the poor, but to her who makes no application all is issued . . .

As we walked to the Civil Supply Office, with Sadiq and Mohammad Ali, the clouds were so low we could hardly see the Rock and each tree bore such a bulky burden that its not slipping off seemed unnatural. Snow has an interesting psychological effect on the Baltis. Today it was possible to be out without gloves at 8.30 a.m., which would be unthinkable on a sunny, blue-skied morning. Yet the locals persuade themselves that it is much colder on a snowy, grey morning, and in all the Civil Supply offices groups of men were huddled miserably around smoking stoves and everybody exuded self-pity. As they snuggled deeper into their blankets, or ankle-length Gilgit cloaks, or ex-army great-coats, they repeatedly told each other that this is the coldest day of the winter, which is almost the reverse of the truth. The explanation may of course be that as the local food supply diminishes, so does the local resistance to cold.

Bureaucracy has not really taken root here as yet and we got our permits within twenty minutes; the same process would probably take at least a month down-country. Of course young men like Mohammad Ali think it proves their grasp of affairs if they make applications in octuplicate; this morning he became quite huffy when I declined to write out three applications each for sugar, flour and kerosene. Evidently my disregard for what he unexpectedly called 'proper procedure' was interpreted as a personal slight. He is a typical example of a semi-literate and not-very-bright young man being hypnotized by inane bureaucratic rituals. But one has to feel sorry for him. Even within the last fortnight his goitre has become more prominent and it is now affecting his voice. (Many male Baltis sound like *castrati*.) He has tried to get treatment, both here and in Pindi, but none of the pills worked. What a pampered minority we Westerners are, taking expert medical care for granted, as part of our birthright!

A major problem here is the food-container shortage; in Coorg last winter we had the same problem on a lesser scale. There the rich 5 per cent could always produce empty tins, jars, bottles or cardboard cartons, but in Baltistan there is no such affluent stratum. The locals carry everything in their blankets or in squares of filthy cloth or – if it's just a pound of tea or salt – tied into their shirt-tails. Luckily our astronaut's blanket and Rachel's snow-suit were both sold in strong plastic bags, one of which now holds our flour and the other our sugar.

When we got home with our spoils my elation ebbed slightly; it is one thing to get a ration of cheap flour (twenty pounds for Rs.15, or seventy-five pence) and quite another thing to convert it into something edible, using a very small kerosene stove. While Rachel went to visit Farida, her local 'best friend' – a ten-year-old Gilgiti girl, daughter of Baltistan's Chief Engineer – I returned to the bazaar and bought a five-pound tin of Belgian ghee for Rs.32 (the same amount of Pakistani-made ghee costs Rs.65), and a large handleless tin frying pan, which was sold by weight and cost Rs.4.75. When Sadiq saw this he said 'N.B.G.' – or words to that effect in Balti – and produced from Hallam's stable a heavy iron griddle coated with horse-droppings. I managed to remove most of the manure and then put it over the heat, whereupon the residual dung gave off a pungent odour which Rachel likened to incense. I thought the simile far-fetched, and not flattering to incense, but I forbore from arguing the point.

By then several spectators had accumulated. Apart from Sadiq and his son and daughter (aged four and two), there were Mohammad Ali, Nazir, an elderly teacher called Sanaullah who comes (I suppose) for indirect English lessons, Shakir Shamin's servant, who simply finds us fascinating, and Mirza Hussain, the neighbourhood's idiot. Mirza – a filthy but lovable character – frequently avails himself of Murphy warmth, squatting timidly near the door like a stray dog who expects to be kicked out at any moment.

Everybody watched critically while I made my first attempt to cope with *ata* which is what we call brown flour. A terrific argument ensued when Sadiq again went to the stable and brought me an antique sieve, obviously much trodden on by Hallam but dung-free and still serviceable. The men insisted that *ata must* be sieved to make it into white flour, while I protested that I did not wish to discard the best of it. Everybody got into such a lather of anxiety at the thought of our eating wholemeal bread that eventually I gave in, carefully preserving what remained in the sieve for future use. They also deprecated my adding ghee and sugar to the mixture, and kneading it with both hands, and they roared with laughter when I shaped a dozen little scones instead of flip-flapping the dough from hand to hand to make chapattis. Then they all had to go because it was almost dark and still snowing. I was quite relieved to have them depart before the moment of truth. Rachel likened the scones to dog-biscuits but I was in the mood to relish anything other than dahl or rice-pudding. Only on my sixth did I begin to notice that they were rather charred on the outside and decidedly soggy in the middle. Better luck next time: it might help to add more ghee.

SKARDU. 30 JANUARY

Today snow fell non-stop, though the sun was visible as a dim yellow disc when we went foraging at noon through the bazaars, seeking what we might devour. Our bag was four minute eggs (Rs.3) and a pound of onions. I made an onion omelette for Rachel and with concealed envy watched her eating it while I chewed my ration of dog-biscuits.

Then we had an unknown visitor, a tall boy of fourteen carefully carrying another minute egg. In excellent English he said that he had heard we were looking for eggs in the bazaar, but when I got out my purse he emphatically refused payment. A handsome lad, he told us his Punjabi father is married to a Gilgiti and has been here six years, working as a *dhobi* unofficially attached to the army. (The difficulties of a *dhobi's* life during the Balti winter don't bear thinking of.) I was much taken by Yakob, who speaks five languages – Punjabi, Urdu, Shina, Balti and English. Plainly he is intelligent above the average and there is a certain *something* about him which distinguishes him sharply from his local contemporaries. It is not that the Skardu folk are unfriendly, but at every level of society (not that there are many levels) one is aware of their being unused to outsiders and in general preferring to keep aloof from the unknown. Even when relaxed relations have been established, as with Sadiq and my many other

regular visitors, one misses some quality that is found among even
the poorest Tibetans, or the most isolated highland Ethiopians, and
which for want of a better term could perhaps be called 'natural good
manners'. Yet that won't do, for it wrongly implies that the Baltis are
ill-mannered. What I am trying to express is something more
negative and elusive: perhaps simply a basic insensitivity to
others, bred by the Baltis' exceptionally arduous struggle to survive, which can leave little over for the development of any social
relationships not biologically or economically essential.

SKARDU. 31 JANUARY

There was a startling change in the weather today – an unmistakable
hint of spring in the air. It was almost mild, with warm sun and soft,
hazy cloudlets floating above diamond-brilliant summits. From now
on the heat of the midday sun will be the predominant force, though
a lot more snow is inevitable.

I have never seen anything more beautiful than the trees this
morning, especially the very tall poplars. Every branch and twig was
encased in frozen snow and to look up at that silver glitter against the
cobalt sky was like a glimpse of Paradise – every detail delicate and
fragile and *perfect* beyond anything humanity could achieve.

On a more mundane level, everyone was out clearing their flat
mud roofs with wooden snow-pushers. We walked through the
bazaars in imminent danger of encountering a mini-avalanche,
while piles of shifted snow, eight or ten feet high, blocked many
passage-ways. Today's foraging was rewarded by a pound of hairy
goat's butter which greatly improves the dog-biscuits. A daily forage
is well worthwhile because small quantities of food trickle into the
bazaars at irregular intervals. The weather has made most approach
tracks to Skardu impassable, so the price of firewood has gone up to
Rs.60 a maund. The price of kerosene has followed suit, and also the
price of a cup of tea in the *chai-khanas*, where all cooking is done on
wood-stoves. While taking a short cut from the Old to the New
Bazaar I saw a frozen corpse in a disused hovel; every winter there are
a shocking number of deaths from exposure in Skardu town.

We heard today that trouble continues in Gilgit, where troops have had to open fire on rioting sectarian mobs. On the road to Hunza the Pakistani army halted 5,000 Nagar Shiahs who were marching to support the Gilgit Shiahs, and on the road to Juglote they halted 3,000 Chilas Sunnis who were marching to support the Gilgit Sunnis. Nazir and Abbas Kazmi both found the situation humiliating and declared that all concerned were disgracing their faith and their country; the Chinese road-workers have had a grandstand view of the whole fracas and will now say, 'What sort of religion is this, that makes men into barbarians?' To ease their embarrassment I gave them an outline of recent Irish history.

Abbas Kazmi also reported that yesterday a jeep loaded with petrol went into the Indus twelve miles east of Thowar. There was of course no hope for the driver or his four passengers, whose perching on top of the load is said to have caused the accident by upsetting the vehicle's equilibrium.

SKARDU. 1 FEBRUARY

Last night I was baffled and not pleased to find a large wet patch on my sleeping bag. I peered apprehensively at the ceiling before remembering the week-old kid who had accompanied Sadiq's children on their afternoon visit. This charming creature is very much a member of the family but not yet house-trained.

I must say I have never before lived in such unmitigated squalor. A well-maintained mud floor can be swept, but we have a half-inch carpet of fine dust identical to what one would find on the track outside in summertime. Therefore the floor is by now profusely littered with cigarette ends (most Baltis are heavy smokers), matches, broken apricot kernel shells, lengths of straw and lumps of horse-dung. Every move raises a cloud of dust and all our possessions are pale grey; to live permanently in such quarters must be very bad for the lungs.

Today from 10.30 to 3.30 the sun felt as hot as on a good May day at home, though it was again freezing hard by 5.30. We went for a long walk with Farida – a fluent English speaker – and her eight-year-old brother. I have never been asked to meet her mother, who possibly disapproves of mysteriously wandering females, but her father is an entertaining and erudite character. Farida often asks us in for tea and enjoys riding Hallam; she is a most self-possessed young lady, with a keen interest in the Wide World, and she seems likely to discard numerous taboos as she matures.

On our way home we found a young man sitting doubled up with pain on a boulder beside a stream under a solitary *chenar*. Beside him sat a friend, with ginger hair and bright blue eyes, who jumped up on seeing us and begged for pills. The patient was sweating weakly and on his companion's instructions he pulled up his *kamez* to show a truly horrific bulge above the abdomen. I urged him to go to the hospital but his companion scornfully dismissed this suggestion and continued to beg for pills. I agreed then to provide a few pain-killers, but emphasized that they would do nothing whatever to cure the disease. At once the patient struggled to his feet and set off towards our house, leaning on his friend's arm. I tried to dissuade him from making this effort but he persisted – and then suddenly began to vomit blood on to the glittering snow. As he collapsed, and lay with his eyes closed, his friend made a gesture of despairing resignation and signed to me to leave them. (I had already directed the children to go ahead.) There seemed nothing else to do but – illogically – I have never in my life felt so callous. When I looked back at the prone dark figure on the snow, with that sinister stain beside it, I saw that Ginger was walking away too, in the opposite direction – presumably to fetch help. Near our house I met a group of Punjabi government clerks and asked if a jeep could be provided to take an emergency case to hospital; but even as I spoke I realized that my request was just plain silly. The young men shrugged and said that on Saturdays the hospital is closed and anyway government jeeps are not for the use of villagers.

A medical survey team has concluded that at least 30 per cent of Baltis need prolonged hospital treatment which cannot be provided owing to the lack of staff, medicines and equipment. Hallam is luckier. He has been responding well to his injections (or the passage of time) and we plan to leave for Khapalu on the 5th, doing the sixty-five miles in easy stages.

SKARDU. 2 FEBRUARY

Today every path was like an ice-rink because after yesterday's hot sun it froze hard last night. Nor was there much thawing: when the sky clouded over at noon a cold wind sprang up.

This morning I called at Sadiq's house to photograph his children and found his young wife sitting in the sun in their small compound knitting a sock. Her seat was a Balti stool – a piece of wood some eighteen inches by twelve, on two six-inch legs – and on her lap sat the miserable little daughter of the house. This child's whole person is ingrained with filth, her fair hair is hopelessly matted and her chin is covered with small, inflamed sores. I know that people inside glass-houses, and etc., but surely children's faces and hands could be washed once a day, and their hair combed. Mamma is equally filthy and bedraggled. She is also very pregnant and has a ghastly yellow pallor and dreadfully bloodshot eyes; at twenty-one she could pass for forty. What a setting for another baby to be born into! And if she survives she will very likely have ten or twelve children, though she makes it plain the third is unwanted.

Rachel had a riotous time with the livestock – especially her friend the incontinent kid, and his mamma. Goats make worthwhile friends; compared to sheep they seem full of intelligence and personality. On the whole the Baltis are kind to their animals in a rough and ready way. When the usual dirty apricots were produced they had to be guarded against the kid, his mother, two other goats, a calf the size of an Irish sheep, *his* mother, four quarrelsome hens and a cock who was by far the most aggressive raider. All these ravening creatures were given an apricot apiece and then rebuffed good-naturedly, not cruelly.

As I photographed the three children Mrs Sadiq turned her back to the camera; though Sadiq had urged her to face it she was very determined to do no such shameless thing.

SKARDU. 3 FEBRUARY

After all my waffling about spring in the air – tra-la-la! – this has been our first downright disagreeable day in Baltistan. It was heavily overcast and penetratingly cold, with a savage rawness in the air. We gave Hallam a four-mile walk and then retreated into our cell. When I went for water at sunset I noticed that all day there had been not the slightest thaw.

This afternoon Rachel unconsciously embarked on literary criticism. From Farida she had borrowed a palaeolithic copy of the *Reader's Digest* and having read a true, very badly written story about two young men who were drowned in Canada she looked up, puzzled, and asked, 'Why don't I feel sad about these two young men the way I do about poor Prince Andrei? I know they were real and he was only a pretend person, but I don't really *feel* anything about them.' It is interesting that even Rachel can see the difference between one of the greatest of writers and other kinds of printed matter.

SKARDU. 4 FEBRUARY

Another overcast day, but quite mild and hence slushy. Hallam is now in great form and we are all set to leave tomorrow. I baked twenty rounds of *roti* this morning, to eat on the way, and today's discovery in the bazaar was a little box of apples. I bought the lot (fifteen) for Rs.5 and Rachel says they are the best she has ever eaten: this valley is famous for its apples. Shopping takes a long time because the stalls are so tiny and dark and higgledy-piggledy. Some are scarcely bigger than hen-coops – wooden cubes on four short legs – and it was in one such that we discerned today's treasure-trove.

This morning I had a rare (for me) complaint – severe heartburn, undoubtedly caused by too much pungent goats' butter on my thrice-daily dog-biscuits. However, some of Hallam's tonic soon set me right. It is a marvellous mixture of aniseed, ground black pepper, bicarbonate of soda, cardamom, ground ginger and sundry other unidentifiable seeds, powders and spices. It cost Rs.70 for half a seer but Hallam spurned it: so my economical soul is eased by the discovery that it also makes excellent human medicine.

8

Skardu to Khapalu

We set off . . . in real winter weather, going up the Indus . . .
Our first stage was uncommonly long; the march between
Skardu and Gol is famous for its length . . . The porters had
been sent ahead and made the march in two stages . . . Where
the road cut across the steep slopes we had to look out for
stones rolling down from above; this danger would be greater
later on; at present the stones were mostly frozen fast to the
rocky walls. But one of the caravans which followed us did
have a horse killed by falling stones and one of the porters had
an arm broken.

Fillipo de Fillipi (1914)

GOL. 5 FEBRUARY

The few people about when we left Skardu all stopped to stare at the
dotty *ferenghis*; and one young policeman, who speaks some English,
informed us that we are unlikely to reach Khapalu alive because of icy
or disintegrating paths, rockfalls, blizzards, avalanches and landslides. Had I not known that the hazards of this route are considerably less than those of the M1 I might have been rattled. Like many
simple peoples, the Baltis delight in exaggerating local dangers. For a
people so little affected by tragedies when these do occur, they are
extravagantly gloomy about potential disasters.

It was such a mild morning that I needed no gloves and left my
parka unzipped. The first seven miles were tiring on an icy track:
then, where the land rises, it became sandy underfoot and remained
so until we left the Skardu Valley. Just past the turn-off for Shigar
Rachel suggested an early lunch, and while Hallam ate his barley
ration we sat on black rocks amidst the snow, sniffing the scent of
wild thyme and eating one dog-biscuit each. I at least could have

devoured half-a-dozen, but in Baltistan one soon gets into the way of eating to keep alive rather than to achieve repletion.

From this point the Indus was invisible, hidden in its gravelly bed, but when we continued towards the narrower eastern end of the valley it reappeared directly below us. In the bright noon sun it was a most glorious shade of green – a clear sparkling emerald between glistening snowy shores. Here we looked back to say *au revoir* to the Skardu Valley before the track swung around the base of a chunky grey mountain to take us into another sort of world.

Over the next ten miles we were separated from the Indus by a snow-covered expanse of rocky scrubland. There was no trace of humanity on our side, but on the right bank two tiny hamlets marked narrow clefts between high dark mountains. All the surrounding mountains were too sheer for snow to lie on their grey-brown flanks and when the sky suddenly became overcast, at about one o'clock, the landscape acquired an aura of menacing desolation. A razor-keen wind rose, blowing against us, and I tightened my scarf, zipped my parka and put on my gloves. We were the only travellers on a track covered with the sort of frozen slush which jeeps hate. Nor did Hallam like it much. He soon began to flag – and when he flags he flags. We had covered the first twelve miles in three and a half hours but the last nine took five hours; yet Rachel walked about six miles, both to spare her mount and to restore her circulation. Apart from our kit, Hallam is now carrying over forty pounds of food: flour, sugar, milk, rice and dahl. However, we are spending two nights here so he can have a day off tomorrow and devote himself to eating the abundant (though inferior) hay supplied by the chowkidar at Rs.10 for a man's load.

Gol is almost at river level and one first sees it from a height, before the track drops abruptly. Where the mountains recede from the left bank of the Indus, to leave an oval of hilly but cultivable land, groups of houses and orchards of fruit-trees are scattered over an area some three miles by two. It was 5.30 when we arrived but not yet very cold. The wind had dropped at sunset – luckily, because we had a forty-five minute wait, standing outside the Rest House, before the chowkidar could be unearthed. 'I suppose he's hibernating,' said

Rachel resignedly as dusk faded to dark and our fascinated entourage expanded rapidly. She has become completely adjusted to the oriental way of life and no longer expects anything to happen promptly. The crowd around us was a friendly one, but so unaccustomed to foreigners that our every move provoked excited comment and much laughter. I was just beginning to doubt the chowkidar's existence when a tall, broad-shouldered, elderly man loomed out of the darkness behind a lantern and asked for my chit. When it had been laboriously read to him by a younger man he again vanished, in quest of the key, and did not reappear for twenty minutes – by which time it was freezing hard and we were shivering miserably, though our devoted admirers evidently felt no discomfort. Apart from mislaying the key, this pleasant chowkidar seems quite efficient. But then we are no great test, being independent where food, fuel, bedding and illumination are concerned. All we need is a roof over our heads and a bucket of water.

This Rest House was built by the British about a century ago as one of a series on the old pony-trail from Leh to Skardu. It has its own set of stables at the back, enclosing a courtyard, but unfortunately these are now roofless, so Hallam is again in a kitchen – where once throngs of servants built enormous fires to heat the bathwater and cook four-course dinners for their Sahibs. From the track the whole place looks such a ruin that at first I had refused to believe it was our destination. But in fact this room is very comfortable: small and windowless (a great advantage in mid-winter), with a real fireplace, unused for thirty years, instead of a tin stove. And the thunderbox in the bathroom is vastly preferable to the waterless modern lavatories of Thowar and Satpara.

When we were at last admitted to our room seven men followed us, oozing friendly curiosity and taking up so much space that I had no room to unpack. As Rachel was almost asleep on her feet I had to ask them to leave after ten minutes, though they were obviously longing to examine our belongings and see how and what we ate for supper. On this last score they were not missing anything. Rachel had already had her supper of dried apricots while we were waiting outside, and mine consisted of two dog-biscuits and a kettle of tea.

It is now (10 p.m.) much colder than in Skardu because we were gradually climbing today. There is only one charpoy here and I had intended sleeping on the floor, but as our kerosene stove cannot be kept burning all night it might be wiser to doss down beside Rachel.

GOL. 6 FEBRUARY

It was a cold brilliant morning when we left the Rest House at 8.30. Within moments we had attracted a drove of ragged children who squealed with delighted excitement at our every word and deed. Whenever I looked around they clutched each other nervously and a few of the more craven spirits actually ran away, but as soon as I withdrew my gaze curiosity impelled them back.

Our destination was the nullah above Gol. First we climbed a 'stairway' of narrow, snowy, neatly-terraced fields which led to a scattering of flat-roofed dwellings set amidst the inevitable fruit-trees – some ancient and gnarled, some saplings with tender trunks wrapped in rags. Here a new mosque, built on traditional Balti lines, was by far the biggest building. Two friendly adolescents, who had joined our following, opened the main door to allow me a glimpse of an interior decorated with wood-carvings of great beauty. (Before committing this indiscretion they glanced around furtively to make sure no bigoted mullah or orthodox elder was in sight.) The developers from Pakistan grumble incessantly about the impossibility of importing modern raw materials into Baltistan, not realizing that this is one of the region's greatest advantages. Of very few countries can it be said, in 1975, that their new buildings are as pleasing as their old.

Our boy attendants were on their way to school and one of the senior students, who spoke scraps of English, invited us to visit their 'college'. We were conducted to an old two-storeyed house, the ground floor of which was a stable, ankle-deep in dried dung. A shaky, almost perpendicular ladder led to a landing from where, on our approach, three women fled in a flurry of shawls over faces. This floor was littered with fresh poultry-droppings and having negotiated these we went through a low door in a thick stone wall and found ourselves in the open air. Threadbare goat-hair rugs had been laid on stony ground swept clear of snow, and here Gol's scholars sit in rows imbibing what passes locally for education. Each child brings his own wooden writing-board but no other equipment is used; no abacus, no books, not even a home-made blackboard. An undersized twenty-two-year-old with a lean, pallid face and shifty eyes came forward to greet us. 'I am passed Matric. with Skardu College,' he introduced himself. 'Please you draw picture of me with your camera? What is your town in America? Please you take rest on this stone. What is your business here? I am Principal teacher in this school. I teaches this boys Urdu, English, pysix, matmatix and the good history of Pakistan.'

By speaking very slowly and repeating each question at least three times I elicited from this teacher of English the information that Gol school was founded in 1947 and now has 140 pupils and two teachers. Possibly it makes its pupils barely literate in Urdu, but even this seems doubtful.

A group of small girls had gathered beyond a low stone wall to stare shyly at us, their tattered shawls covering the lower halves of their faces. When I provocatively asked the Principal, 'Do you have no girl pupils?' he gazed at me for a moment in astonishment, then glanced contemptuously towards the group and said, 'Women cannot learn! We will not have them here!' In reaction to his glance the little girls giggled, completely covered their faces and scuttled away. 'I have one wife, two sons,' continued the Principal, 'but I will not want her if she read.'

Having gone as far up the nullah as snow and ice permitted, we returned to the track by another route and Rachel proposed trying to find a way down to river level. This was easier said than done, though from a distance Gol looks so close to the Indus, but eventually we made it to the untrodden snow by the edge of the swift green water.

Here the Indus is about eighty yards wide and on the far side a mountain wall, mottled grey and light brown, rises sheer from the river-bed. Upstream, colossal boulders stand in the water, causing it to foam furiously as it dashes past them, and not far downstream a wider, shallower stretch is all noisy and white. But where we were the water flows deep, smooth, silent and strong. While Rachel built a

snow-dog and a snow-cat I sat in warm sun on a flecked granite
boulder and wished politics had not so successfully taken over the
twentieth century. But for the politicians one could try to follow the
Indus to its source in Tibet and what a journey that would be! Two
wild ducks flew overhead, with black and white barred wings, and one
giant kingfisher – blue, black and scarlet – flashed across the river to a
hole in the opposite cliff. Apart from *chikor*, choughs and a few
magpies, one sees very few birds in Baltistan.

On the long climb back to village level Rachel, who was ahead,
suddenly yelled, '*Look*! Come quickly!' She was bending over
something at the sheltered base of a terrace wall and when I had
joined her we crouched down together, looking with speechless
reverence at a few inch-long spikes of fragile new grass. 'It's green
and it's growing!' marvelled Rachel incredulously.

It is not easy to convey what this sight meant to us. I stood up and
gazed around at the vast barrenness of our world – all dark, lifeless
rock, and austere miles of snow, and bare, gaunt orchards. And I
wondered how many other minute, hidden stirrings of spring were
already responding to the sun's new warmth. At home spring is
something romantic and gay; here it seems solemn and sacramental. I
watched Rachel very gently touching these tiny heralds of renewal: it
seemed that in her inarticulate way she too felt awed by this miracle
of green.

In Gol's mini-bazaar I bought six eggs. These were half the price
and twice the size of Skardu eggs so we both had omelette for lunch
before setting off to cross the Indus by a handsome new suspension
bridge not yet open to jeep traffic. The massive yet graceful towers
are of well-cut local granite and the chowkidar tells me they were
designed by a young army officer.

We walked four miles upstream towards Kiris, around a low,
reddish-brown mountain of shale, scattered with sharp, fist-sized
stones. Beyond the river the Khapalu track was like a straggle of
thread at the foot of high, dark-grey mountains, their slopes deeply
scored by the passages of rockfalls and landslips. Below our track,
beside the Indus, lay many silver-grey sand-dunes, curved and fluted
by the wind. But Rachel's yearning to build sand-castles had to be

frustrated: the afternoon, as yesterday, was cloudy, windy and much colder than the morning.

GWALI. 7 FEBRUARY

A blissful day, apart from two brief but nasty 'incidents'. Hallam was in fine form, the track was neither icy nor snowy (though sometimes rather slushy) and the weather was ideal for walking. We covered eighteen miles and the traffic consisted of two army jeeps and one peasant carrying a sack of grain. For fifteen miles there is no trace of humanity on this south side of the valley, though we saw several settlements beyond the Shyok.

About five miles from Gol, at the junction of the Shyok and Kharmang Valleys, we had to leave the Indus. In pre-Partition days the main trade route followed the river between the Deosai Plains and the Ladak Range, but now this area is closed to foreigners for military reasons. Having accompanied the Indus up the Kharmang Valley for about a mile we came to a military road-block and had to cross the Hamayune suspension-bridge, built twenty-four years ago in two months by the Pakistani army, and double back to where the mighty Shyok River – which also rises in Tibet – meets the Indus.

As we were approaching the bridge, on a narrow stretch of track hewn out of the precipice, several stones the size of footballs came hurtling down just ahead of us. One of the largest barely missed Hallam's nose, causing him to shy towards the edge of the track, which at this point directly overhangs the Indus. Seconds later another barely missed my own head, but Rachel's escape had shaken me so badly that I scarcely noticed it. Fortunately she herself seemed unaware of the danger she had been in so I hastily camouflaged my state of shock. It was as well that I could not then foresee a much more unnerving incident also scheduled by Fate for today.

Looking up the steep Kharmang Valley from the bridge, one sees the Indus rushing through a narrow gorge – and the sun caught it where it leaped into sight around a sharp bend, so that the water glowed like molten metal. Then suddenly it calms down and broadens, as though composing itself for its union with the Shyok, which at their confluence looks the more important river. A traveller without maps or local information would assume the Shyok to be the continuation of the Indus, and the Indus a major tributary.

As we continued east, the Ladak Range was on our right and on our left flowed the Shyok, broad and deep. Then for a few miles it vanished, as the track climbed to avoid land that is under water during summer, and when it reappeared it was shallow and frisky, racing and sparkling over pebbles between spotless expanses of snow.

At noon we came to one of those intimidating stretches where the track has been built up on stakes driven into a rocky wall rising sheer out of the Shyok, which swirls rapidly past, hundreds of feet below. Here a jeep came over the highest point of the track, some twenty yards above us, without warning. (We had been unable to hear it over the roar of the river.) Hallam snorted with terror and reared up and I looked around to see him on his hind legs with Rachel poised over the water far below. Even to recall that vision now makes me feel sick. There has been no nastier moment in my entire forty-three years. As the jeep-driver jammed on the brakes Hallam recovered himself, Rachel dismounted and I beckoned the driver to help me unload, since a loaded animal could not pass the vehicle. Then I slowly led Hallam – still trembling and with ears laid back – along the edge of the precipice and over the top. There the track mercifully widened, allowing us to re-load in safety. Meanwhile Rachel had dissolved into tears of fright and if ever an occasion called for loving maternal reassurance this was it. But I am deeply ashamed to relate that I rounded savagely on the poor child and told her to stop behaving like a baby. Human nature can be very unattractive.

On regaining level ground we stopped for lunch and found that in Gol the chowkidar had mistakenly included our picnic-bag in the load, so it was now out of reach. Therefore while Hallam complacently munched his barley – carried in my nylon waterproof anorak, for lack of anything more suitable – we feasted our eyes instead of filling our bellies.

Four miles further on, the track descended to the broad valley floor and passed through acres of ancient orchards: we haven't seen so many trees together since leaving home. A hamlet of stone cubes adhered to the dark mountain directly above us and beyond the orchards, towards the again invisible river, many poplars and willows grew between huge, snow-sheathed boulders. Here we saw a magpie flying purposefully with a beakful of cow-hair: another sign of spring.

The next climb took us up a colossal spur of rock that thrusts out from the towering southern mountain wall towards the Shyok, forcing it into a U loop. On this 'plateau' we rested briefly, looking back the way we had come to the confluence of the rivers, now ten miles away, and picking out our track which from here seemed like a thin line feebly scratched along the snowy base of the mountains.

Even by local standards the descent to Gwali was extraordinarily steep, besides being mud-slippy. Again I felt very aware of our own puniness, in relation to the gigantic surrounding confusion of mountains, gorges, cliffs and crags. I thought of myself as an ant as I slithered along beside a faltering Hallam, whose loud breathing marked his disapproval of such an outrageous gradient. There were groups of dwellings on various unlikely ledges, and two startled inhabitants stared wordlessly at us as though we were ghosts.

Having heard that Gwali offers a '*chota* hotel' I was looking for something like The Hotel in Thowar, but instead we found an isolated new building at the foot of the spur, where Gwali's long oasis begins. This 'Hilton' was opened last month and has two rooms: a small kitchen and a large dining-room/dormitory/lounge containing four charpoys with comparatively clean bedding, two crudely-made wooden benches, an unsteady small table and the statutory tin stove. It has thick stone walls, an untreated earth floor and a flat mud roof. Safarhad, the proprietor, is an agreeable middle-aged man who has lived in Gilgit and may therefore be considered much-travelled. He is slim and brisk, with bright eyes, naturally good manners and a quick smile. He also seems an excellent cook, though admittedly our palates were not critical today. When Hallam had been unloaded and watered we each drank four large cups of tea and I wolfed three thick, grease-sodden *paratas* while Rachel devoured a six-egg omelette.

Then Safarhad produced a 'host' for Hallam – a pleasant young man named Hussain, with Mongoloid features, who led us across two snowy fields to his home. This dwelling consists of one long, windowless living-room and three stables on the ground-floor, while an outside ladder leads to a loggia with three walls of woven willow-wands, ineffectually mud-plastered. Many Balti houses have these roof-shelters, open to the south, which enable the maximum benefit to be derived from the winter sun's light and warmth.

In one corner of the loggia Hussain's sister-in-law was trying to cook *roti* over a few reluctant flames which were being fed with twigs and shells of apricot kernels; absolutely nothing is wasted here. In another corner his wife sat rocking to and fro, her face distorted with grief, her eyes reddened and swollen by hours of weeping. It was explained to me that her baby died last night – a three-month-old son. The bereavement seems to have left Hussain unmoved, though he shows much affection towards his other children. These, aged about two, four and six, were crouching near their aunt and staring at their stricken mother with bewildered, frightened eyes. All wore threadbare, shapeless, homespun shifts that left them naked from the waist down, and they were shivering wretchedly from a combination of cold and distress. Their round little Mongoloid faces, with infected eyes and malnutrition sores, took me right back to the Tibetan refugee camp at Dharamsala where I once worked as a helper. Both women have rosy cheeks and wear their hair Tibetan-style, in countless thin braids. If clean and not so haunted by misery they would look most attractive. Nobody spoke a word of Urdu but the Gwali dialect of Balti seems much more like modern Tibetan than the Rondu and Skardu dialects. As we sat on two mangy fox-furs, which formed the seat of honour beside the pathetic fire, our unhappy hostess suddenly pulled herself together and, though still shaking with sobs, reached out for a large wad of sheep's wool and began to spin with automatically nimble fingers. At once, as though reassured by this resumption of normal activity, the toddler rushed to his mother and buried his face in the folds of her filthy gown. When he stood up I could see his grotesquely distended belly – obviously crammed with worms. Yet despite this family's acute poverty Hussain presented us with two eggs, and filled Rachel's pockets with apricot kernels.

On our return to the 'hotel' we found four fellow-guests who have just settled down for the night on two of the charpoys, leaving the other two for us. They each have a rifle, so perhaps are soldiers or police in mufti. All were much puzzled by my industrious scribbling; one forgets what a weird habit diary-writing must seem to members of an illiterate society. Now I can hear a rat rustling loudly among the dried leaves of the ceiling – or perhaps it's a mongoose, fancying a drop of Irish blood for supper.

GWALI. 8 FEBRUARY

At 6.15 I was roused by Safarhad lighting the stove a couple of feet from my head. Then our room-mates got up, loudly slurped tea, shouldered their rifles and were on the road before 7. As eggs are gloriously plentiful here we each had a monster omelette and two *paratas* before setting off to explore Gwali.

It was snowing lightly and pale clouds were low on the mountains; but I love this Himalayan world seen through a flimsy, mobile curtain of falling snow. The great gaunt peaks appear and disappear through drifting cloud, while the nearer crags and precipices and gullies and cliffs and ravines all have a new sort of mysterious, softened beauty. We climbed high, using as our starting point that massive rocky spur we crossed yesterday, but however high we went there were always a few more minute hovels around the next corner, the majority indistinguishable from the stony mountainside until one was almost beside them. At our highest point, which cannot have been lower than 10,000 feet, we came on an inexplicable sight. We had been following a frozen irrigation channel around and around the contours of a succession of mountains, when suddenly we saw six men, young and old, standing up to their knees in green glacial water treading on blankets. Their *dhobi*-pool was artificial and had a three-foot stone wall on which they leant, with heads down, while stamping vigorously. We watched them for some moments before they noticed us: then they roared with laughter when I conveyed by pantomime that it gave me cold feet even to look at them. Snow-flakes were whirling around us, while icicles six feet high and as thick as oak-trees stood all about the pool: and naturally we wondered why these representatives of a spectacularly filthy race had chosen to wash their woollies so enthusiastically and masochistically on this insalubrious morning. Such baffling details make the language barrier very frustrating.

Gwali extends over an area some five miles long by two miles wide and there are about a dozen quite separate groups of dwellings, on various levels. A few houses have splendidly carved windows and doorways but most are primitive structures from which the inhabitants were just beginning to emerge as we strolled past. Many babies and toddlers were being carried out – tied Tibetan-style to the backs of parents or older siblings – and held over the snow to do their morning duty. I fear we seriously disrupted this routine for they tended to panic at our approach, yelling and wriggling in a manner not conducive to the functioning of the lower bowel. I cannot say that we were made to feel welcome. Everybody was too overcome by astonishment to do more than stare silently and our greetings were rarely returned. Apart from a few derelict ex-army sweaters, used as smocks by small children, the entire population wears home-spun garments and I noticed a number of Tibetan-style felt boots.

At lunch-time it stopped snowing but the afternoon was exceptionally cold, with a penetrating rawness in the air. We explored upstream by the Shyok, often leaping from boulder to boulder to avoid the deep snow. On the far side we saw that a recent landslip has obliterated a quarter of a mile of the old trade route, which we hope to use on our return journey from Khapalu. But perhaps there is an alternative route, or an easy fording spot nearby, or the track may have been remade by then. The Baltis have long been renowned as the best, bravest and fastest road-builders in the Western Himalayas, possibly because they have had more than their fair share of practice.

Not far from our hotel we came on a scene of great activity around seven little water-mills, now just beginning to work again, having been frozen since early December. Each consists of a low, circular, stone shelter built over the mill-stone, which is rotated by water from a nullah caught in a hollowed-out tree-trunk set at an acute angle to the wheel to increase power. Above the wheel hangs a conical wicker basket with an appropriate hole in its base. This contains a curious species of barley, without chaff, which grows from 8,000 feet upwards and at lesser heights resumes the characteristics of ordinary barley. Marco Polo mentioned finding this convenient variety in Afghanistan; no cleaning is necessary and the Baltis, like the Tibetans, parch the grain in special furnaces as soon as it has been threshed. Thus the flour is pre-cooked and an ideal form of nourishment for long journeys through terrain where no fuel is available. The Tibetans and Ladakis mix it with butter-tea to form a tasty and sustaining dough known as *tsampa*, which is their chief food; but in this region of meagre soil it is a delicacy, known as *satu*. It smells like toast and our mouths watered as we bent to peer through the four-foot high entrances into the noisy gloom. No doubt it was just a coincidence that each mill was being tended by an aged, bearded man and a young girl. The man supervised the flow of water into the tree-trunk, clearing away extraneous matter caught by a wooden grille, while within the shelter the girl crouched – a figure made ghostly by flour-dust – rhythmically gathering the precious *satu* into a dirty square of cloth. The mills of Gwali ground slowly today, for the thaw is only beginning, and every mill-watcher wore that look of pinched misery peculiar to those who accept that there is no alternative to being cold.

Near the mills, on a sandy level space that had been shovelled clear of snow, a young woman squatted beside a rug-like expanse of sheep's wool which she was beating energetically with two thin willow-wands some three feet long. Occasionally she stopped to sprinkle the wool lavishly with fine sand and I deduced that this ritual cleans it without removing the natural oils. She was still tirelessly beating and sprinkling as we were on our way back an hour later: but time is among Baltistan's few plentiful commodities. And at least wool threshing keeps one warm. I get the impression that here women feel the cold more than men, possibly because of excessive child-bearing on a poor diet.

BARA. 9 FEBRUARY

I wished today's trek could go on for ever; I have never anywhere enjoyed a day more. It puzzles me that so many of the early travellers in Baltistan complained about the monotony of the landscape.

There was quite a blizzard last night and we set off at 8.15 into the unique silent brightness of a world freshly laden with snow. The sky was dove-grey but a patch of blue to the south-east rapidly widened as we climbed towards the Khardung La. Safarhad and Hussain had insisted on tying the load *their* way so when it fell off half-way up the pass I was not surprised, though considerably dismayed. It takes two people to lift it into place and in this context Rachel cannot yet be counted as a person – or so I thought. Since leaving the hotel we had not even glimpsed a fellow-being in the distance, nor was there any possibility of jeep-traffic today, with new snow deep on the pass. Cursing myself for having been too polite to Safarhad and Hussain, I undid their idiotic knots and re-roped the load according to the system I had been taught in Thowar. Then I somehow dragged it on to a flat-topped rock, half-way between ground-level and saddle-level, before manoeuvring Hallam into position beside the rock and enlisting Rachel's aid. Without her unsuspected strength I could not possibly have coped: she took much of the sack's weight at that crucial moment when I was pushing the canvas bag over the saddle. Hallam's co-operation was no less important: had he moved an inch at the wrong time we would have been back to square one. But he is an animal of great understanding. From his point of view it is obviously much nicer to have the load lying by the wayside, yet he stood as still and steady as any of the surrounding rocks while I heaved and swore and struggled, leaning against him like a back-row forward. His physical condition may leave a lot to be desired, but temperamentally he is a jewel. When I at last got the bag over the saddle, after a final prodigious effort, he looked around at me with what seemed very like a congratulatory gleam in his eye.

Then off we went again, steeply up and up, with the Shyok returning to view far below and Gwali's wide white valley stretching away behind us. From that top we could see the next two miles of track curving level around a complex of mountains, before rising for the short, severe climb to the true pass. Now only a few clouds remained, over the Khardung La, and the sun felt almost warm. A thousand feet below us the Shyok was looped like a green satin ribbon around the base of an isolated rock-mountain whose summit was lower than our track, and directly above us golden-brown crags glowed richly against a dark blue sky. Hallam moved cautiously through knee-deep snow, aware of black ice beneath the new fall, and I decided to picnic on the pass. For him the descent would be even more difficult than the ascent and best coped with after barley.

Our own lunch of hard-boiled eggs and chapattis was demolished in five minutes and for the next half-an-hour, while Hallam methodically munched, we marched to and fro across the level, circular bowl of the Khardung La. On that exposed height it was far too cold to remain immobile for an instant. All around were snow-peaks, some obscured by fast-moving clouds which also obscured the sun. We could see nothing beyond those peaks and were enfolded by the peace of high places – that indefinable, incomparable quiet which at once soothes and excites as nothing else can do.

For the next hour we were slithering down slopes that even without snow and ice would have taxed Hallam's agility. Before us lay another fiercely desolate chaos of shattered rock, turbulent water and brilliant snow, dominated by the peaks from which we were descending. Here the Shyok again loops and swirls wildly, in its efforts to find a way through the dark tangle of angular mountains, and we tried in vain to discern the continuation of our track. 'Which way next?' makes a good guessing game in these parts; irrespective of the direction of one's ultimate destination, the track can turn at any time towards any point of the compass.

Below the pass lies another populated oasis but we saw only two people – a cheerful young woman with baby on back, leading a lame goat, and an ancient little man with a long wispy beard who was vaguely shovelling earth on to the track at the foot of the mountain. Looking at him, and then at the barrier we had just crossed, he appeared to be engaged on some mythological task rather than on a routine P.W.D. job. Many yak and dzo were out for their midday airing, ever hopefully sniffing the thick snow and whisking their great bushy tails irritably at the negative results.

Then our track climbed a cliff-face to switchback spectacularly beside the river for a few miles. The noon sun had wrought havoc here and even Hallam slipped twice. On one of my numerous falls I came down awkwardly and twisted my knee, but not seriously.

Back on the wide valley floor we enjoyed a few miles of easy going through level, neatly planted orchards. Beyond the Shyok to the north-east a side-valley was dominated by improbably symmetrical twin peaks, their gleaming triangular summits rising superbly above a jumble of lesser mountains. As usual the ranges beside the river were comparatively low and too sheer to be more than dusted with snow; their red-grey-brown ruggedness had an intoxicating beauty as they reflected the golden sunlight. I often looked back, too, at the mountains we had just crossed: the western sky was filled with their wild, shining magnificence.

At about 2.30 a piercingly cold gale sprang up, mercifully behind us. It powerfully swept the dry, fine snow into drifts and then shaped them – like a restless, invisible sculptor – into countless ever-changing, elegantly-curved mounds.

Where the Shyok swings south we climbed high above the river-bed and the surface again became hideously treacherous. Rachel cheerfully remarked, 'If Hallam slipped over the edge here we'd both be drowned. Would you try to rescue me or would that be a waste of time?' The other day's terrifying experience has not spoiled her nerve for these perilous paths, as I greatly feared it would. Perhaps when I treated her so unsympathetically afterwards I did the right thing for the wrong reason.

Around the shoulder of this mountain we were sheltered from the gale and looking up the Khapalu Valley, which is some ten miles long, a mile wide and 8,500 feet above sea-level. At its head stands an overwhelming array of dazzling, sword-sharp peaks and this afternoon the valley floor was a flawless sheet of white, broken only by the several channels into which the Shyok divides during winter. Towards sunset the high cliffs on the far side of the valley were reflected in the Shyok and it became like a roll of shot-silk flung across the snow, its swift rippling surface dark gold with strange glints of carmine.

By that time we were down to river level, amongst Bara's poplars, willows and fruit-trees. Most of the houses are high above the track though one large group of dwellings stands beside it; many Balti settlements should really be described as scatterings of hamlets, rather than villages. Only one man was visible, driving two black dzo across the whiteness from the river, and when I called out to ask if there was a '*chota* hotel' he came hurrying towards us. He was elderly and bare-footed, wearing a tattered *shalwar-kameez* under a once-fashionable scarlet lady's coat. His big grin revealed crooked, broken teeth. In response to my question he indicated a small building standing on its own amidst apple-trees and I at first mistook this for a Rest House. Red-coat delightedly appropriated us, leading Hallam into the orchard, tethering him to a tree and helping me to unload. When he pointed to a half-open door I entered the building and recognized an abandoned school, put up before the keen young Pakistani government had learned that school-buildings solve no-body's educational problems. If the doors and windows were ever glazed all the glass has long since been removed and the roof leaks so badly that one-third of the earth floor is at present under water. The Urdu alphabet is still faintly legible on a wall-blackboard – the only item of furniture.

'I don't think this is a very suitable floor to sleep on,' said Rachel, who has never before been known to complain of sleeping accommodation. I could not but agree, so I hinted to Red-coat that a charpoy would be acceptable. He nodded vigorously and hurried off into the dusk, taking Hallam with him to a stable.

Our arrival had transformed the deserted village into a seething mass of men and boys; it seemed incredible that so many people could erupt from so few houses. As they milled around the little school-house, jockeying for the best vantage points, they created such an excited hubbub that Rachel and I had to converse in shouts. The deep snow on the pass had got into my boots so I quickly unpacked the stove, bared my agonizingly cold feet and sat on the food-sack to thaw my toes and dry my saturated socks. Meanwhile Rachel was crouching in a corner beside a candle as completely absorbed in *William The Fourth* as though she were sitting by the fire in her own home. The adaptability of the very young never ceases to astonish me. Often these days I have occasion to bless her abnormally small appetite. After riding eighteen rough miles through crisp mountain air most children would not unreasonably demand food, but she looks first for printed matter.

My toes had just thawed when a hush fell on the mob outside. Then a tall, very thin old man appeared in the doorway, wrapped in a ragged blanket and holding up a lantern which showed him to be toothless, with deep-set, beady, kindly eyes and an unmistakable air of authority. He said that a windowless, leaking schoolroom was no fit place for Bara's guests to be entertained and directed a bevy of lads to carry our half-unpacked belongings to his home. As we followed him through the orchard the whole juvenile population cheered and sang and wolf-whistled deafeningly. Never anywhere else have I caused such good-humoured turmoil.

In pitch darkness we stumbled through a labyrinth of narrow passages between dwellings, crossed a short footbridge of unsteady tree-trunks over a frozen nullah, and groped our way through still narrower passages, uneven with humps of old snow and full of the warm smells and sounds of livestock. Then I bent my head to pass through a low doorway into a stable where our unfamiliar scent made invisible dzo snort nervously. A wobbly ladder led to the roof of the stable, off which two doors opened into the kitchen and living-room. We are now installed in the latter apartment, which is about ten feet by twelve and unfurnished except for a high wooden cupboard along one wall. All evening I felt *too* hot, as the pampered stove was augmented by dozens of men, women and children crowding in to see us. The small unglazed window is sealed with sheets of a Japanese newspaper and one wall is decorated with advertisements from *Time* and *The Observer* colour supplement. How cosmopolitan can you get . . . A few strips of filthy matting on the mud floor add to the warmth and the stone walls are over three feet thick; even now (11.45 p.m.) the air remains warm though the stove has been out for a couple of hours.

Rachel was soon asleep on the floor, after a supper of two hard-boiled eggs, and an hour later I was given four small chapattis and an enamel soup-plate of very hot curry gravy. Our host, the Headman of Bara, is a charming old gentleman whose thoughtfulness and graciousness could serve as an example to many more fortunate men. This family's poverty is extreme. A nine-year-old grandson with a hacking cough wears only a frayed blue cotton shirt, of European provenance, which reaches almost to his ankles, and everybody seems in some way diseased.

Soon after 8.30 our host withdrew, followed by the rest of the family, who first took from the cupboard bedraggled quilts, and bits of goat-skin sewn together, and shreds of blankets. Obviously this room has been sacrificed to us and I only hope the family is warm and comfortable in the kitchen.

As I write I have a major problem on hand – or rather, in bladder. A natural consequence of having drunk several plastic cupfuls (made in China) of salt tea . . . The snag is that our host has carefully locked us in, obviously imagining that this would make me feel more happy and secure. (Our door cannot be locked from inside.) So there is nothing for it but to unpack our *dechi*, making a mental note to sterilize it before cooking the next meal. Although now I come to think of it, we are none the worse for having drunk some urine one dark morning in Skardu (I had thought I was adding water to our tea).

KHAPALU. 10 FEBRUARY

We were awakened by our Bara host removing a small section of the *Tokyo Times* from the window, to admit a pale glimmer of dawn greyness and a draught of icy air. His daughter-in-law, with a four-month-old *bungo* on her back, brought a tin of glowing embers from the kitchen fire and got our stove going after much persistent blowing, which sent clouds of acrid smoke into the eyes of both mother and baby. Once the sun was up a surprising amount of light – reflected off the snowy slope behind the house – came through that little gap in the *Tokyo Times*. Our bed-tea was sweet and black – none of the family indulged in this luxury – and breakfast was served after a very long interval. It consisted of salt tea, two chapattis and a minute omelette for which our host apologized, explaining sadly that the women could find only one small egg.

Meanwhile we had been inspected by numerous locals, including a group of twenty-four young women. These came laughing into the room *en masse* and sat packed on the floor with expectant expressions as though they believed we would at any moment start performing strange rites. One unfortunate girl had a large goitre, a badly pock-marked face and a blind eye – this last a rather dreadful sight, though we should be used to it by now as the loss of one or both eyes is such a common Balti affliction. However, most of our visitors were healthy and happy-looking, with rosy cheeks and handsome features. The quality of their silver, turquoise and coral headdresses indicated that these were the elite of Bara and their faces – though not their clothes or their habits – seemed cleaner than the average Balti's. So many babies were having breakfast that the background noise reminded me of a litter of suckling piglets and Rachel greatly admired the stoicism of those mothers who were nursing hefty toddlers with mouthfuls of sharp teeth. After the departure of this contingent several little pools were to be seen on the floor so daughter-in-law scattered a few fistfuls of wood-ash as blotting paper.

Then Red-coat arrived and settled down in front of the stove to chat to our host. When another man offered him a cigarette he casually opened the stove, took out a red-hot ember with his bare fingers, leisurely lit his cigarette and dropped the ember back into the fire. 'Is he a conjurer?' asked Rachel breathlessly.

While we were breakfasting our host called his wife and asked her to find something. She selected a key from a bunch in her pocket, removed a little padlock from one section of the wall-cupboard and after much rummaging handed a wrist-watch to her husband. He carefully handed it to me, plainly expecting me to be able to set it going by some Western magic, and the whole family watched tensely while I examined it. As the spring had gone I was unable to help; what baffled the disappointed owner was the fact that the hands could still be made to go round.

By 10.15 we were on our way, followed by scores of deliriously cheering youngsters. After a very frosty night progress was slow, up and down the icy mountainsides, with Khapalu's pale brown orchards and white terraced fields gradually coming into view on our right.

This oasis is roughly fan-shaped and climbs 1,000 feet from river level to the base of a semi-circular wall of glittering snow-mountains. Beyond it the Shyok does another U-turn, having been deflected by a gigantic outcrop of brown rock which rises 2,000 feet above the valley floor. A few miles north-east of this rock one can see the opening of the Hushe Valley, overlooked by a dramatic phalanx of slender, pointed, grey-white peaks. Masherbrum stands at the head of the Hushe Valley and we hope to get as far as Hushe village towards the end of the month, if the track is clear by then.

Khapalu's solid, British-built, well-maintained Rest House stands at right angles to the brown outcrop and about two furlongs from it. Through our window we look past the majestic *chenar* in the garden, across the Shyok – scarcely fifty yards away – and up the widest stretch of the valley to those pointed peaks. Behind are cosy stables, and then orchards and terraces with icy paths leading steeply to the bazaar. These are short cuts; the jeep track finds a more gradual gradient.

Bazaar prices are lower here than in Skardu, despite additional transport costs; Khapalu's merchants do not automatically raise their prices when a foreigner appears. This afternoon we got ten fresh eggs for Rs.5 and a seer of onions for one rupee. Moreover, a load of hay costs only Rs.2, and the elderly chowkidar tells me that tomorrow he can provide oats at Rs.1.50 per seer. He is a splendid character, intelligent, discreet and courteous – the first genuine chowkidar-type we have met in Baltistan. Short and sturdy, he has a square nut-brown face with twinkling blue eyes; he and Rachel fell in love at first sight.

Khapalu is much colder than Skardu and this room has such a high ceiling it is virtually impossible to warm it with one small oil-stove. I am now wearing every garment I possess, including a glove on my left hand, and the stove between my feet is turned up full – yet I am shivering.

9

The Nurbashi Influence

Beyond Daho, Khapolor stretches twenty-five miles further down the Shayok, the whole length of the chiefship being sixty-seven miles. As the mean breadth is about thirty miles, the area will be 2,010 square miles. The mean height of the villages is about 9,000 feet. The chiefs of Khapolor have for several generations acknowledged the supremacy of the Gyalpos of Balti but their ancestors most probably had possession of the country for several generations before the rise of the Balti dynasty, whose very title of Makopon or General betrays that they are the descendants of some military chief.

Alexander Cunningham (1852)

The Balti Wazir of Khapalu . . . was, like all Baltis, a mild and biddable creature and did what he was told. His equipment included an umbrella and a sword, the sword to show his rank, though I am perfectly certain he could never have used it, even in self-defence.

C. G. Bruce (1910)

KHAPALU, 11 FEBRUARY

Roti-making takes far longer on our own tin pan than on Sadiq's iron griddle. It kept me busy for two hours this morning and I have now perfected a formula – using lots of ghee and some sugar to give us energy – which produces a Balti shortbread.

Today we followed the jeep-track to 10,500 feet. The sun was warm when we set off and the light had a clarity extraordinary even by local standards. Every colour seemed alive and every breath tasted like sparkling wine as we climbed gradually through scattered hamlets, poplar groves, rich orchards and hundreds of tiny terraced fields. Khapalu's population (about 9,000) is so spread out that one has no sense of being in even a small town. The atmosphere is completely 'village' and the people are much more welcoming than in Skardu.

From afar one sees a large building near the foot of Khapalu's semi-circular, southern mountain wall, where the jeep-track begins to climb steeply. This is much the biggest edifice in Khapalu, and perhaps in all Baltistan – apart from Skardu's fort. 'It must be the Raja's Palace,' observed Rachel, already wise in the ways of the Karakoram. The eccentric, white-washed pile of wood and stone and carved balconies has a slightly Tibetan air, though its walls lack the characteristic Tibetan inward slope. It is wildly ramshackle, yet handsome in its simplicity and undeniably imposing as it dominates the valley. Two small circular summer-houses are conspicuous on the enormous expanse of its flat roof, from the edge of which several midget-like figures were studying us with the aid of binoculars. The usually docile Hallam was so determined to leave the jeep track here that I feel sure he once formed part of the Raja's polo team. When Rachel at last got him past the turn-off we were walking parallel to the polo-ground, distinguishable because of its area – about ten times that of the average field.

An hour later we were on the rim of an oval plateau some three miles wide and six miles long. Here was mountain beauty in all its perfection: the flat land aglitter with new snow, the light crystal, the blue sky faintly streaked with wispy cloud, the silence profound. But as we walked on Rachel wanted to know what uranium is, how gems are mined, why different races speak different languages, where numbers were invented and when the Himalayas were formed. At times I itch to push her over the nearest cliff.

On our way home we were at one point overlooking a small hamlet and could see all the life of the community on the rooftops: men, women, children, yak, dzo, sheep, goats and poultry. Many Balti houses are built either around or right beside an ancient apricot, mulberry or *chenar* tree. On these clothes are hung to dry, having been washed by laughing women in glacial streams with ice a foot thick along the edges. Most of the local women go unveiled – being

Nurbashi rather than Shiah – and are remarkably good-looking. To everyone's amusement Rachel is exactly the same physical type as the majority of the local children; they, too, have round faces, rosy cheeks – now somewhat the worse for windburn – dark brown eyes and straight, light brown hair. This afternoon some of the older boys tried to upset Hallam; obviously they long to see Rachel falling off. Their elders attempted to control them, but without much success. This sort of hooliganism is unexpected here.

KHAPALU. 12 FEBRUARY

It was a grey morning, with more snow in the air and thick ice on the bucket of water that had been in our room all night. After breakfast we set off on foot to follow an interesting little path around the flank of the nearby outcrop mountain, but it soon proved too interesting to be wholesome. It was about eighteen inches wide, covered with frozen snow and directly overhanging the Shyok. As we turned to retreat we found the way blocked by a dozen goats who showed no inclination to move politely aside; both above and below this apology for a path the cliff face was unattractive, even by goatish standards. However, the drop into the Shyok was scarcely thirty feet, and no rocks were visible, so our chances of survival seemed quite good. Then the goatherd appeared, a cretinous-looking youth with feet bound in leather thongs. He shouted angrily, whether at us or at his animals was not clear to me. But the goats took it personally and came straight towards us. I seized Rachel and forced her into a providential crevice I had just noticed in the rock face. Then I spreadeagled myself against the cliff and hoped for the best. As the goats passed, one young male – probably unnerved by our strange smell – did go over the edge, to the youth's fury. But having been swept twenty yards downstream he was able to scramble out more easily than we could have done.

Further wanderings along the base of this mountain brought us to a leafless thicket of some unidentifiable shrub where a flock of exquisite little birds was feeding on I can't think what. We stopped, enchanted, to listen to their tentative end-of-winter song. It sounded very sweet – and brave – against the enormous snowy silence of the valley. They had white caps, black collars, crimson breasts and black and white barred wings in flight; they were finch-sized but their song was thrush-like. We also saw one large black and white wild duck feeding in the Shyok.

At noon we came on a hamlet high above river level where everybody gathered along the edges of the roofs to observe our progress and wave and smile and shout greetings. Then a man addressed us in English, asking the standard set of Balti questions – 'Where is your city? What is your age? How much you pay for horse?' When we accepted his invitation to drink tea a door was opened in the high stone wall beside the path and we followed a shy girl along a dark, wide passage – evidently a stable – from which led a boulder-stairway of shallow steps, specially constructed for cattle. The roof was divided into two sections and we sat on shaky home-made wooden chairs in the open-air parlour under a *chenar*, while a yak and three dzo gazed disbelievingly at us through a decrepit wall of woven willow-wands. From a higher roof – that of the kitchen and bedrooms, which led off the 'parlour' roof – sundry tiny white and brown sheep, and long-haired grey goats, peered down at us in comical astonishment. A fine cock and his harem flew to and fro – Balti poultry are great fliers – and the fascinated women of the family, themselves looking not unlike roosting hens, squatted in a row on a single tree-trunk 'bridge' linking two roofs; had they toppled backwards they would have fallen twenty feet.

Our young host introduced himself as Khapalu's 'animal dispenser' and despite limited English managed to tell us the sad story of three New Zealand rams which he progressively acquired five years ago. For some reason they did not get the Balti ewes in lamb and last week all three died of a mysterious fever. It seems that yak and dzo are immune to T.B. but very prone to brucellosis, and almost all the local animals harbour a variety of worms. Our *chai*, when at last it came, was unwontedly elegant – Chinese jasmine tea (which costs Rs.24 per pound in Gilgit), served in Pyrex cups made in France.

After lunch we paid our respects to the Raja; on the way it began to snow and it hasn't stopped since. By giving Hallam his head we were shown how to enter the Palace courtyard through a wooden double-door – fifteen feet high and beautifully carved – in a twenty-five-foot-high stone wall. A wide passage-way between two-storeyed stables and granaries leads under an archway to a secluded quadrangle, and on the far side stands the many-storeyed Palace, built about 140 years ago by the present Raja's great-grandfather. The off-white, fortress-like façade is broken at irregular intervals by ten windows of very unequal size. In the centre, built on to the main structure like enormous bay windows, and now in a sad state of disrepair, is a handsome set of four wooden balconies. As the main entrance is no longer in use we climbed a flight of broken, ice-encased steps to a side door where two lovely-looking but very shy young women were obviously awaiting us. The Raja's daughters, I assumed, though they spoke no English. Smilingly but in silence they guided us along interminable twilit corridors with mud floors and mud walls no different from any peasant's hovel. Then a low doorway led into almost total darkness and we both stumbled frequently while groping our way through further low doorways, with invisible raised thresholds. When a startled hen squawked and fluttered beside us in the darkness, Rachel emitted an understandable yelp of alarm and gripped harder on my hand. At last we saw a glimmer of light ahead and stepped into a small, low-ceilinged room with a tiny window near the floor. The temperature was around freezing point and the only furniture was a charpoy, a threadbare Bokhara rug and a much-dented tin stove. Two rifles stood against the wall in one corner and a razor and shaving brush lay on the window ledge. The young women gestured towards the charpoy, on which we duly sat. Then they seated themselves on the rug – still silent – and a beaming, excited-looking maidservant hurried in to light the stove. Despite our companions' resolute silence I felt bound to attempt some bright social chit-chat, in my best hybrid English/Urdu/Balti, but mercifully the Raja soon arrived.

Stud Yabgo Fateh Ali Khan is a tallish, well-built man in the mid-sixties who wears dark glasses and a home-spun gown. He looks completely European, though one of his grandmothers was a member of the Ladaki royal family, and when we had introduced ourselves he sat on the floor near the stove, leaning against the mud wall, and launched into a spell-binding dissertation on his ancestors. I already knew that for generations this family has been producing most of Baltistan's few scholars and he is certainly keeping up the tradition. He was educated at a Srinagar college – where the headmaster was an Irishman, one Mr MacDermot – and before Partition he represented Kashmir in India's embryo parliament. He is descended from a branch of the Seljuk Turks that settled in Baltistan just before their more ambitious fellow-tribesmen pushed west into Persia and Turkey, and he emphasized that his family has never intermarried with the Baltis. Yet throughout the centuries there have been many marriages between the men of his family and Buddhist women of the Ladaki ruling family, though never vice-versa. (A good example of class mattering more than creed.) The wives usually remained Buddhists, while their children were brought up as Muslims. The Raja's family, like the vast majority of the people of Khapalu, are Nurbashis – the most liberal and unorthodox sect of Islam. So it was easy for them to ignore the Islamic ban on marriage with those outside the Peoples of the Book. Nurbashi tolerance also explains Khapalu's natural ratio of unveiled women to men, which comes as quite a shock after the exclusively male-populated streets of Gilgit and Skardu.

The Raja's deposition is too recent to have made the slightest impression on his subjects. To the people of Khapalu he is still their beloved 'Raja Sahib', a man very nearly as poor as themselves in material possessions, but full of wisdom, and of concern for their well-being, and surrounded by the irreplaceable aura of some seven centuries of inherited authority. He himself is altogether without bitterness towards the Pakistani government; he is too dignified and profoundly self-assured for petty resentment, and too intelligent to imagine that any inhabited corner of the world can escape 'Progress' in the 1970s. But he does not disguise his personal antipathy to the trappings of Progress and it delighted me to hear him referring to jeeps and aeroplanes in a tone that put them on a level with disease-carrying insects. I laughingly remarked on this and he promptly pointed out that such machines *are* disease-carriers. Thirty years ago, when it took three weeks to walk in from down-country, smallpox, typhoid, T.B. and measles were virtually unknown here: now they are common.

As we talked, the two beautiful daughters and a selection of ragged servants and retainers sat cross-legged around the stove and for their benefit the Raja often paused to translate. There was a distinctly medieval quality about the atmosphere, created by the extreme discomfort of this 'Palace', the numbers of under-employed but cherished retainers and the autocracy-cum-informality of Raja–subject relationships. I found the whole scene wonderfully congenial.

At four o'clock tea was served in a monumental tea-pot of solid silver. The eldest unmarried daughter now appeared, her beauty enhanced by a delicate flush because she had been busy cooking delectable savoury and sweet tit-bits. Only when I tasted them did I realize that since leaving Islamabad we have not eaten anything else cooked in a civilized manner.

KHAPALU. 13 FEBRUARY

It snowed all night and was still snowing when we woke. After breakfast Rachel went off to make merry in the chowkidar's quarters while I baked, greased boots and tack, broke apricot kernels, crushed rock-salt and attended to other trivial but time-consuming domestic chores.

At noon, when we went egg-hunting, the beauty of the snow-laden valley was dream-like. There was no one to be seen and on reaching the first straggle of bazaar booths we found them all locked; evidently most denizens of Khapalu simply stay in bed on such days as this. However, at the far end of the Sadar Bazaar the 'Karakarom [*sic*] General Stores' was open. Khapalu's most ambitious shop is run by Haji Abdul Rehman and his son Ghulam, a burly young man with light brown hair, hazel eyes and such a flair for languages that he managed to acquire intelligible English at the local school. Ghulam befriended us within hours of our arrival and today invited us to sit on the shop verandah, where a tiny fire of wood-chips was burning in half an old kerosene tin. Five passers-by who had happened to notice this hint of warmth were crouching around it, their blankets covering everything but their dark eyes, which rested on us with varying degrees of wondering friendliness. Unsteady stools were provided for us and as snow continued to swirl down Ghulam questioned me yet again about Ireland and Europe and Pakistan, which last country seems to him almost as remote as Ireland, despite its being only an hour's flight from Skardu.

On the way home we were invited to drink tea in the Post Office, which consists of one room about eight feet by six. The Postmaster, a middle-aged Punjabi named Akbar, is remarkable for the fact that he *likes* Baltistan. Khapalu acquired a Post Office just two years ago and Akbar begged me to use it; with no local tradition of letter-writing through public scribes, business is very slow. So I bought three aerogrammes and spent the rest of the snowy afternoon using them.

KHAPALU. 14 FEBRUARY

A sunny morning, though fat clouds were still sitting on the surrounding mountains. We set off early to visit our Bara host, as we had promised, but were side-tracked on the edge of that wide-spread settlement. An agitated young man with severe conjunctivitis begged me urgently to look at his ailing son and though I am well aware of the futility of amateur medical intervention I hadn't the heart to refuse. So Hallam was tethered and we followed the distraught father far up a steep, snow-slippy path. Just above an old mosque with an elaborately carved portico stood a cluster of wretched hovels, and in a cold, shadowed yard a young woman was nursing an emaciated two-year-old boy who wore only a short ragged shift. He had so many infected open sores on his face that it seemed just one big sore and his meagre buttocks were similarly afflicted; yet the rest of his body was clear and he had sound teeth set firmly in his gums. When next the father is in Khapalu he is to call at the Rest House for a tube of penicillin ointment, which can do no harm (unless the unhappy child chances to be allergic to it, as I am) and may do some good.

As we were admiring the mosque a tall young man came around the mountain and introduced himself as Ghulam Hussain, a teacher in Khapalu's High School. He invited us to drink tea with his wife and outside his brand new house we climbed a steep and shaky ladder to a stable roof, off which were three rooms. In a corner of the smallest an eighteen-year-old girl sat on a quilt nursing a seven-week-old infant the size of a premature baby. The mother herself looked ill and worried and dispirited but managed a wan smile of welcome. While our host was absent another young woman came in, cheerful and rosy-cheeked, with a toddler on her back and a spindle in her hand. She was quickly followed by four young men and three boys; then the door had to be bolted to keep out the curious, laughing, shouting mob who longed to examine us.

We sat on a charpoy – the room's only piece of furniture – opposite a large photograph of Mr Bhutto – the room's only decoration. After twenty minutes Ghulam Hussain reappeared carrying a shiny new tin tray on which were two cups of ginger tea (a most warming and refreshing concoction) and two boiled eggs on a saucer with two teaspoons. Rachel found the tea too spicy so she ate both eggs and I drank both teas while a stream of village sufferers came to the door to beg for medicines. It was hard to explain that although I happened to have something which might help one child I could do nothing for all the rest.

KHAPALU. 15 FEBRUARY

We spent most of this bleak grey day at the Palace, where Rachel was entertained by the three lovely daughters while I talked to the Raja, his younger brother, the Headmaster of the High School and various other callers who wandered in and out. As we were leaving, Raja Sahib unlocked the massive door of the guest-bungalow to show us around. On our first visit he had apologized profusely for not being in a position to offer hospitality during winter and now I saw exactly what he meant. The numerous, sparsely-furnished rooms seem half a mile long and quarter of a mile high and could not possibly be made habitable at this season.

As we had already deduced from internal evidence, Hallam is a native of Khapalu. He belonged to the Raja's brother until three years ago, when he was presented to our Thowar friend. He was not a very good polo pony, being well above the ideal height and with a tendency to cross his forelegs. Moreover, he has only two white feet, which is rather inauspicious; none or four are much preferred. Incidentally, Raja Sahib says that 'polo' is a Balti word meaning 'ball'. He also informed me that during the Raj, English and Swiss Protestant missionaries operated in Khapalu for many years without ever making a convert.

KHAPALU. 16 FEBRUARY

One of the advantages of growing old is that I appreciate a day such as this much more keenly than I would have done ten years ago, when it seemed that the future held an infinite number of days. Now the future is felt to be finite and every flawless experience is valued all the more.

There was spring in the air as we set off to explore that high plateau visited too briefly five days ago. Suddenly the trees are budding, and a few small patches of earth, covered with short dead yellow grass, are appearing through the whiteness. On the climb out of the valley the track was a mixture of frozen snow, running water and greasy mud; but on the level 'highland', as the locals call it, we only had to contend with deep dry snow.

The surrounding mountains were dazzling after the new fall and, as we continued east, a long line of high, jagged, gleaming rock-spires came into view only a few miles away, contrasting dramatically with the curved summits directly ahead. From the edge of the plateau we could see, far below, the unfamiliar Surmo section of the Shyok Valley, where that river meets the Hushe. The descent towards Surmo was easy enough, though snow lay two feet deep. That spectacular row of rock-spires rises straight up from the opposite side of the valley – a tremendous sight – and the track was visible for miles ahead, dropping almost to river level before spiralling up to disappear around a bulky brown mountain. Three-quarters of the way down, we stopped for lunch. Behind us rose a sheer red-brown wall, from which a magnificent pair of eagles came sailing out over the glittering solitude of the valley. The distant Shyok gleamed green in its various meandering channels, which soon will have become one wide racing torrent, and on our right was the amphitheatre slope we had just descended – a wonderful sweep of smooth snow, like one half of a gigantic broken bowl. The bowl's even rim extended for about two miles against a sky where silver shreds of cloud floated in that peculiar high-altitude blueness which to me is the loveliest of all colours. (For some odd reason, just looking up at this sky makes me feel deliriously happy.) Beyond the rim rose curved mountains, backed by a medley of still higher peaks of every conceivable shape; and on our left, behind the spires, was an endless desolate confusion of gaunt, white-streaked summits – the heart of the Karakoram, beyond which lies China.

During the homewards climb up the side of the 'broken bowl' we saw a magical 'rainbow cloud' and back on the plateau the afternoon sun was dazzling. Here I dawdled, reluctant to leave the beauty of this 'highland', while Hallam took Rachel far ahead. Theirs was the only movement on all that brilliant expanse, which stretched away to the south until it merged with snowy, rock-flecked mountain flanks below stern grey peaks. To the north was a long wall of brown rock – so regular it seemed artificial – beyond which rose the 'spires'. And ahead were all those radiant peaks and gloomy precipices which overlook Khapalu from the west.

The descent was treacherous after hours of hot sunshine, but in the bazaars we found the evening's new ice already forming over fetlock-deep mud.

KHAPALU. 17 FEBRUARY

Today's first task was to have a broken girth strap repaired. No problem: an ancient cobbler did the job in five minutes and refused payment. Like many local craftsmen he operates in the open air with the few primitive tools of his trade on the ground beside him. Khapalu's scribe, jeweller, tinsmith, welder and tanner all have their sites near merchants' stalls, into which they retreat to thaw when business is slack. The same applies to two barbers and several tailors. One of the tailors – a wizened old man who wears only cotton rags under his blanket – sits on an exceptionally exposed ledge of ground, where he keeps a small patch clear of snow, and works away with his machine as happily as though he were on Mediterranean shores.

I cannot understand the Baltis' lack of adequate clothing. Even with the limited resources at their disposal, every Balti could be as warmly clad as the poorest Tibetans traditionally were. But Raja Sahib tells me there has never been any sensible Balti national dress.

We lunched at the Palace, where a most engaging four-year-old boy was successfully provided for Rachel's entertainment. The meal consisted of omelette, a few bits of very tough curried mutton, delicious pickled cabbage and chapattis. When I commented on the lack of dogs in Khapalu Raja Sahib explained that many years ago they were all wiped out by some epidemic (rabies?) and never reintroduced. Certainly there is no need for watchdogs, local standards of honesty being so high. But this situation may soon change, now that the region is about to be invaded by Pakistani government officials who will import the inferior moral standards of the plains. As I myself saw when working with the Tibetans, unsophisticated people are very easily corrupted, just as their bodies have no resistance to alien bacteria.

On the way home we stopped to buy new bootlaces when I saw some hanging from a nail in a tiny stall standing by itself near the track. There was no merchant in sight, but I reckoned he would soon appear, alerted by the crowd we had attracted. When he did not, I asked the crowd how much bootlaces cost and was told fifty paise; but I had no coins, so a ragged young man pointed to a tin box at the back of the stall and told me to get my own change. That box contained at least Rs.500. And when we went on our way the crowd dispersed, leaving box and stall unguarded. It is regenerating to be in a land of such innocence.

KHAPALU. 18 FEBRUARY

Today Hallam had a rest while we explored a short-cut footpath to my beloved highland. An advantage of having Rachel on foot is that she has less breath for talking. Today's walk took us to 11,500 feet and though the climb was gradual enough most of it was blessed by silence.

After an hour on slippy pathlets, we came to a long stretch of treeless, uncultivable, boulder-strewn land, fissured by many gullies.

We stopped often, for Rachel to rest and me to be ecstatic, and as we sat on one boulder, sweating in hot sun, a frail, sweet sound suddenly came to us through the intense stillness of the heights. Immediately that song swept me back to the Tibetans on a wave of nostalgia, but for some moments we could not locate the singer. Then my eye was caught by the movement of distant goats, beyond a snow-filled gully, and at last we saw the goatherd sitting on a rock, wrapped in his rock-coloured blanket and singing his timeless song. It seemed at once robust and plaintive, merry and poignant, and each note came to us distinctly through the thin, pure air.

There was heavy traffic this morning because Khapalu's meadows are on the highland. Fodder is stored there, in semi-underground circular stone shelters, and is carried down as required, either in wicker baskets for straw (which the Baltis call hay) or in colossal roped bundles of hay (which the Baltis call grass), worn on the shoulders like monstrous rucksacks. Occasionally yak or dzo are taken up, but it is reckoned that the extra feed they need before this trip makes their use uneconomic. We met several mixed groups of men and women coming down: they must have left home at dawn and travelled fast. The women were well-built, handsome and high-spirited, with clear skins, strong white teeth and glossy hair in many small braids. They all stopped to greet us and Rachel was given sweet juicy pears and home-made Balti biscuits disinterred from the recesses of rarely-washed garments but instantly devoured by the delighted recipient. These light-hearted women and girls were carrying loads that would prostrate the average twentieth-century European male and I could not help comparing them to their puny-looking sisters in Skardu and Gilgit.

We were ravenous when we came out on the jeep-track, beyond which our path continued to climb steadily to the foot of the southern mountains. Before following it we picnicked near a convenient 'summer residence'. Many of these one-roomed huts are surrounded by fodder stores which now look like ill-made igloos dotting the highland. We followed new footprints through deep snow and behind the hut found an endearing ten-year-old boy diligently feeding a flock of eight minute sheep. In the background a shaggy she-goat with a manic-depressive air was for no evident reason repeatedly ramming her horns against a stone wall. Possibly she was protesting against her lunch as best she knew how, for it seemed to have consisted entirely of dried leaves. In Baltistan there are no autumn bonfires: every leaf is hoarded for fodder. We sat on a snow-free edge of a roof to eat our hard-boiled eggs – throwing the shells to the goat – and watched Hassan at his task. First the sheep, too, were given an armful of dried leaves, and then a bundle of some aromatic herb that looks like sage but isn't, and then a basket of barley-straw, and finally a twist of hay smelling strongly, as all the best Balti hay does, of wild thyme. It was not surprising that the she-goat felt jealous. We later discovered that Hassan had driven the animals up to feed them because all the adult members of his family are ill and he himself is too small to carry down enough fodder. While his flock was eating he set about clearing the shelter roofs of snow with a heavy shovel: otherwise the imminent thaw would destroy both buildings and fodder. This was no easy task for a little boy but he is a sturdy lad and seemed happy as he worked.

The sun felt very hot when we left Hassan alone amidst the white silence of his fields. Rejoining the footpath, we climbed steadily towards those severe grey summits whose snowy skirts merge into the highland. As we approached the base of the crags the afternoon cloud began to gather, though without lessening the sun's power; it was just a vast, symmetrical fan of silver vapour, its handle pointing east. Rachel eyed it for a moment and then observed, 'I suppose that's the mist we saw being drawn up from the Shyok this morning.' It is odd how unalike we are. I revel in the morning's mist and the afternoon's cloud formations, but left to myself I would never connect the two.

Then suddenly, as we sat on a rock amidst all that brilliance and stillness and changeless beauty, I thought for some inexplicable reason of 'Outside'. And I felt an absurd spasm of disbelief in the existence of that busy, noisy, ever-changing turmoil from which we have now been completely cut off for two months. Never before have I felt so detached from the rest of the world and from my own past and future. Here the present is so simple and satisfying and undemanding – and so full of peace and beauty – that one is more than willing to pretend nothing else ever has existed or ever can exist. Each day I seem to feel more deeply content and inwardly stronger, as though the uncomplicated joy of travelling through these mountains were a form of nourishment. If we settled here I suppose I would eventually become restless and anxious to be reinvolved with all the people, places and activities that make up my normal life. But as yet I feel only enrichment.

On the way down to the jeep-track junction we were accompanied by five young men carrying fodder. Then Hassan joined the party, driving his little flock home and staggering under a load of 'grass' as big as himself. He was finding it hard to manage his heavy shovel, too, and to keep pace with his flock, so I took the shovel over my shoulder and Rachel went bounding ahead of us down the path, shouting Balti swear words at any sheep who showed an inclination to stray from the straight and narrow. (Actually it was crooked and narrow.) The sun still shone warm on our side of the valley and in places the path had become a shallow stream. Twice I slipped and sat down hard, reducing our companions to paroxysms of mirth. My pidgin Balti provoked more laughter and when we were joined by the singing goatherd his obstreperous animals occasioned further mirth by repeatedly trying to steal from Hassan's load. One could not wish for more accepting, heart-warming companionship. As I deposited Hassan's shovel outside his home Rachel received three precious little pears from a gnarled and half-blind but very gracious grandad.

KHAPALU. 19 FEBRUARY

Today we returned to Bara and found our friends sitting on their roof in the sun, guarding an expanse of golden-brown barley which needed to be aired before being ground. Nearby their daughter-in-law was shelling apricot kernels while a granddaughter – aged nine but smaller than Rachel – knitted a balaclava for her baby brother; she was using home-made wooden needles, so progress was slow. Balti females of all ages are ceaselessly industrious. Tiny girls wash clothes in icy streams, and spin wool or knit while sitting on sunny roofs laughing and chatting. Opposite our friends' roof half-a-dozen young women were struggling to mend a primitive loom which hung from the next roof up, where several men sat weaving wicker pannier baskets. As always, animals and poultry scampered or flew from roof to roof, being formally abused by everyone but never ill-treated. And amidst the goats and sheep, and the newborn kids and lambs, and the coy hens teasing randy cocks, wandered innumerable human young with bare bottoms and runny noses. I could have sat there happily for hours but the object of the exercise was to repay hospitality, not to receive it, so having presented our little gift of biro pens we stayed only briefly lest a meal might be prepared for us.

Near Bara we saw a magnificent woodpecker – olive green with a crimson head and speckled breast. He flew just ahead of us, from tree to tree, tapping experimentally – the picture of a harassed house-hunter, with his mate impatiently scolding him from a tree on the other side of the track.

Every day now the sound of water is louder throughout Khapalu as the ice relaxes its grip on countless streams and torrents. This afternoon we followed tumultuous irrigation channels, bridged by great slabs of rock, and then penetrated a labyrinth of old houses and stables and granaries and mills – such an unplanned jumble of stones that the buildings seemed an integral part of the mountainside. Three of the young women we met yesterday on the highland path invited us into a 'Wendy-house' mill, fragrant with the aroma of roasted barley. We were given fistfuls of *satu*, which can enjoyably be eaten dry – a little at a time. Then a small girl came forward from a shadowy doorway, slipped three bracelets off her wrist, presented them to an astonished Rachel and ran off smiling shyly over her shoulder. The generosity of these people is very moving. Round the next corner a toothless old woman, with a gay sparkle in her eye, signed us to wait and reappeared a moment later with two new-laid eggs; and from the kerosene merchant Rachel received a handful of walnuts.

On our way home we met Raja Sahib, strolling through the bazaar with his elder son – recently appointed a police officer – and followed at a respectful distance by a group of elderly henchmen. When I told him that we were planning a trek to his ruined ancestral fort he said the path would be too difficult for Rachel and invited her to spend tomorrow at the Palace.

KHAPALU. 20 FEBRUARY

As it was a grey morning, with more snow threatening, I postponed my fort trek and instead we explored Saling village, north of the Shyok.

At this season animals ford the river about a mile downstream from the Rest House, while humans use the two low footbridges which are constructed in September and dismantled in May, by families who have been responsible for the task from time immemorial. The larger is near the Rest House, a swaying contraption of rounded tree-trunks that seem only loosely tied together. It is long for a home-made model – some forty yards – but on the way over Rachel was taken pick-a-back by a young man who crossed specially to help us. This was a great relief: I found it difficult enough to keep my own balance while seeing the clear green water racing beneath my feet. (There is a six-inch gap between the tree trunks.)

Saling is on the sunny side of the valley and today, for the first time in six weeks, we saw snow-free acres of brown earth, over which flocks of crows and choughs circled and squabbled, swooping down at intervals for feasts of worms and giving a novel air of animation to the scene.

At some time in the past this group of hamlets seems to have been much more important and prosperous than it now is. There are some half-ruined but quite elaborate fortifications, a few handsome though decrepit mosques, numerous substantial dwellings and the Raja's winter residence. This fine house is the largest in the village but has not been used for years though it must be incomparably warmer than the Palace.

On our return Rachel went first over the bridge while I firmly grasped her left hand. The worst moments were at the maladjusted junctions of tree-trunks where one had to manoeuvre on to another level while the whole wretched device swayed like a hammock. 'Isn't this fun!' exclaimed Rachel delightedly. 'Great fun!' I agreed hypocritically between clenched teeth. As we landed a little group waiting to cross to Saling cheered ironically before briskly tripping over with enormous loads on their backs and awkward bundles in each hand. 'Aren't they clever!' said Rachel.

KHAPALU. 21 FEBRUARY

Today's climb towards the old fort was not really difficult, apart from one stretch where the neglected path was crumbling over snowy rocks a hundred feet below. I certainly could not have faced that with Rachel. I never found the ruins, which presumably are now under snow, but they served their purpose by giving me an excuse for climbing the mountain. From river level it looks a mere hill, because of the surrounding giants, but when one is on it it feels what it is – something the height of Mont Blanc and very steep.

Much of the path is vague, but the Raja's younger son had showed me where it should be and I lost it only once, which led to an exhausting scramble through waist-deep snow, as fine and dry as caster sugar yet hard to manage on such a gradient. At first the Palace was visible, shrinking to doll's house proportions with tiny dots watching my progress, the tiniest dot of all being Rachel. Then I rounded a rocky bulge and was out of sight of spectators, which was rather a relief.

The gradient became easier as I passed – even here! – a stairway of mini-fields. No one can accuse the Baltis of wasting land; they manage to grow crops where even the Nepalese would give up. The path crosses this mountain by a saddle some 200 feet below a craggy, snow-free, brown summit and a rounded snow-laden summit which this morning bore the neat tracks of ibex. From the saddle one looks down into a high, shallow side-valley, on the lap of tremendous peaks and approached by a precipitous stairway of boulders covered with thick glassy ice. Two hamlets are visible, one near the foot of the path and the other high up on the opposite mountain.

This valley must contain a pocket of Shiahs: in the first hamlet all the women fled before I had been identified as female. Then I was recognized as Raja Sahib's new friend and everybody wanted to know where my *bungo* and *ghora* were; I had to promise to bring Rachel another day, by the easier track that runs around rather than over the mountain.

From a little distance the higher hamlet looked a mere huddle of heaped stones, with handfuls of mud shoved into the larger crevices. The permanently-shadowed passageways between hovels were stairways of frozen snow, neatly shaped by shovels, and so many tree-trunk ends were protruding from the walls that I had to walk bent almost double. It was hard to distinguish between the 'public highway' and the corridors that lead from one part of a dwelling to another, and for once no curious inhabitants appeared. Yet I was all the time aware of being watched as I hesitantly made my way through the twilit passages, towards the snow slopes beyond. I could not, however, get very much further. Soon the path petered out, amidst a strange array of weirdly shaped snow-drifts, and icicles like cathedral pillars, and to have gone on without mountaineering equipment would have been unwise.

On the way down I met three worried-looking elders who had decided it was their duty to warn me against going higher. Having established that I was female they led me on to a rooftop – one of the few in this bleak hamlet to get some midday sun – and invited me to rest on a goat-skin. An ancient woman with black teeth and dim eyes abandoned her weaving the better to study me: and then suddenly a mob of excited women and children came swarming on to the roof from every direction – several small boys along the branches of a tree, out of which they dropped like so many monkeys. At once the women began to laugh and joke with me as though we were old friends; amongst these extrovert Baltis the language barrier is not allowed to matter. Everybody looked filthy, but healthy enough apart from eye diseases. (I have seen few goitres around Khapalu.) A saucer of neatly-shelled walnuts and apricot kernels was produced and the party continued for over an hour, watched by half a dozen men who sat on adjacent roofs attending to their winter chores of basket-weaving, spinning, kernel-pounding (to extract oil) and felt boot-making.

On the way back over the saddle I made a detour to follow the footprints of an ibex-hunter. These led me up to the rounded, snowy summit – where I would not have dared to go had there been no prints – and at the highest point I rested on a flat rock littered with apricot kernel shells. (Blessed is the country where litter takes this form!) As I was relishing the luxury of unbroken silence I noticed a diverting phenomenon. I was pouring sweat after the hard climb and in the cold air the hot sun was drawing clouds of steam off me, so that I looked like a boiling kettle.

The descent took longer than the climb: every step had to be carefully judged on rapidly thawing snow. As I came into view of the Palace a faint yet very clear call floated joyfully up through the stillness – 'Mummy!'

Salted tea and crisp *paratas* were awaiting me and Raja Sahib had hot news from the high village of Hushe – our next objective. Much of the path is still under four feet of snow but the thaw has started and it should be possible to take a *ghora* to the village within a few days. So I have decided on the 26th as our departure date – In'sh Allah.

KHAPALU. 22 FEBRUARY

Another hot spring day, though in shady places the slush had frozen anew by 3 p.m. I can easily believe what the locals say about Khapalu's average summer temperature being between 80° and 90°F.

Today we again visited Bara and saw how the thaw at once brings the Balti landscape to life. A few days ago the only visible activity was the noon watering and airing of cattle; now there is a positive bustle of work, all centred on fertilizing the fields. By the side of the track stood many mounds of manure seven or eight feet high and thoroughly mixed with wood-ash. *Hundreds* of tiny donkeys were carrying this mixture in wicker pannier-baskets to the flat land by the Shyok, where it is again piled in mounds ready to be spread on the fields the moment the snow melts. No time must be lost if a crop is to be harvested from the rich river soil before the summer floods. This enormous donkey population astonished me; I have never seen them out with the other animals. Many are jet black, while others are a most attractive smoky blue and all are as furry as cuddly toys.

Small children drive the donkeys, leaving their elders free for the heavy shovelling work which is done by both sexes. Obviously everybody was rejoicing to be out and active after months of enforced idleness. The very smell of the manure was spring-like, though not exactly fragrant, most of it being human excrement. Baltistan in winter is strangely odourless, apart from an occasional whiff of dried thyme in some areas.

KHAPALU. 23 FEBRUARY

This has been a foul day, most untypical of Baltistan and hard to describe. It was not exactly snowing, or raining, or hailing, or sleeting; a very fine snow, which seemed to melt as it touched the ground, probably best describes it. We walked to the bazaar at noon, through a pale grey twilight, and when I called to the Post Office for aerogrammes I found that it was Sunday. But a cheerful little boy soon located the Postmaster who says he will probably be sending a bag out next week – by mail-runner to Skardu, where it will await a plane to Pindi.

On the way home we met a young teacher from Saling – he entertained us there the other day – and got into conversation about what passes here for 'local politics'. Our friend lavishly praised Mr Bhutto for helping the Northern Areas in practical ways and declared that his is the first Pakistani government to take any real interest in Baltistan. I don't know how true this is, but most Baltis seem to be enthusiastically pro-Bhutto and those not impressed by his efforts belong to the tiny educated class. Elsewhere one would say that this is because his reforms have interfered with local vested interests, but no such interests exist here. Some critics argue that subsidized foods sap the peasants' pride and could – as with aid to refugees – quickly get them into the way of regarding cheap food as their right. However, having glimpsed the extremity of poverty that prevails in most Balti villages, one cannot but commend any effort to relieve it by any means.

Mercifully Khapalu has so far been spared the worst degree of poverty. The people are perceptibly better fed, healthier and less filthy than elsewhere. Yet post-Partition political developments have withered their natural trading life, which depended on the ancient routes to 'Outside' via Leh or Srinagar. Traditionally Baltistan's links with Gilgit, Hunza or Chitral were few and tenuous: communications

were too difficult and the Baltis looked steadily east, to Ladak and
Kashmir. So in times past many Baltis were more prosperous than
they have been since their country became an artificial politicians'
cul-de-sac.

KHAPALU. 24 FEBRUARY

Another holiday for Hallam, while we walked *around* the mountain
behind the Palace, into that side-valley I visited alone the other day.
The long climb took four hours and we passed through three hamlets,
the highest distinguished by an imposing square wooden mosque
with a pagoda-like roof. By 10.30 we were dripping sweat and had
our jackets off, yet we were glad to put them on two hours later,
when we stopped to picnic at about 10,500 feet. Below us the valley
lay glittering in bright sun and the remains of yesterday's cloud was
draped about the high peaks. Directly opposite was poised the
17,000-foot summit of Marshakma, virgin-white against the cobalt
sky, solitary and serene, cut off from its base by a cloud bank. 'It
makes me feel queer,' said Rachel, staring across the valley with a
hard-boiled egg in one hand. 'In what way?' I asked. 'Nice queer,' she
replied, 'but I can't describe it.' Nor can I.

While we were eating there was a terrific BANG! as though
someone had fired a gun in our ears, followed seconds later by the
uncanny booming crash of an avalanche, evidently quite near. A
primitive fear stirs below the level of rationality, as the habitual
silence of the mountains is shattered by this tremendous muffled
roar. For long moments it echoes and re-echoes through valleys and
ravines, seeming to bound almost visibly from one colossal rock wall
to another. We have been warned to take great care on the Hushe
track, between 11 a.m. and 3 p.m. This is also the season of rock-falls.
Near Bara we saw a fearsome cascade of boulders and stones hurtling
down a steep slope alarmingly close to the nearest dwellings.

From river level our objective had seemed not very far and not
very high, and the intervening slope had looked smooth and simple.
Yet it was far from being either smooth or simple: at times the path
dived into ravines, or had to wriggle around or climb over considerable hills. One doesn't notice these from a distance because they are

dwarfed by the sheer, massive, brown rock walls enclosing this side-valley, which in turn are dwarfed by the mighty snow-peaks at its head.

We came home through the bazaar, and were yet again invited to drink tea by the Postmaster. As we sat sipping near the stove the door swung open and a tall, youngish man appeared: he was streaming sweat and carried a sack over his shoulder. Around his waist was a broad leather belt with an enormous brass medallion announcing MAIL RUNNER. And he must indeed have run, for he left Skardu – sixty-two miles away – at 7 a.m. *yesterday* and arrived here thirty-three hours later. The Postmaster told us that jeep-drivers occasionally stop to offer him a lift, but he holds it a point of honour never to accept. A remarkable attitude nowadays. Today he brought the first mail to come in from Pindi since 4 January and we watched it being solemnly unsealed and sorted. His burden had not been heavy. Even after such an interval, Khapalu's post consisted of only one parcel (a copy of the Koran for the High School), one magazine (for the Raja), and about forty letters.

KHAPALU. 25 FEBRUARY

A gloomy day of farewells to favourite people and places; we both hate the thought of leaving Khapalu, though one could scarcely have a more alluring destination than Hushe. In the course of our good-bye visits we received much conflicting advice. We have been told that the trip to Hushe will kill Hallam; that the track will certainly be quite clear by tomorrow; that the cold when we get there will kill us all (but this seems unlikely), and that by now avalanches must have destroyed the track in many places. We shall soon see for ourselves. At least Hallam will be carrying a much lighter load on these next stages; I used the last of the *ata* this morning and we have very little of anything else left in our food-box.

It was horrid saying goodbye to Raja Sahib; he has become one of the dearest of the many friends I have made over the years in several countries.

10

Vanishing Paths

> The larger part of the way is on the sides of the highest and most frightful mountains; as a rule there is no room to walk save with the greatest caution and in single file; in some places, the mountain being broken down, now by the weight of the snow, now by the force of the waters, it comes about that the path is totally lacking.
>
> Fr. I. Desideri, S. J. (*c.* 1720)

> In valleys like the Shyok . . . paths are more imaginary than real.
>
> Giotto Dainelli (1914)

MARZI GONE. 26 FEBRUARY

This evening I am in a position to state that Hushe is at present inaccessible. We had to turn back at 4 p.m., but it was an honourable defeat. Having negotiated two of the avalanches that now lie across the track, we were thwarted by a third.

Our good friend Ali, the chowkidar, volunteered to get the Murphy expedition across the Shyok. Hallam was unloaded and unsaddled at the footbridge and Ali twice crossed with the load and a third time with Rachel. (He even offered to give me a pick-a-back, but I am not quite anile enough for this.) Rachel and I then sat on a pile of stones in brilliant sunshine while Hallam was ridden downstream, in search of a fording place; there is no permanent ford because the beds of Himalayan rivers change annually. After three-quarters of an hour we began to feel anxious and Rachel suggested a walk down the valley to see if anything had gone wrong. Scanning the level, unbroken miles of snow – still two feet deep – we at last saw poor Hallam, gallantly struggling towards us, with Ali beaming triumphantly though wet to the knees. Soon scores of icicles were hanging from the long hair of Hallam's belly, but like all Baltis he seems indifferent to immersion in glacial water. Ali said he gave no trouble, despite having to swim the deep central channel because no true fording-place could be found. Only as we approached the bridge did I realize that I had not thought twice – or even once – about leaving our gear unattended. To be in such an honest region is very relaxing – and simplifying.

Saling this morning was a bog of mud in which the track often became indistinguishable from the surrounding fields, paths and streams. At this stage of the thaw land and water merge in a most confusing way, but always there was someone around to put us right when we strayed. Then we were climbing gradually towards the junction of the Shyok and Hushe Valleys. Because the Shyok Valley here turns sharply, this seems like the junction of three valleys; and for a mile or so, before one turns north towards Hushe, the landscape has a spaciousness rare in Baltistan.

As we left the Shyok Valley the slope on our left was marvellously coloured: green, pink, yellow, rust-red, burgundy, white. I have never seen such a variety of rock colours on one mountain. We had been warned about this stretch and the track was indeed littered with newly-fallen chunks of rock, some almost large enough to block the way. Below, on our right, the Hushe River appeared occasionally where its winter 'lid' of snow and ice had begun to thaw. Then after a few miles we descended abruptly to the valley floor and found beside the track a swift narrow stream from which we all drank gratefully, for the sun was hot. Soon we were again climbing steeply, until we came in sight of a hamlet on a high spur, its hovels apparently piled one on another above tiny terraced fields and tall spreading trees. Ice and slush formed a grim mixture underfoot as we crossed the spur, leaving dozens of astounded natives behind us. But then Masherbrum appeared, looking every inch of his 25,600 feet, and in the presence of such a regal mountain all minor discomforts were forgotten. This mighty white triangle so decisively dominates the valley that the landscape seems almost stage-managed. As we plodded on a tall, elderly villager came hurrying after us, begging me to photograph him. When I had done so he almost wept to find that I could not immediately produce his picture from my camera: obviously he is accustomed to the polaroid magic of mountaineers.

From here the valley floor was invisible; we were on a wide ledge of cultivable mountain and the track ran level for a mile or so before dropping to another hamlet. There we lost it temporarily, in a wilderness of mud, and the young man who put us right begged as usual for medicine and cigarettes. What is not usual is the number of small boys who beg for money in this valley, sometimes quite aggressively. Nowhere else in Baltistan have we encountered begging; it must be a side-effect of mountaineering expeditions.

Here the valley narrowed and became melodramatically rugged, its walls varying from sharp spears of grey rock thrusting into the blueness, to brown, fortress-like ridges; and several rounded snowy summits above steep white slopes looked as though they might at any moment release an avalanche – but we were not then in a danger-zone. The thaw has made little impression at this height and our path was a channel of mud through thick whiteness. Many trees stood out darkly against the snow, interspersed with colossal rocks, so we knew another village must be close. It was, and our arrival caused an uproar. Several men wearing tattered expedition garments (so squalid compared to their own graceful 'toga' blankets!) warned us against going further. I assured them that we would take no risks and return to the village for the night if the path proved too difficult.

Hallam had to be unloaded to get him through the narrow laneways between the hovels, as the alternative route round the hamlet was too icy for a *ghora*, and two young men roughly demanded payment for carrying the load 200 yards. A few young women followed us for a little way, good-naturedly trying to dissuade us from continuing, but they soon realized that the lunatic *ferenghi* was determined to go as far as she could. Slowly we crackled and sloshed through iced mud below a tremendous wall of serrated rock which threw back the roar of the river – now a rushing, leaping torrent, amidst a cataclysmic disarray of boulders. We had left the mid-valley concentration of hamlets behind and when next we lost the track there was no one to guide us and we had to learn by error that the steep path up which we struggled was only a goatish cul-de-sac. Returning to river level, I scouted among the boulders and eventually found traces of footprints. Hallam followed me with feline agility through a wilderness of uneven rocks, but when we came to the first of two deep, narrow gullies Rachel had to dismount while I led him up and down hellish gradients which caused the load to slip forward on to his neck. It then had to be removed and re-roped before we could go any further. Both gullies contained racing streams with beds of loose stones that were difficult for a *ghora*, though we humans crossed easily enough on stepping-stones only slightly immersed. Emerging from the second gully we could see the Hushe close by on our right – a foaming waterfall between giant, glittering rocks, its greenness vivid amidst the otherwise unrelieved white-grey-brown of snow and precipice.

We were on an unexpected snow-field which stretched for half a mile to the base of the valley's western wall. There a definite track could be seen climbing sharply before levelling out to continue north far above river level. Some five or six miles away the valley became a mere cleft and a faint brown blur of trees marked Gande village. Masherbrum seemed very close, a sublime medley of crags and peaks, eternally armoured in ice and snow. Across the snow-field we followed the not-quite-obliterated footsteps of the obliging gentleman who had been our absent guide for some time past. He had been carrying a load of hay and periodically a few wisps appeared reassuringly. Reaching the path we found it strewn with the remains of several new rock-falls, including one jagged hunk the size of a sofa, and I was glad of this excuse to tell Rachel not to talk, lest the vibrations of our voices might bring disaster on us. When we had climbed to the level stretch we found it narrow and very snowy but not unduly dangerous if handled with care. The steep white slopes directly above might have been unsafe earlier in the day but this shaded side of the valley was already re-freezing. Then we rounded a slight curve and Rachel exclaimed, 'Look! Is that an avalanche?' It was, fair and square across the path – but only a minor one, some fifteen yards wide and evidently quite 'stale', with our guide's footprints proving it could be safely traversed, at least by humans.

Not that I much liked the angle of it – or the drop, should one slip. By our present standards that drop was nothing to get excited about (perhaps 150 feet), but it would be an unimpeded fall to the stony valley floor. Moreover, how would Hallam react to the feel of an avalanche beneath his hoofs? And – even more pertinent – how would the avalanche react to Hallam's weight? But, as I was thus dubiously contemplating the situation, Rachel took command. 'I'll dismount,' she said briskly, 'and go across first. Then you can lead Hallam over.' I looked at my ewe-lamb with fresh misgivings; the mere act of dismounting on this narrow path seemed to me rather unhealthy. But already she was down and handing me the reins and the non-maternal half of me thoroughly approved of her attitude. I watched in silence as she crossed, coolly and carefully planting her boots in our guide's footprints and steadying herself with my *dula*. Then it occurred to me that we had no alternative but to continue, since it would be impossible to turn a *ghora* where we were. This realization cheered me illogically as I led a faintly protesting Hallam across. Once he stopped suddenly, and as he laid back his ears I loosened my hold on the reins, fearing for a ghastly moment that he was going to panic himself over the edge – thereby fulfilling the prophecy of our more pessimistic Khapalu friends. But when I spoke soothingly he recovered his nerve.

Rachel continued on foot, as there was no room for her to remount, and about 200 yards further on, around the next curve, we met the twin of the first avalanche. 'Here's another obstacle!' cried Rachel gleefully. Over she went, as before, and this time Hallam gave me a very reproachful look; but after much head-shaking and many grumbling snorts he at last responded to my coaxing. Beyond this obstacle the path widened considerably but Rachel chose to remain on foot and scampered far ahead, with the result that I got a nasty shock when we came to Obstacle No. 3, around yet another curve. This avalanche was quite a different matter: wider, steeper and definitely not negotiable by man or horse. But it had left a fifteen-inch (I measured it) strip of path free, and while out of sight Rachel had strolled along this ribbon of frozen snow above a jumble of boulders far below. I concealed my horror and rapidly reviewed the situation. The alternatives were for Rachel to return on her own or for me to cross and hold her hand on the return journey. Remembering my nightmare experience near Thowar, I reckoned that the former was the only sensible course. Then, looking beyond the avalanche, I saw that some thirty yards ahead the path had been not merely blocked but completely demolished by a landslide. Hundreds of tons of rock had simply swept it out of existence – evidently very recently, since our guide's prints were one-way.

I stood feeling sick while Rachel returned. On her way she glanced down at a fearsome conglomeration of fallen boulders and called out cheerfully, 'I don't think anyone could survive if they slipped here.' It's only February, but I am backing that remark as this year's most blinding glimpse of the obvious.

Mercifully it was now easy for Hallam to turn – I haven't attempted to work out what we might have done otherwise – and he re-crossed the two smaller avalanches without even a token protest. Both Rachel and I felt deeply disappointed about missing Hushe. But no one could say we hadn't tried.

The return to Marzi Gone was austerely beautiful, as the cold blue light of evening filled the desolation of this valley. And Masherbrum was more than ever commanding, his high snows reflecting the setting sun above a world long since drained of brightness. I vowed then that somehow, sometime, I would return to Baltistan at a season when it is possible to become more intimate with the giant peaks.

We got back here at sunset (six o'clock) and the whole village turned out to greet us. In the van were those two young men who earlier had carried our load and now seemed determined to monopolize us. When Hallam had been stabled with an evil-tempered yak we were conducted up a ladder to this small room where they and two other young men share three charpoys. Tonight Rachel has been allocated one charpoy, for a fee of Rs.5, and I have spread my bedding on a floor carpeted with thick straw matting.

For an hour or so after our arrival the scene was past description as dozens of men, women and children physically and verbally assaulted each other in their efforts to enjoy a close-up view of the Misses Murphy. The passage of expeditions certainly hasn't quenched their

Balti thirst for observing foreigners, probably because most expeditions choose to camp at some distance from settlements. It saddens me to see how the mountaineers have unwittingly sown the seeds of greed all along their route. Five men barged into the room to try to sell me Balti jewellery for ridiculous sums and became quite abusive when I pointed out that their 'treasures' are shoddy imitations of Tibetan work and not worth a rupee each. An even more discordant note was provided by three powerful Japanese transistor radios, given to our hosts last summer. When these were switched on simultaneously I had to exercise all my self-control not to ask their owners to switch off. No doubt I over-reacted, but these raucous sounds were literally physically painful, after so many weeks of Himalayan quiet. Until that moment I had not fully realized what an integral part of the local beauty this quiet is. Apart from an occasional jeep, one hears nothing mechanical or loud in Baltistan. Even the people's voices are low and soft, and Balti, like Tibetan, is a lulling, gentle language. (Except in rare moments of over-excitement, as during the *Muharram* procession in Skardu, or when Murphys descend on small hamlets.) It is ironical that the remotest valley we have visited is the most spoiled by outside influences. Happily, however, the Baltis retire early. By eight o'clock our room-mates had switched off their hideous contraptions and gone to sleep.

MUNDIK. 27 FEBRUARY

I was comfortable without gloves as we left Marzi Gone at 7.45, having been grossly overcharged for Hallam's fodder. The recent rise in temperature means a much longer day; if need be, one could now trek from 7 a.m. to 6 p.m. But the thaw also has minor disadvantages. When we stop to picnic it is no longer possible to cool Rachel's tea with fresh snow and I *sorely* miss my snow-ball loo-paper. Stones have quite a different effect.

This morning was tinged with regret as we retreated down the valley from Masherbrum, yet no one could possibly feel depressed in such surroundings, breathing air of intoxicating crispness and with a long day's walking ahead.

By eight o'clock swarms of villagers were carrying manure to the fields – we saw no donkeys up the Hushe Valley – and the routine seemed to be for the men of the family to stand by the dung-heaps with wooden shovels, filling the large baskets roped to their womenfolk's shoulders. The women sat on the ground while this was being done and then struggled unaided to their feet and went to the family fields. There, with a swift parody of a deep bow, they deposited their reeking load without removing the basket and at once turned back for a refill. The numbers of small children engaged in this work, wearing mini-baskets, showed the importance of child-labour hereabouts and the consequent impracticality of setting up schools which are attended only when the pupils have nothing more important to do.

Many of the young women had beautiful faces surmounted by silver ornaments and filthy shawls. The majority walked barefooted on ground still hard with frost and were clad in rags – scraps of cotton and bits of blanket and shreds of goatskin clumsily sewn together. Frequently people sought medicine for themselves and their children and – being used to expedition medical 'aid' – rather resented my inability to help. But, however young or old or ill-looking, everyone carried their heavy loads apparently effortlessly, often up mile-long precipitous paths.

We were back on the floor of the Shyok Valley by 10.30, before it had become too mucky after a night of hard frost. Half-way through Saling we were briefly held up when Rachel took her mind off her work and the load caught on a poplar sapling and was dragged to the ground. It is not easy to ride a laden *ghora* on narrow, tree-lined paths.

At noon, when we were within hailing distance of Khapalu's Rest House, we turned west down the right bank of the Shyok. Until we get back to Gol we will be on an old pony-trail which was the main trade route before the building of the left bank bridle-track (recently converted to a jeep-track) in the early 1920s. Soon we came to another foot-bridge, only about two feet above the Shyok. Here I had to adjust the load again, before Rachel rode Hallam through belly-deep water, and the next stage was a toilsome trudge over a mile of soft, dry sand where ravenous and wildly irritating sandflies followed us in clouds – the first insects of any kind that we have seen in Baltistan. Near the unlikely-sounding village of Youski we picnicked by a sparkling stream in the shade of stately walnut-trees and within moments were surrounded by excited, smiling women, carrying manure-baskets and/or babies. As we ate they squatted in a row in the sun to watch us, and the nursing mothers took advantage of this lull in fertilizing activities to produce breasts for the refreshment of avid infants, most of whom had infected eyes.

Beyond Youski the track climbed and for about two miles was hewn out of the mountain. The Shyok flowed wide and green at the base of the cliff and above us towered stark rock-faces, which support neither snow in winter nor growth in summer. At no stage was this an easy route, but its initial complications did nothing to prepare us for the horror of a stretch where to all appearances the track simply ceased to exist. Here Hallam was required to ascend a steep pile of rocks on a narrow ledge overhanging the Shyok about 100 feet below. I would have turned back had we not met, near Youski, two heavily-laden pack-ponies coming from Dhagoni. As they must have used this path it was evidently the sort of thing Balti ponies take in their stride. But they had been loaded in a suitable manner, with bulging sheep-skins piled high – not protruding on both sides, like our load. So when Rachel had dismounted – on the wrong side, for obvious reasons – and been wedged into a safe crevice in the cliff pro tem, I set about cautiously unloading. Then I led Hallam over – every moment expecting him to break a leg – tethered him to a rock and returned twice for the load. My third trip was to unwedge Rachel and guide her over. This was not an alarming stretch from my point of view – there was plenty of room for humans – but it was a *climb* rather than a walk and I therefore judged it best to keep a firm grip on her, lest in her inexperience she might trust her weight to a chunk of friable rock. By the time I had reloaded Hallam I was beginning to feel my age.

When the track again descended to river level it became a wide channel of deep mud into which Hallam and I sank exhaustingly at every step. Sometimes we walked on the snow where it was still firm enough to bear us, but in most places it had already thawed underneath. Then up we went again, on a gradient of lung-searing severity, to another large, straggling village. I was about to seek shelter when we were hailed in English. Looking around in wild surmise we saw a slim young man standing on the edge of a nearby roof wearing maroon and white striped pyjamas and cleaning his teeth. He waved his toothbrush vigorously and yelled, 'Come ladies from Ireland and be our guests!'

'How does *he* know we're ladies from Ireland?' marvelled Rachel. 'You don't *look* like a lady from anywhere!'

We soon found that Liaqat Ali and his colleague, Ali Hussain (in blue and white striped pyjamas), are Health Inspectors from a small town in the Gilgit Agency and had heard of us through Mazhar. They remain in a village for six weeks, trying to teach the locals elementary hygiene, but as neither speaks Balti, and the villagers speak no Urdu, the language barrier is a serious difficulty. They are charming young men, immensely kind and clearly dedicated to their work, but conversation is something of a strain because their English is almost as feeble as my Urdu. They obviously believe in practising what they preach and are the first really clean people we have seen for a long time, with smooth-shaven faces, beautifully groomed hair, manicured hands and impeccably laundered clothes. I prefer not to imagine what they must think of the depths of personal filth to which the 'ladies from Ireland' have sunk. But I believe we are wise in our dirt. These two skinny young men complain of incessant colds and coughs, whereas we have been completely germ-free since leaving the plains – Allah be praised! Undoubtedly the best protection against the mid-winter Himalayan cold is that natural oil produced for the purpose by one's own skin. Not for nothing did the Tibetans grease themselves all over instead of washing.

Our friends share a tiny bed-sitter and it was difficult to dissuade them from sacrificing their charpoys to us. We are now installed in the even tinier adjacent kitchen, where their local servant cooks for them. He is not over-extended, their menu consisting of the famous Balti specialities of *roti*, onions, dahl and eggs, with rice for special occasions. This evening we had rice and dahl – about quarter the amount I could have eaten, after walking fifty-four miles since yesterday morning on three Balti shortbreads, two hard-boiled eggs and a pocketful of dried fruit.

A narrow charpoy with sagging ropes was moved into the kitchen when the servant had cleared up after supper, and because the mud floor is so wet (post wash-up) I shall have to share this bed with Rachel. I am writing on the floor beside the glowing wood embers in the mud stove, by the light of a string wick immersed in an ink-bottle of kerosene. This is Baltistan's most popular form of illumination – *not* designed for the convenience of itinerant authors.

In some of these villages the people remind me of the Ethiopian highlanders: at first they are very wary of foreigners, but gradually they thaw out into great friendliness. This afternoon, the usual crowd gathered to stare and were initially quite dour. Yet half-an-hour later I was being shown the best method of removing nits from hair (which demonstration may yet come in handy), while Rachel was in one of the cattle-shelters being introduced to a new-born yak calf, and was then given day-old twin kids to mother. All Balti women are very worried by my refusal to cover our heads. I am not sure whether this is on moral or health grounds, but if they were less rigid about keeping their cloaks wrapped tightly around their heads they might not have to expend so much time and kerosene on lice-hunts.

KURU. 28 FEBRUARY

What a day! What a country! What a track! We covered only fifteen miles – but what miles those were!

I had an uneasy night beside Rachel, who is almost as active asleep as awake, and we were up at dawn (6) to get out of the kitchen before the servant arrived. I suspected from our map that the Rocky Road to Kuru might pose some problems; but it would have seemed impolite to hurry away before breakfast and it took two hours to light the stove and prepare four *paratas*, four hard-boiled eggs and a pot of tea.

Our friends were appalled to discover that we had washed our faces and hands in the ice-festooned torrent behind the houses; they wait for hot water from the stove. And we were equally appalled to observe them going to the distant latrine, at 7 a.m., wearing only thin cotton pyjamas – which they were still wearing when they came down to the track at 9.30 to see us off. As no grain was available I had had to buy hay for Hallam's lunch – very awkward to carry, but a comfortable back-rest for Rachel when at last it had been securely roped on to the load.

At first our track was a wet mess, winding through level, cultivated land from one hamlet to another. Then it did a Cheshire Cat and we paused on the edge of a sea of mud, wondering which way to turn. I knew that somewhere here we had to cross the Thalle – at this season an insignificant tributary of the Shyok – but the thaw-devastated expanse in front of us was several miles wide and having lost the track it was impossible to guess where the fording place might be. (Our map – the only one available – is a U.S. Air Force effort and does not concern itself with such petty terrestrial details.) However, we were soon rescued by a courteous old man who abandoned his dung-heap to lead us through acres of mud and slushy ice. We came suddenly on the Thalle – only about twenty yards wide, and shallow, but very fast and full of small boulders which made it nasty for Hallam. Rachel crossed by the footbridge of two slender, unsteady tree-trunks, not even nominally tied together, and our guide signed to me to follow her, leaving him to deal with Hallam. At the same time he tried to borrow my *dula*, indicating that he would need it to thrash the *ghora*, so I firmly took the bridle from him. As I stepped on to the bridge he looked around hastily for some other weapon, and found a branch sticking out of the water. His bewilderment was considerable when I ordered him to move away and leave us on our own. Hallam at first resisted strongly, standing on the bank with braced forelegs and rolling eyes. But he is unfailingly responsive to patient persuasion (and praise after the event) and within five minutes he was over, sans curses, kicks, beatings or stonings, to the extreme astonishment of our guide. It baffles me that a people as generally amiable as the Baltis, who live in such intimacy with their livestock, have never realized that animals are more easily controlled by kindness than by violence.

Here our path was again visible, if one looked hard enough, and we went sliding and squelching on our way, between small fields divided by miscellaneous gullies and ditches. I had just crossed a particularly mud-slimy ditch when I heard a grunt from Hallam and an unfamiliar sort of squeal from Rachel. Turning, I saw Hallam scrambling up from his knees – and on one side of him lay the load and on the other Rachel, face downwards and completely still. I was not as alarmed as I might have been since the mud was deep and her riding-hat had been kept in place by its chin-strap. As I bent over her Hallam, too, turned towards her, with a look of almost human concern. She lifted a grinning face and said, 'That was my first fall! Joan says you must fall off seven times before you're a real rider – is Hallam all right?' He was, and so was the load – when I had disentangled the jerry-can of kerosene from the bag of books, and our bedding from the sack of cooking equipment, and everything from the bale of hay.

When our path turned towards the Khardung La we stopped for a sad farewell look at Khapalu. (But not really farewell, I feel. It is impossible that one should come to love a country as much as I love Baltistan and not return. And Rachel – entirely without prompting – announced the other day that this is her favourite place, where she plans to spend her honeymoon.)

We were still out of sight of the Shyok, amidst level orchards of apple and apricot trees standing in a foot of snow. The track was now unmistakable but it remained treacherous until we left the broad valley floor. Although it was noon the sun had not yet appeared and snow could be seen falling over the Khardung La, while an icy wind blew against us. It reached gale-force, and stung our faces with fine sand, as we began to climb on a rough, steep path that soon levelled out to take us through an arid expanse of dark, tumbled, shattered rocks, some bigger than a barn. Under a bleak grey sky this landscape showed the Himalayas at their most grim. When we met a small herd of goats and three laden ponies the two youths accompanying them almost fell into the bottle-green Shyok, so astonished were they to see us. Then we turned the flank of this mountain and were suddenly out of the wind, directly below the Khardung La. Half a mile of level, firm sand came next – our most comfortable walk for weeks – and here we met a black woolly pony, hardly bigger than a Shetland, carrying a long-legged mullah wearing a black turban. Without halting the mullah shouted a warning of rockfalls ahead, where our path climbed to wind around a steep shaly mountain overhanging the Shyok. We found the surface strewn with small boulders – the larger ones end up in the river – but Hallam as usual picked his way cleverly between them and Rachel as usual gazed serenely from the saddle at a swirling Shyok 300 feet below. Meanwhile the sky was clearing rapidly and by the time we had again descended to river level the sun was shining. Another mile, across a semi-desert of grey sand, grey thyme and grey rocks, took us on to the base of an immense brown mountain. Then we came to a small, shadowed village enclosed on three sides by colossal rocky ramparts. When I asked for the path to Kuru the astounded inhabitants pointed silently to a 12,000-foot summit. At first I thought this must be their little joke. But, as Rachel remarked, 'To get out of here you have to go over *some* mountain and that's the lowest.'

For at least 3,000 feet our path zig-zagged towards the sky and we soon had iced snow underfoot. At every other 'hairpin bend' I called a halt and we gazed down at a splendour that I cannot attempt to describe. Then we would gaze up instead, to where the cleverly packed stones that reinforced our path could be seen winding on and on and on, like some giant grey serpent. We wondered where it went over and down; it was impossible to guess because above us, filling the sky, was an apparently endless complex of peaks and spurs and snow-slopes. After a time we could see – far below us on the left, beyond the invisible river – that jeep-track over the Khardung La which had seemed so high when we were on it.

Underfoot conditions became trickier as we climbed and there was only one set of footprints for Hallam to follow. On either side of these the snow was two feet deep and it was impossible to distinguish between the true edge of the track and the beautiful but menacing cornice. Then a very steep stretch confronted us, apparently leading to The Top, and Rachel dismounted as Hallam had begun to blow. I led him slowly up and we were all three 'panted out' by the time we reached level ground. But 'The Top' proved to be no such thing; we were merely standing on the uneven rim of a shallowish bowl about a mile in diameter and full of snow. It also contained gigantic time-smoothed boulders, looking like a herd of prehistoric monsters, and on the far side, where the rim was much higher, we could see our track resuming its climb.

From the next pseudo-top we were overlooking another, similar bowl – and also the magnificent Ladak Range, lying south of the Shyok, which we had been unable to see as we crawled along its base towards Khapalu. Now the sun was shining on the highest slopes – graceful sweeps of snow below the triangular rigidity of grey and white peaks – and on our side of the valley the immense cliffs above us glowed golden-brown against a violently blue sky.

Having climbed strenuously out of this second bowl, we paused on its rim to rest. Thirty yards ahead another track joined ours, descending from who-knows-where along the ultra-precipitous slope of the mountain on our right. Off that track had just come a laden yak who could be seen in the distance – on *our* track – traversing a completely snow-covered and obviously avalanche-prone mountain. I thanked Allah then for not having allowed the sun to shine this morning. And I was grateful, too, for that yak, whose owner presumably knew enough about local conditions to be followed confidently.

Rachel remounted for the next stage, a gentle descent to the flank of a rocky mountain too sheer to be snowy. On reaching that flank, we found ourselves looking into a ravine so profound that one's first reaction was incredulity. The shadowy chasm was very narrow and perhaps half a mile long. It lay between the brown mountain we now stood on and the white mountain ahead and at a conservative estimate it was 1,500 feet deep, with absolutely sheer sides. This scene was the very quintessence of Himalayan drama – vast, beautiful, cruel – belonging to a landscape that has no time for the paltry endeavours of men.

Our narrow path was in a state of considerable disrepair where it rounded the ravine. Having ordered Rachel to dismount I remembered her propensity for achieving the impossible and added firmly, 'We'll go first.' I then roped the load high and hoped for the best. As we moved into the shadow of the white mountain the ravine seemed suddenly sinister – seeing it as a threat to Rachel I could not simply revel in its grandeur. The psychological effect of height is extraordinary. If she fell 150 feet she would be killed as surely as here, yet that awesome drop, added to the friability of the neglected path (our passage sent bits of it into the ravine every few yards), was noticeably unsoothing.

I led Hallam at his own pace – he prefers to deal with such paths fairly quickly – and in places the rock overhang was so low that I had to bend my head. I never looked behind, having once warned Rachel to keep close to the cliff. (She has a perverse tendency to walk along the edge of precipices, no doubt the better to savour the depths below.) At the head of the ravine, where the path did a V-turn on to the snowy mountain, it was blocked by a small landslide. But the slope below the V-turn was of course not sheer and a dozen careful steps took us on to a path no longer crumbling but hair-raisingly slippy with frozen snow. Here I began to have nasty feelings in the pit of my stomach and these did not abate when we turned a corner to find a forty-yard avalanche sprawled across the path. By now the drop was again sheer but the yak's deep, definite prints were our salvation. Actually the sloping mass of snow was quite firm and safe, though it looked as if it were about to go thundering down into that unbelievable chasm. Soon we were climbing steeply and another hundred yards took us away from the ravine on to a plateau so high that it seemed almost level with the lonely peaks of the Ladak Range.

Here, Hallam and I waited for Rachel – a tiny red figure toiling gallantly up the steep white slope, with frequent pauses to lean on my *dula* and regain breath, for the air was exhaustingly thin. At that moment I felt very proud of my daughter. She may talk too much at all the wrong times, but she'll do . . .

We walked on across a billowing snowfield, to which slanting rays of pale golden light gave a magical sheen. Ahead we could see no end to it, but it was scarcely half a mile wide. On our right rose the rocky lower slopes of an invisible snow-peak and on our left was a long, rounded, snowy ridge, cutting off our view of the valley – but not of the Ladak peaks. These were so beautiful, against the paling blue of the evening sky, that I could scarcely bear to look at them. And the configuration of this landscape, with its long enclosing walls of brown cliff and white ridge, reinforced that unique sense of isolation and tranquillity felt only on such heights.

Rachel, again in the saddle, suddenly exclaimed, 'Doesn't Hallam look like a fiery steed!' – which he did, with the golden radiance of that hour on his light chestnut coat. Then we saw a black dot ahead and had soon overtaken the yak, a superb specimen with a tremendous spread of horn. His elderly companion, who had hide-bound feet and wore only a ragged homespun *shalwar-kameez*, stared at us as though we were ghosts and was too startled to return our greeting.

I had been worrying slightly lest we might find ourselves on some lethal precipice as darkness fell but the descent was comparatively short because Kuru is only half-way to river level. I scarcely noticed our surroundings as we struggled downwards; my whole attention had to be given to the narrow path. When not wriggling between high, jagged rocks that threatened to catch the load it was winding around slopes where an ill-judged step might well be one's last. The final stretch was so steep that the load slipped on to Hallam's neck: this is becoming a familiar crisis. As I was dismantling it on the outskirts of the village a marvellous old character appeared on the roof of his house and a moment later was beside me, offering help and hospitality.

While the family conferred about their unprecedented guests Rachel and I sat in a little yard, on a flight of steps that led up to the latrine, and watched Hallam munching vigorously. I could see that we were exactly opposite, but much higher than, our Gwali Hotel, which was invisible because of an intervening foothill. The sun had just set and the whole south-western sky was a strange dusty pink, through which Venus glowed golden. As Orion appeared overhead our host opened a low wooden door in an otherwise blank stone wall and beckoned us into a pitch-dark stable from which an even lower door led to this windowless room. It is about ten feet by eight and strips of woven goats' hair cover half the floor space. The other half is bare mud and under a hole in the roof is a 'fireplace' of three stones on which a *dechi* can be balanced. One wall is lined with handsomely-carved wooden cupboards – the only furniture, apart from a pile of filthy bedding. These are the living quarters of our ancient but sprightly host and his endearing old wife; the younger generations live upstairs. On arrival we found another old man squatting in the dark by a tiny fire of twigs, meditatively smoking a hookah. But we have been spared the usual throng of curious locals and I had just room to get our own 'kitchen' organized by candlelight and cook a *dechi* of rice on our oil-stove. This was transformed into rice pudding by the addition of a little sugar and our last tin of Dutch condensed milk; and no meal ever tasted better.

It is wonderfully convenient to have a child with a small appetite; this evening was the first time I have ever heard Rachel saying, 'I'm hungry!' Despite her big frame and formidable expenditure of energy she seems to flourish on about two hard-boiled eggs every thirty-six hours. She was already in her flea-bag as we ate and the instant she had put down her empty bowl she turned on her side and went out like a light. I envied her then: diary-writing at the end of a strenuous day severely tests one's will-power. As Alexander Cunningham noted, while exploring Baltistan some 125 years ago: 'The generality of travellers get too much fatigued with their exertions by day to be able to make any observations at night.' But having brewed myself a kettle of strong black tea I came to and now I feel quite lively.

This is a very Tibetan-looking family and our host has a splendidly benign face, wrinkled and browned by wind and weather, with a wispy grey beard, bright humorous eyes and a big smile that shows a mouthful of sound, even teeth. His wife – who has borne twenty-two children, of whom sixteen survive – suffers greatly from rheumatism but is nonetheless a cheerful character and full of concern for our welfare. We have been given the carpeted half of the floor and two hours ago the old couple spread tattered goat-hides on the mud half, laid their wretched bits of bedding over these and went to sleep. Just now another elderly couple and three adolescent girls came in and took their bedding from the pile in the corner. So we have a full house and are not likely to feel cold – as we might have done, during the small hours, had there been only four (or three and a half) people sleeping in a room of this size.

KIRIS. 1 MARCH

My night was mildly disturbed; sandflies are not the only Balti insects to have come out of hibernation and we were both bitten all over.

I woke at 5.45 to hear a familiar sound which I could not immediately identify. Then I poked my head out of my aptly named flea-bag to see by firelight our host churning Tibetan tea in a hollowed-out tree-trunk. The Baltis add a little milk as well as rancid butter, salt and bicarbonate of soda, but the result is much the same. Although we had enough rice left over for breakfast, the old couple insisted on my sharing their tea and *tsampa*. For themselves they poured four cups of tea, two for mixing with their *satu* and two to be taken straight. As an Instant Food *tsampa* wins; apart from its convenience it is much more palatable and very much more sustaining than rice. The despised (by conservative foreigners) butter-tea is also sustaining on its own, and extraordinarily warming; it has an almost whiskey-like effect on one's inside. But unfortunately Rachel's adaptability breaks down when it comes to food. She is one of the conservative foreigners who won't touch Tibetan tea or *tsampa*, bored as she is by the monotony of our diet.

It would not have done to tip our host so I tried to think of some suitable gift and was inspired to give him my gloves, which I am unlikely to need again, and one of our two hideous orange plastic mugs, which his wife much admired last night. Then off we went at 7.30, when the sun was already warm and the sky cloudless.

The first hour was tricky as the steep narrow track wound between dwellings or five-foot stone walls, neither of which left an adequate margin for Hallam. In our host's house, on the periphery of the settlement, I had not grasped Kuru's size; when he told us that in British days it offered a one-room Rest House (now demolished) I had diagnosed delusions of grandeur. But this morning I reckoned the whole settlement – scattered over many high ledges, separated by narrow gullies – probably supports five or six thousand people. It is a savagely beautiful place, with its bewildering network of ravines, dark overhanging crags and loudly leaping torrents. As in Saling, I had the impression that it was once a good deal more prosperous. These right bank villages must have been much livelier when on the main trade route; now they rarely see even a Balti outsider.

Platoons of men, women and children were briskly carrying manure to the fields and I find that as the sun gains strength the aroma of human manure becomes less and less romantic, even on a fine spring morning. When at last the track began to level out – going towards the next mountain-flank instead of towards the invisible river – I sighed with relief to have Rachel and baggage still *in situ* on Hallam. (Despite the gradient Rachel had not dismounted because then the load might have again come forward on to Hallam's neck; if she sits on the connecting rope across the saddle this helps to keep it where it should be.) But my relief was premature. Just beyond Kuru the track has to traverse a horrifying bulge at the base of a 20,000-foot mountain. It overhangs the Shyok for a quarter of a mile about 700 feet above the water and is worse than anything else we have met in Baltistan; I remember looking at it from the left bank and deducing that it could only be a goat-track. On a good day it would be demoralizing and today was *not* a good day; during the night two landslips about fifty yards apart had blocked the path. Luckily there were plenty of people around to warn us and we were taken under the wing of a kindly mullah, who was also going to Kiris and spoke a few unexpected words of English. He beckoned to two of the many youths who had accumulated behind us and told them to unload Hallam and carry the load across the slips, which were about half a mile further on. I followed with Hallam, leaving Rachel in the care of the mullah and his party. This consisted of another mullah, who was (oddly) a deaf-mute, his veiled sixteen-year-old daughter, a wiry little Mail-Runner with ginger hair and two gloomy elderly peasants entirely lacking in oriental fatalism. They were convinced that Allah had it in for us and that we would all be pulverized by falling rocks long before we reached Kiris. Personally I have stopped worrying: once embarked on a trek in Baltistan one becomes either a fatalist or a nervous wreck. Towing the faithful Hallam I strode across the two slithery new slips as though in an Irish field, and then looked back to see Rachel standing in the middle of one gazing earnestly up at the mullah and saying, 'No, not Holland – it's Ireland – a small island called *Ireland*.' If being rescued from a blazing building she would hold up the firemen to have a chat.

Beyond the slips we all continued together across the bulge, Rachel still walking (and talking) with the mullah. The Mail-Runner trotted ahead as our scout and once had to hold us up while a minor rock-fall went hurtling from the heights far above to the river far below. (It might not have seemed minor had we been in its way.) Where we came off the bulge the path at once widened to jeep-track proportions as the mountains receded, leaving us on a wide ledge of undulating semi-desert not far above river level. Here we said goodbye to our companions as Hallam had not yet had his breakfast.

Kiris is only ten miles from Kuru and the rest of the way was comparatively easy going, apart from a few stretches of soft sand or skiddy mud, and one tough climb to the village of Gone, three miles short of Kiris.

This fertile oasis lies a mile upstream from the confluence of the Shyok and the Indus. Three young men returning from their fields and reeking of excrement guided us to our destination across a brown expanse of squelchy, muddy ploughland. Evidently this Rest House has been used rarely (if at all) since Partition. The chowkidar could not be found, and there seemed to be some confusion about his identity, but eventually an ancient little man came fumbling along with an enormous key and admitted us to a building which, apart from its British fireplaces and glazed windows, might be one of the larger village houses. Our room, approached by an outside stone stairs, is directly over Hallam's stable and has bare boards, a small table and chair and one unsteady charpoy. Off it is a totally unfurnished bathroom with a door leading on to another roof, equipped with four circular holes. As this latrine lacks even a token surrounding wall one has to bare one's bottom in full view of the entire village – which of course matters not at all, in a society where such behaviour seems decent and normal. One of our windows overlooks a small courtyard, dominated by six poplars far higher than the house, and from the other we can study local life, which this afternoon consisted mainly of a few yak and many male cross-breds with spring in their blood. There is something wonderfully comical about a frisky yak. With their heads down and their great bushy tails curved over their backs they go bounding and racing around like so many lambs – until they meet a female. Breeding seems completely uncontrolled, though cattle-products are important in Baltistan.

We have just heard that last night the track between here and Gol was blocked by a massive rock-fall. The Kiris P.W.D. coolie-gang does not expect to have it clear in less than three days but this leaves me undismayed. I am very willing to linger in Kiris, which seems a most attractive and friendly village.

11

Kiris to Skardu

The dryness of the climate is such that in the whole of the Trans-Himalayan region there are barely six inches of rainfall in the year. Were it a plain it would be like the Sahara. Fortunately, however, the highest ridges condense into moisture whatever snow escapes being caught upon the Himalaya, so that, whenever the exposure and the slope of the mountains allow it névés and glaciers are formed which permit the scanty population to support life in spite of their inhuman surroundings.

Fillipo de Fillipi (1909)

KIRIS. 2 MARCH

I hate writing the word 'March': it reminds me too forcefully that our days in Baltistan are numbered. I have over the years become attached to many places and peoples, but I realized this morning, as we climbed high above Kiris, that my feeling for Baltistan is less an attachment than a passionate love-affair. And it is emphatically a feeling for the *place* rather than for the *people*. The Baltis are likeable, dependable, cheerful, welcoming and pathetically generous with what very little they have. But they lack that complex quality inadequately described as 'personality'. This may be because they are neither ethnically homogeneous nor culturally distinct: not truly a race, but a mosaic of many different strains, none of which has been strong enough to impose its character on the whole area. Comparing them only with the peasants of other regions, they seem to lack the vigour of the Pathans, the graciousness of the Persians, the serenity of the Tibetans, the dignity of the Amharas, the subtlety of the Hindus, the enterprise of the Nepalese. Their struggle to survive in these merciless valleys has left them with nothing to spare for the evolution of arts and crafts, apart from essential skills, such as terracing. And their geographical remoteness, combined with the absence of a rich leisured class, has prevented the development of even the most rudimentary intellectual life. Things may of course have been different in the pre-Islamic era; Cunningham quotes a persisting tradition that at the beginning of the seventeenth century all the temples and monasteries of the country were destroyed and their libraries thrown into the Indus. Now the nearest thing to 'an educated class' consists almost entirely of bigoted, power-loving mullahs, adept at distorting Islamic theology to suit their own ends. And so, as I have said, it is with the *place* that one forms a relationship. Sir Francis Younghusband spoke for a lot of travellers when he said, 'The more you see of the Himalayas the more you want to see.'

Behind Kiris we ascended a narrow nullah and passed many busy water-mills, attended by groups of friendly women who presented us with fistfuls of *satu*. The powerful torrent sprang noisily from ledge to ledge and was being joined on our side by sparkling streams of newly-melted snow. Yet the opposite precipice was hung with sheets of ice like plate glass, and with icicles the size of telegraph poles – one of which killed a goat-herd yesterday, when the ledge under which it had formed collapsed. The natural hazards of Baltistan are gruesomely varied.

At noon we overtook a herd of seventeen goats and sheep, attended by three small boys. We were now in an oval valley scattered with hay-shelters, massive boulders and a few 'summer residences'. Sitting in the sun by the torrent, we watched the little herd being directed across a slender tree-trunk 'bridge' to the far bank, where patches of short yellow-brown grass have just been exposed. Then the three boys tentatively approached us and for ten minutes stared in perplexed though not unfriendly silence. But they never forgot their responsibilities; every few moments one of them found it necessary to shout a warning or an order to some member of his flock, and I was fascinated by the promptly obedient responses of individual animals. These long-distance commands explain why three children are tending so few animals at this busy season:

obviously remote control can only be exercised by a member of the animal's own family. There is more to shepherding than meets the eye.

It will break my heart to leave the beauty, the silence and the endless variety of these mountains. Yet I shall be taking with me some of this strangely fortifying Himalayan peace. And it will endure. There is nothing ephemeral about the effects of a journey such as this.

KIRIS. 3 MARCH

A fascinating day, despite disagreeable weather – grey with a harsh wind, like a nasty March day in Ireland.

To explore an area of weird, pale brown clay cliffs, noticed en route from Kuru, we took a path beside an irrigation channel built around the base of a mountain. Here we came on a puzzling sight; three men, using a crowbar, a mallet and all their strength, were hewing long, flattish slabs of rock off the cliff-face. With so many thousands of tons of loose rock lying all over the place I should have thought there was no need for such exertion. But when one looks more closely at these terraced fields one sees that their embankments are constructed not of any old stone that comes to hand, but of neatly shaped wedges. The labour involved in making and maintaining each tiny patch of fertile land is quite staggering; and often at this season, when all the labour-force is needed for fertilizing, embankments collapse as part of the general thaw havoc. Then the unfortunate cultivator has quickly to repair the damage before his precious patch of earth is washed away. Those down-country folk who scornfully refer to 'the lazy Baltis' should try farming here for a few seasons.

The hamlet near the clay cliffs had a startling Middle Eastern look, being built of mud-bricks instead of the usual Balti stone. Some dwellings stood on the cliffs, apparently growing out of them, but most of those were in ruins, their foundations having been partially eroded – a measure of how rapidly these curious cliffs are disappearing. They are honeycombed with exciting-looking caves which seem to have been troglodyte dwellings in the not too distant past. Rachel longed to explore these but I was less keen, in a region where the landscape is so mobile. This hamlet was also remarkable for the most gigantic vines I have ever seen – fantastic growths, some like a multitude of serpents intertwined, some growing right *through* the roofs and walls of houses, some forming foot-bridges over the broad irrigation channel and some extending for fifty or sixty yards, linking several apricot and mulberry trees.

Beyond the cliffs we found ourselves on an uncanny little plain, still partly snow-covered, where the uncultivable spongy soil was strangely resilient and broken up into many dark chasms too deep to be fathomed with the eye. Some were circular pits, at least 100 feet in diameter, others were long, narrow cracks and all had crumbling edges. Between these scores of death-traps the barren ground wobbled underfoot, like a bog, and I suddenly noticed that not one path crossed it at any point. I decided then that I did not like the feel of the place, either literally or metaphorically, so we departed from it as speedily as was prudent, sliding on our bottoms down a 500-foot cliff to an area of orchards and fields just above river level.

The district of Kiris is about sixteen miles long by ten miles wide and like every Balti oasis of any consequence it has a Raja – who I believe speaks some English, but unluckily is at present in Skardu. On our way back to the Rest House we passed his Palace, a square, three-storeyed house on the very edge of a cliff overlooking the Shyok. Apart from its being by far the largest building in Kiris it is unremarkable, and a young policeman from Shigar, who saw us walking around it, explained that 'most good house in Kiris is big mosque – you come, I show'. So we went and were shown.

This mosque is close to Kiris bazaar – if six small stalls with three-quarter empty shelves can be so described – and by Balti standards it is indeed magnificent. In design it resembles the ordinary stone village mosque, which is square, flat-roofed and usually rather wretched-looking, with a wooden portico. But its scale and proportions give it a simple sort of grandeur, despite its state of disrepair. A close row of high wooden pillars supports the portico, and the spacious interior, which we were allowed to glimpse from the doorway, is divided into naves by austere, symmetrically arranged columns. Straw mats are scattered on the earth floor and four lamps hang from the high ceiling. Shiahs and Nurbashis – who interpret the Prophet's teaching so very differently – worship here together. Northern Ireland Christians please note.

In an enclosure near the mosque are two broken-down tombs which at one time must have been quite impressive; the remains of their carvings show a degree of skill quite alien to modern Baltistan. Our guide identified them as the tombs of those intrepid missionaries who converted the Baltis to Islam. Maybe. But I am cautious about accepting as fact the historical data on offer hereabouts.

We saw five major rock-falls today and heard several more. At present there is little traffic on the jeep-track, visible from here across the river; otherwise accidents would be frequent because jeep-drivers, unlike riders or walkers, cannot hear the warning rattle of pebbles. The steep, smooth slopes above this stretch of track are classic rock-fall sources and massive boulders hurtle down from the heights at meteoric speeds.

Kiris is rich in rats. I am sleeping on the wooden floor and last night as I lay reading by candlelight they had the audacity actually to scamper over my flea-bag. Then when I blew out the candle they came along to eat the wax and I could hear them gnawing by my ear.

KIRIS. 4 MARCH

We woke at dawn to see a world newly white under three inches of snow, but by 8 a.m. this had turned to the first rain we have seen for three months. It continued all day, occasionally becoming sleet, and the cold damp kept everyone indoors By 5 p.m., when the sky began to clear, Kiris must have had most of its annual ration. Rachel spent the day painting and doing sums while I attended to my customary bad-weather chores.

SKARDU. 5 MARCH

Our toughest day. The weather compelled us to do a forced march of twenty-six miles in seven and three-quarter hours with one five-minute stop. From which you may rightly deduce that Hallam and I are pretty fit by now, despite (or because of?) the limitations of the Balti cuisine.

At dawn the weather was difficult to judge but by 7.30 the sky had begun to clear and at 9.15 we set off. As we approached Gol more cloud could be seen gathering around the peaks ahead but for the next six or seven miles conditions remained tolerable – dry underfoot, and not too cold. The track switchbacked across a wide ledge between a dark chaos of mountains on the left and the deep gorge of the Indus on the right. When we came this way a month ago the whole area was white but now the thaw is complete. Beyond the Indus stark cliffs rose sheer from the water and at a little distance seemed to have the texture of brown velvet. We watched three spectacular rock-falls on these but our track was rarely at risk. Over the uninhabited twelve-mile stretch from Gol to Gomo Thurgon we saw only one other person – a mail-runner jogging along with a small sealed sack on his back. He looked at us with a strange expression, as though he didn't believe it was true, and never for an instant altered the rhythm of his jog-trot.

I feared rain when the clouds thickened and sank lower and the wind blew more strongly and coldly against us. However, as we turned into the Skardu Valley it began to snow instead; not the attractive dry snow to which we have become accustomed, but dreary wet 'Irish' snow that melted as it landed. With every mile we became wetter and colder and soon visibility was down to fifty yards and liquid mud lay six inches deep on the track. Frequently through the gloom we heard the uncanny booming of avalanches and despite the extremity of my discomfort I rejoiced to have known Baltistan in this mood, too. One doesn't expect one's beloved to be always amiable. Sadiq tells us that throughout the Skardu Valley it has been snowing thus for four days and nights non-stop.

It was exactly 5 p.m. when we arrived back at Skardu and I thrust Rachel – soaked and shivering – into our cold little room. First I got Hallam unloaded (not easy with numb fingers), rubbed down and fed. Next I unpacked the load, got the stove going, undressed Rachel, wrapped her in a quilt, made tea – and discovered that our bedding, too, had been saturated. Therefore I had to settle down at once to the excessively laborious task of drying our flea-bags by the stove. And so to bed – not a moment too soon.

SKARDU. 6 MARCH

Today in Skardu nobody could walk ten yards without becoming mud to the knees and I found a stick essential to keep upright. The grey sky hung low and our ceiling has sprung so many leaks that there is hardly space between them for charpoys, while our floor has become a milder version of the ground outside; and poor Hallam's ceiling is even worse. Four schoolboys spent the afternoon on the roof but I fear their shovelling will have further damaged the disintegrating mud. Many Skardu households have the same problem at present.

We spent the day calling on friends, all of whom warned us against leaving for Shigar before the weather improves. Despite Skardu's unattractiveness just now, it feels good to be back in our Balti 'hometown' where we are welcomed so warmly by so many families – and by traders in the bazaar, and neighbours met at the stream, and policemen on the barrack verandah. Skardu may lack the Instant Friendliness of Khapalu, but once it has accepted you all is well.

SKARDU. 7 MARCH

There was a great improvement in the weather today, with disastrous consequences for us. The hot sun melted so much snow on our roof that when we got back from a kerosene-hunt we found all our bedding sodden. But it soon dried when hung outside. The early afternoon was repeatedly punctuated by the cracking and booming of avalanches. Rachel spent the forenoon at the local girls' school with some of her young friends; she finds it very difficult to keep upright while walking around Skardu under these conditions. The kerosene shortage is now acute because no jeeps are able to get through from Juglote, the track having been blocked by seven major landslides.

SKARDU. 8 MARCH

This morning we called on the Chief Superintendent, who told us that throughout Baltistan a tragic amount of fertile land is destroyed by erosion every year, which partly explains why many villages give an impression of having once enjoyed greater prosperity. If the Baltis were trained in methods of do-it-yourself flood-control enormous tracts of land could be saved. Obviously peasants who are capable of farming these mountainsides would profit by such training, though now they fatalistically accept the destruction of their most fruitful (literally) lowlands as the 'will of Allah'.

During our conversation several jeep-owners, the majority Pathans, came into the office to plead for an issue of petrol, but all had to be refused. It was not clear to me why the Chief Super-intendent of Police was responsible for petrol-rationing, rather than the Civil Supply Officer in the next room. But such is life in Skardu. Then it occurred to me to mention that I could find no kerosene, though the C.S.O. had given me a chit. At once Raja Karim Khan attempted to solve our problem by despatching a young recruit to search for the precious fluid – complete with our jerry-can, chit and Rs.9. It is now bedtime and the youth has not reappeared: but undoubtedly he will, one day.

Tomorrow we are going to Satpara for a day-trip, weather permitting.

SKARDU. 9 MARCH

When we set off after breakfast there was some cloud on the peaks but much blue overhead, yet by 2 p.m. it was snowing again steadily. The whole Satpara Valley is still snow-bound and the lake is completely covered in thick ice which supports a blanket of snow, so that one could pass it without even suspecting its existence. The jeep-track has long since been obliterated and the locals have tramped out for themselves an independent footpath which became so uncomfortable – and eventually dangerous – for Hallam that we had to turn back a mile short of the hamlet. By then a steady pre-snow wind was blowing and the clouds were down; I am fated not to see the head of the Satpara Valley on a clear day.

The regular habits of avalanches astonish me. As we were walking around the invisible lake we heard today's first 'gun-shot', followed after the usual moment of tense silence by a terrific rumbling boom –

the loudest we have heard – seeming to come from the far side of a mountain on the west shore of the lake. I looked at my watch: it was 11.58. It is quite extraordinary how the first avalanche each day is heard between 11.55 and 12.05.

Deep grooves and long brown earth-stains were visible on the steeper snowy slopes and while coming from Skardu we had noticed fresh blood stains on the white path – a curiously melodramatic combination of colours. After about two miles we came to the scene of the accident, where the stains continued up a snowy slope to an expanse of bare scree. At one point high on the snow there was a wide patch of crimson, from which the victim had rolled down to the path, bringing a small rock-fall with him. Later we heard that he had been traversing the scree, searching for a lost sheep, when a rock hit him on the head. But like a true Balti he picked himself up, tied his shirt around the wound and walked four miles to the hospital – where he found no one on duty, because this is Sunday. So he tightened the tourniquet and walked another eight miles home. A few months among the Baltis make one realize how perilously effete we Westerners have become. After a few more generations of pampering and motor-transport our bodies will no longer be capable of normal functioning.

SKARDU. 10 MARCH

This morning saw a historic event of enormous interest: the removal by the Misses Murphy of their clothes, after almost three months. Rachel was disappointed – 'Our *bodies* don't look dirty! It's all on our vests!' Apparently one does not get progressively dirtier in a very cold climate. That protective coating of oil which establishes itself on the skin seems to repulse dirt. There was of course nothing to be done with our underclothes but drop them on the midden outside, from where they will soon be retrieved by some fuel-hunter. I decided against washing before putting on clean garments. Who knows what temperatures we may encounter up the Shigar Valley?

Today's weather has been vile. It snowed wetly and continuously, the low sky was almost black and the icy damp seemed to chill one's very marrow. Walking around the town was neat hell, with deep sticky mud trying to drag one's boots off, or skiddy mud making it impossible to keep upright even with a stick.

This evening I am seriously worried about the kerosene crisis. For days we have been desperately borrowing from friends – a pint here, two pints there – and the young policeman was unable after all to find any. At this rate we shall have to go to Shigar without our stove and depend on the precarious local supply of firewood.

SKARDU. 11 MARCH

Today's weather was fractionally less dismal than yesterday's; and our horizons were brightened by the discovery of four gallons of kerosene, which means that we can return what we borrowed and leave for Shigar as soon as the sun comes out. I also found a few potatoes in the Old Bazaar – expensive at Rs.2 a seer but they made the best meal we have had for months.

Satu was available in the Kiris bazaar at Rs.1 a seer and I bought four seers for our Shigar trek; mixed with thermos-hot tea it provides a warm picnic lunch, instead of our usual hard-boiled eggs on a good day and dried apricots when times are hard.

12

Spring comes to the Shigar Valley

The Shigar Valley had no mean glories of its own. It is a broad,
flat, open valley: but it is bounded on each side, and at head
and at base by lofty mountains of the ruggedest type,
culminating in needle peaks or covered with eternal snow.

Sir Francis Younghusband (*c.* 1888)

Happiness depends on the taste, and not on the thing, and it is
by having what we like, that we are made happy, and not by
having what others consider likeable.

La Rochefoucauld

SHIGAR. 12 MARCH

A blissful day, weather-wise and every-otherwise. By 8.45 we were
on the road, looking and sounding like tinkers as we jogged along
with kettle, pan and *dechi* rattling in their tattered sack. This cheerful
cacophony has become our Karakoram signature tune.

For seven miles we followed the Khapalu track, which has just
been reconstructed with gravel and sand. (The local P.W.D.
employs one coolie to every mile.) Then we crossed the Indus
by an oldish suspension bridge, where the river is about one
hundred yards wide. Its smooth green flow is broken only by a
few colossal, weirdly-shaped boulders; other gigantic lumps of
granite lie tumbled along the banks and the bridge's steel cables
are anchored to some of these. On the right bank the thaw is
almost complete and our track at once climbed to a long, wide shelf
of silver sand, dotted with low clumps of a tough desert plant not
relished even by goats. Towards Skardu this plain becomes a series
of elegantly curved sand-dunes, and ahead of us a long wall of
dark rock was lavishly veined with white marble. At its western

end rose a solitary, sharp, red-brown mountain and our track squeezed through a gap between this and the dark wall. Beyond the gap we were looking into a shallow valley where a distant goatherd was taking his animals away from us towards some invisible pasture.

After crossing a level semi-desert the track swung north to wriggle steeply up between arid, shattered mountains that looked as though some giant vandal had been venting his ill-temper on them. Higher and still higher we went, on to a long, narrow saddle where snow still lay deep and the air had a crispness I welcomed after the hot climb. Ahead were unfamiliar snow-peaks, wearing ribbons of pale vapour, and on either side rose gaunt black cliffs curiously pitted with round holes. We took it easy here, ambling along under a dark blue sky amidst the sort of fierce beauty and infinite silence that make me feel I never want to leave Baltistan.

Then we were looking up the tranquil Shigar Valley to its junction, some thirty miles away, with the much narrower Braldu and Basna valleys; and on our left Skardu's Rock was again visible, presiding over the confluence of the Shigar and the Indus. The long descent ended on a wide ledge scarcely eighty feet above river level. This flat land, at the base of dark, barren precipices, was covered with rocks, boulders, stones and pebbles of every size, shape and colour; we recklessly collected until my parka pockets were bulging. Next came orchards and dwellings, with women weaving on roofs and yak standing around looking imperious. I noticed here some unusual shades of grey-blue and cinnamon-brown among the cross-bred cattle. When the track became too muddy we followed footpaths across fields and passed through a string of hamlets before skidding and squelching into the centre of the town. I at once recognized the conspicuous mosque, and all the tiny houses and giant trees around it, from the photographs taken by the Duke of Abruzzi's expedition sixty-six years ago. Where else have the chief towns changed so little since 1909? No wonder my reactionary heart throbs with love for Baltistan.

In the main bazaar I glimpsed some fine wood-carvings on the balconies of several houses. I say 'glimpsed' because had I taken my eyes off the mud-slippy track for more than an instant I might have broken the ten eggs I had just bought. Beyond this bazaar a pompous new notice points disconcertingly to 'Government Servants Colony: Civil Hospital and P.W.D. Rest House'. Looking past the pleasant little Rest House, we saw the 'colony' – a row of abandoned half-built bungalows. Such aborted projects are characteristic of modern Baltistan: this 'colony' was probably conceived by some Islamabad bureaucrat who has never been further north than Murree. But happily it is behind the Rest House and from the verandah we look towards a radiant semi-circle of snow-peaks.

One of the many small boys in our entourage was sent to fetch the chowkidar by Ghulam Nabi, the dispenser at the Civil Hospital. Ghulam in fact runs the hospital, aided by an elderly nurse who comes, most improbably, from Rangoon. To serve a population of about 30,000 there are six beds and doctors rarely visit Shigar. But some 200 patients attend the clinic daily, the majority suffering from goitre complications, tuberculosis, bronchitis, eye diseases and worms.

It is hoped, by the Pakistan Tourism Development Corporation, that this valley will soon become Baltistan's Costa Brava. The British-built Rest House has recently been redecorated, lavishly furnished and fitted with electric switches and modern plumbing, neither of which seem likely to work in the foreseeable future. There is only one (very superior) charpoy in our room, but the thickly carpeted floor may be counted as a second bed. When the chowkidar appeared Ghulam told him to bring tea, which arrived half-an-hour after I had supplied it to the company. By now it takes me hardly fifteen minutes to unload Hallam, unpack, assemble and fill the stove and brew a kettle of *chai*. Practice indeed makes perfect.

SHIGAR. 13 MARCH

During our morning's exploration up the Shigar I had an unpleasant experience with quick-sand: fortunately Rachel was being geological just then and failed to notice. To avoid this hazard we had to go far out of our way, until the sand allowed us to dash across it to the safety of a cliff-face – which promptly proved to be not-so-safe, for a hunk of earth the size of a cottage fell across our path fifty yards ahead. There's never a dull moment, when you go for a short walk in the Karakoram.

At the top of this cliff we passed a group of houses amidst muddy fields and three young women, with tense, pleading expressions, insistently beckoned us. Following them, we were led through stables into a cramped, filthy, twilit, smoke-filled room in which an old woman lay on a heap of straw, naked but for a tattered quilt and coughing painfully. Her forehead was fever-hot and her hands, when she clutched mine gratefully, were wasted and trembling. Yet as she lay there, amidst the sort of squalid poverty our affluent society can scarcely imagine, she had an air of indestructible dignity. I sat beside her for half-an-hour, while Rachel was fed with dirt-encrusted apricots. Almost certainly this much-loved granny was dying, but I asked a grandson to accompany us to the Rest House and gave him a dozen antibiotic capsules, hoping he understood my instructions for their use.

After lunch we crossed the mountain torrent that races past the Rest House and followed narrow pathlets above irrigation channels, stopping often to gaze on the ferocious, jagged, glistening beauty of the Karakorams, with just an occasional plume of cloud floating near their summits. We returned through a huddle of ancient houses and saw many diminutive donkeys, and also quite a few dogs – collie-sized but more heavily-built – with short, off-white coats, blunt muzzles and cropped ears.

Shigar has always been the most prosperous of Baltistan's major valleys and some of its domestic architecture is slightly more sophisticated than the average – influenced perhaps by those Kashmiris who came to work on the town's main mosque. This was built 'a few hundred years ago' and the delicate open-work of the cornices is unexpected in a region where crude improvisation is the architectural norm. The pyramidal three-tiered roof looks incongruously pagoda-like and I am told the interior is impressive. As the locals are strict Shiahs we females were not allowed even to peep through the doorway.

SHIGAR. 14 MARCH

Overlooking the bazaar are three rock-peaks – named 'The Three Bears' by Rachel – and the tributary that passes the Rest House comes tumbling through a cleft between the small bear and the middle bear. We took off early to explore this narrow side-valley and near the edge of the town came on a novel (to me) anti-erosion device. Where the summer floods are at their most violent, scores of giant wicker baskets – about eight feet high and five or six feet in diameter – have been placed against the substantial embankment and filled with stones to break the force of the water. Immediately above these is a small pagoda-type mosque, very decrepit and seemingly inhabited by large numbers of quarrelsome poultry. Nearby, on higher ground, stands the Raja's old palace, a grey, four-storey, fortress-like building, overshadowing the impeccably traditional new palace – a two-storey, whitewashed structure with an outside wooden ladder-stairs and a simply-carved balcony facing south. Nobody can accuse Balti potentates of pampering themselves.

When our path entered the cold, shadowed cleft between the 'bears' we were amidst an intimidating conglomeration of boulders. Looking up, one could often see from where, exactly, a certain chunk of rock had fallen. The summit of the small bear seemed to overhang the path and I said, 'Doesn't it look like a bear's head sticking out!'

'It doesn't to me,' replied Rachel. 'It looks like a bit of mountain that's going to fall down any minute now.' And we both instinctively quickened our pace, though that 'bit of mountain' may not fall for another 500 years.

Beyond this short gorge the path climbed gradually towards a towering glitter of snow-peaks. On our right, across the torrent, smooth white slopes led up to a long line of rugged rock summits; and on our left were gentler, boulder-strewn slopes, already snow-free and flowing with thaw-water. This valley cannot be one of Shigar's summer pastures for only a few patches of land promise to be grassy. Yet the path is surprisingly good for much of the way, which puzzled me until we came to the remains of many little terraced fields, far

below us. This evening I was told vaguely, 'There used to be a village
there – we don't know what happened to it.' The Balti's lack of
interest in the past, either recent or distant, can be maddening. That
village must have existed within living memory, as here neither
paths nor fields survive very long unattended. Of course the path is
not consistently good; in several places it has dwindled almost to
nothing where it overhangs the deep gorge carved out by this
nameless (on my map) torrent.

For five hours we saw no other creature, though beyond the nullah
many animal tracks were visible in the snow. We often looked back to
where the mighty peaks beyond the Shigar rose shining above the
darkness of 'the three bears'; but luckily I was not looking over my
shoulder when the track ended abruptly on the edge of a profound
chasm, evidently recently created by some slight shudder of these
restless mountains. Here we seemed very close to the snows at the
head of the valley. Judging by the wind's keenness – despite the hot
noon sun – and by our sense of intimacy with the surrounding
heights, I would say we were at about 11,000 feet. It is unusual to
find a completely unpeopled nullah, so doggedly do the Baltis make
habitable the most unlikely places, and I relished the vast solitude.
Yet those tiny deserted fields were rather poignant, as was a grove of
gnarled fruit-trees opposite our enforced resting-place, where the
vanished village most probably stood.

I should of course have said '*my* resting place'. Even after a six-
mile uphill walk Rachel is not prone to immobility and while I sat
she pursued stones; by now the Rest House looks like a badly-run
geological museum. On the way up we had passed many expanses
of multi-coloured, shattered rock – great chunks of red, green,
white, pink, orange, black, purple, and huge blocks with several
colours in layers. Large lumps of white marble lay beside the path,
as though some Rennaissance palace had collapsed nearby, and mica
glittered everywhere like gold dust. We paused by one of the many
soft, rust-red rocks and literally took a boulder to pieces with our
bare hands.

Truly that lonely valley was perfection, with its long, graceful
snow slopes, and its arid sweeps of grey-brown scree beneath

soaring buttresses of tawny rock, and its all-dominating snow-giants. What an incomparable place Baltistan is! And how futile are all one's attempts to describe it! A pen can no more than hint at its glory.

SHIGAR. 15 MARCH

Today was rather disjointed, in a very pleasant way. After breakfast Ghulam Nabi begged me to inspect the hospital and as we had been invited to lunch by the Tahsildar there was time then for only a short wander around muddy fields. We saw the first ploughing of the season, on an exceptionally sunny terrace that had been spread with manure by women. Two yak-cow cross-breds were pulling the crudest possible wooden plough, without even an iron tip; leather thongs held it to the bamboo yoke and the ploughman had to exert considerable force to make any impression on the new-thawed earth. As each strip was ploughed, four men, wielding wide, clumsily-made wooden rakes, broke up the large lumps. Then the women reappeared and used bare hands to blend the manure with the rich brown soil, as though kneading some gigantic cake. Meanwhile the rakers had joined a small group of men at the edge of the field and were enjoying a few drags on a hookah and keeping their hands warm over a tiny fire of twigs and grass-roots.

To enter the Tahsildar's house we had to climb a steep ladder and struggle through a flock of dark brown mini-sheep who were lunching on the sun-warm roof. Then, in the entrance-hall, our way was blocked by two billy-goats fighting and a cock and hen mating. We were conducted out of the hot sun into a dark, chilly, low-ceilinged room, furnished only with a charpoy and a goat-hair carpet; it is a local status symbol to sit by a stove, burning scarce and expensive wood, instead of depending on the sun for warmth.

The young Tahsildar is taller than the average Balti and much given to emphasizing the importance of his job. His English is poor yet he insists on talking non-stop, very fast, and the results are not unlike those dotty conversations that come about with ancient deaf people.

Self: Do fishermen here use nets, or traps, or dynamite?

Tahsildar: Yes, Government plans a big dam to give electricity everywhere in Baltistan. To make it the engineers must use *much* dynamite.

Self: When was the village up that nullah (pointing) destroyed? When did the people leave?

Tahsildar: No, our people do not leave this valley. It is rich – all Shigar is rich. No one is destroyed.

I acquired from our fellow-guest (one of the High School's twelve teachers) the information that significant quantities of gold are found in the Shigar every summer. It is melted in the villages and sold (at night!) to smugglers who take it to Afghanistan via Chitral. I cannot help feeling that our informant was exaggerating the significance of the quantities, but it is a good story.

To entertain us during a prolonged pre-lunch hiatus, our host suggested visiting the nearby Girls' Primary School, founded in 1909 by the then Political Agent for Baltistan. I have never seen a more feeble educational establishment. The Tahsildar could come no further than the low door in the surrounding wall – Shigar takes purdah very seriously – and we entered unescorted to find two shy young women trying to teach thirty little girls the Urdu alphabet and simple arithmetic. The pupils sat outside a disintegrating school-building – the floors of which were inches deep in melted snow – and wrote on their dyed mulberry-wood boards with sharpened reeds dipped in a mixture of chalk and water. This chalky powder can be picked up by the handful on many mountainsides and when the water evaporates it leaves a clear deposit – so why squander money on ink? I tried to exchange words with the teachers, but they were too overcome by this visitation from Outside even to attempt to utter. And what was the point of it all, I wondered, as we left those meek little scraps struggling with their Urdu. As Shigar's future wives and mothers, what they most urgently need is advice on child-care and hygiene.

Back at the house lunch was still not ready and as we waited numerous men called to discuss business with our host. Each time the door opened I could see three menservants with anxious expressions squatting around the kitchen fire. At intervals one would go out to fetch more wood, which then had to be chopped with a too-small axe; as the fire tended to go out during chopping sessions a lot of blowing was required to set the large *dechi* of rice boiling again. All this effort at last produced excellent thick chapattis, soggy rice, watery gravy and the toughest – beyond doubt the toughest – meat I have ever eaten. There was no question of chewing it: one simply gulped the hunks whole and hoped for the best. Yet after three months in Baltistan this meal seemed a banquet.

On our way home we called on the Police Superintendent, who is married to the Raja of Khapalu's sister. No womenfolk appeared: Indian tea, and cream crackers imported from Pindi in ages past, were served by a ragged, bare-footed youth who also had to attend frequently to his master's magnificent jewelled hookah. Now and then the door was pushed open by a silken-haired young goat with glowing amber eyes who made the day for Rachel. He was a 'character' and plainly enjoyed provoking the Superintendent's wrath while at the same time being thrown apricots by the bevy of children who had gathered to study us at close quarters. Two boys were ordered to accompany us to the Rest House, one carrying on his back a big bale of hay and the other balancing on his head a big basin of barley. Our host had evidently heard of my unsuccessful efforts to buy grain for Hallam in the bazaar. I am relieved that the gallant creature has had a good feed before we set out tomorrow for Dasso, and possibly Askole. As with Hushe, there is some local uncertainty about whether or not the path is at present *ghora*-worthy. We shall soon see. Dasso is thirty-four miles from here so we reckon to spend two days getting that far.

YUNO. 16 MARCH

It is a long time since I have written my diary in such acute physical and mental discomfort. But I must try to organize my mind and begin at the beginning; and I am not complaining, for it has been a glorious day.

Three miles from Shigar the track began to climb, but so gradually that we scarcely noticed until, looking back, we saw the town's orchards as a reddish-brown haze far below, at the foot of bluish mountains. This valley is the least severe of all that we have seen. Its average width is five or six miles, with hamlets on both sides of the Shigar, which today was mostly invisible. The hamlets lie in hollows between the final slopes of high mountains and one switchbacks from hollow to hollow over desolate expanses of moraine. There is little cultivable land on this left bank, once the Shigar oasis has been left behind, but we could see hundreds of terraced fields across the river, where the snow remains thick. On our right, every few miles, a narrow side-valley allowed us a dazzling view of sharp snow peaks. Beyond the river an unbroken white mountain wall rose abruptly from the valley floor and was almost unbearably beautiful against the vivid blue sky. And at the head of the valley we could see other white giants meeting, where the Braldu and Basna Rivers unite to create the Shigar.

We stopped twice for meagre picnics and sand-castle building, and sun-bathing and nature-worship. Outside of the hamlets we rarely met anybody, but during our first stop a startling figure overtook us. This young man was wearing a cheap sky-blue lounge suit, a bright pink shirt and shiny plastic shoes, which outfit made him hideously conspicuous where everybody else wears garments that match the mountains. Obviously he had come off the plane we saw descending towards Skardu yesterday and was walking home, carrying goodies for the family in a bulging P.I.A. bag. Equally obviously, he was not disposed to fraternize with foreigners. He ignored our greetings and I found his expression singularly off-putting – a hard, sullen face and shifty eyes.

Having seen no jeep since leaving Skardu, our astonishment was considerable when we heard a distant engine at about four o'clock. (This rarely used jeep-track continues to the head of the valley.) Staring at the ridge behind us we saw a blue W.H.O. vehicle bumping into view and it contained two of our best Skardu friends – army doctors on an inspection tour of the area. They expressed great concern at our being twenty-one miles from Shigar and were aghast to hear that we had no idea where we were going to sleep. Then they volunteered to arrange accommodation for us at the next hamlet, but I suspect we would have done better just bumbling along on our own.

The disagreeable atmosphere here is probably partly owing to our being associated with 'interfering Punjabis'. (The Baltis seem to regard all Pakistanis as Punjabis.)

From the top of the next hump we saw Yuno at the foot of a steep, arid mountain with snow still lying on terraced fields below the dwellings. Then we met the returning jeep, being escorted by a score of men and youths. These the doctors not inaccurately described as 'stone-age types' and they handed us over to the least neolithic character. As the jeep disappeared he passed us on, for some inexplicable reason, to this really rather nasty family, who had made it quite plain that they would prefer to have nothing to do with us.

At times the language barrier gives an unreal tinge to events. While we stood under an enormous *chenar*, in the sudden grey coolness that comes when the sun has slipped behind the mountains, our 'guardian' conducted a vigorous and lengthy argument with several shrill-voiced women who glared at us from the edge of their roof as though we had the plague. Everybody spoke so quickly and vehemently that I could gather nothing of what was being said, but obviously we were extremely unwelcome. I was about to suggest to Rachel that we should push on to the next hamlet, visible three miles away, when our 'guardian' suddenly shook both his fists at the women and shouted some infuriated threat which abruptly ended the argument. He then beckoned us up the steep path to their house, which has a new room built on to the original structure and seems to be the poshest in the hamlet. While I was unloading and unsaddling – none of the dozen men standing around offered to help – Rachel found that the new wing is entered through a window. The men whispered and sniggered while they watched me carrying the load and tack to the room, which is about ten feet by thirty and has a big over-fed wood-stove. Soon Rachel and I were sweltering, so accustomed have we become to living in cold rooms and depending on our clothes for warmth. While writing this – on the floor, by the light of my own candle, in a corner as far as possible from the stove – I am dripping sweat; and poor Rachel, though exhausted, is unable to sleep because of the heat plus noise. Everyone in the family seems to have a wracking cough – inevitably, when they exchange this temperature for the Balti cold while clad only in rags.

To revert to our arrival. The first person I saw in the room was Blue Suit, sitting scowling on the edge of the charpoy beside the stove. Our reluctant host and hostess are his grandparents and his return to Yuno is provoking extraordinarily intense emotion; everyone who comes to greet him bursts into tears – men and women alike – as they press him to their bosoms and kiss him fondly.

As I was unpacking the stove to make tea Blue Suit asked brusquely, 'Are you Muslim?', and my reply generated a perceptible current of antagonism. Previously I have experienced this sort of bigotry only in Eastern Turkey; it is far less common than anti-Muslim writers would have us believe, though when it does occur it can make one feel wretchedly ill-at-ease. When I held out our kettle and politely requested *chu* everybody in the crowded room stared at me, without moving or speaking, for some moments. Then Blue Suit said, 'Here there is no water. Why do you not go to the next village? They have water. And there you can find Rest House. It is one mile only.' By this stage I was wishing that we had gone on, but having unpacked – and already paid an outrageous Rs.10 for very inferior fodder – I had no intention of being hustled away. Besides, I know the next hamlet does not have a Rest House and is at least three miles further up the valley.

Rachel's reaction to 'no *chu*' was robust – 'You can't have a village without water!' And picking up our *dechi* she climbed through the window and vanished. Fifteen minutes later she returned, looking puzzled, with the *dechi* packed full of off-white snow. 'It's true,' she said. 'There's no stream, no irrigation channel, no well. I had to go down to the fields for snow. But I dug below the surface so it won't be too dirty.' Daughters have their uses.

All evening no hospitality has been offered us, though in a normal Balti home, however poor, apricots and kernels are at once placed before the guests. At the moment fifteen people are eating a starvation-level meal of chapattis washed down by thawed snow. One can only hope the edge was taken off their appetites by the apricots they have been chewing for hours past. (No wonder the old Chinese geographers called Baltistan 'Tibet of the apricots'.) I am filled with despair because our host keeps on stoking the stove, presumably in honour of Blue Suit's return. By Balti standards this is a rowdy family; so far the conversation has been mainly a series of arguments about money, with the harsh voices of the men and the shrill voices of the women frequently raised. It is now 10.15 – long past bed-time for all decent Baltis – but another hubble-bubble has just been prepared and outside I can hear the dread sound of more wood being chopped. From time to time our host directs towards me a glance that is almost malevolent, or at least seems so, by the light of a flickering wick in a wall-niche just above his head. He is a tall, thin man with an oddly triangular pale face and a straggle of black beard. Like the rest of the family he suffers from grievously diseased eyes and his expression is the most unsmiling I have ever seen; under no circumstances can one imagine his face relaxing its grim lines.

And so to bed, but not – I fear – to sleep.

SILDI. 17 MARCH

What a night that was! Rachel had collapsed into an uneasy sleep just before I squeezed down beside her on a mud floor carpeted only with thick dust. For the next three hours I lay in sweaty misery while the stove was kept red-hot and the hookah continued to bubble and the company continued to argue. Repeatedly I reached the edge of sleep only to be jerked back from it by heat and noise and fleas. At one stage the Kashmir problem was being passionately discussed and I gathered – because Blue Suit was giving all the latest Pindi news – that today there is to be a general *hartal* of Muslims in India, organized by Mr Bhutto.

It was 1.40 a.m. before everyone (except our host) had settled down on the floor. We were nineteen, not counting numerous babies who had contributed their share to the evening's din and continued to give tongue at intervals throughout what remained of the night. I was enduring an agony of thirst, for which there was no remedy, and when I at last fell into a doze I was awakened by a powerful kick on the nose from Rachel. This caused such a spectacular haemorrhage that I had to remove my socks to mop up. It really was quite a night: definitely among my Top Ten for sheer discomfort.

At 5.40 our host rose from his charpoy, dipped his spouted pot into a great cauldron of melted snow beside the stove and went out to perform his ritual ablutions before prayers. He came in just as the sun was rising, turned towards Mecca (more or less) and began to intone aloud. The other males did likewise while I boiled our tea-water, having helped myself from the cauldron despite Blue Suit's muttered disapproval. We were so dehydrated after our sweaty night that we quickly emptied two kettles of black, unsweetened, filthy-tasting tea. For breakfast we had apricots and *satu* while the family had scraps of *roti* and herb-tea.

When everything was packed up, Rachel and I went out together to the latrine. (A diet of dried apricots leads to Regular Habits.) On the way we spent some moments admiring the peaks beyond the Shigar. A trail of soft pearly-rosy cloud was just touching the sharpness of snowy crests – which were rapidly becoming golden, one after another, as the sun rose above the eastern mountains.

Then, as I was loading Hallam, I observed that at least Rs.5 worth of kerosene had been stolen from the jerry-can – our first Balti theft, though our kit has so often been left unguarded for hours. This was a mean trick, when I had already given the family three pints of kerosene for their ink-bottle lamp, a dozen boxes of matches and Rachel's fur-lined anorak, which would cost at least Rs.75 in Skardu's K2 Store (a second-hand shop in the New Bazaar). I let it be seen that I had noticed the theft, but I thought it best not to get too rough. It is most unlikely that these people would have harmed us, yet there was about them an unmistakable aura of degeneracy and one can never entirely trust bigoted Muslims in a primitive region.

Our first stop was to water Hallam near the next tiny hamlet – the last in the valley – where several small streams of muddy melted snow crossed the track. Then we followed the mountains' contours high above the valley floor, and crossed several small landslides. By 9 I was sweating, though a slight descent had taken us on to a snowfield with that curious satiny sheen which precedes the thaw. Colossal angular boulders are strewn over this expanse and around these 'storage-heaters' the thaw is sufficiently advanced for clumps of thyme to have reappeared. These so tantalized Hallam that we halted here and for half-an-hour he tore ravenously at the dry, grey-brown bushes.

The next village was Dasso, some ten miles away up the Braldu Valley, and the head of the Shigar Valley was close – towering bastions of rock all jumbled together in snowy magnificence, leaving just enough space for the Braldu and Basna Rivers to find a way through. I scrutinized the steep, pale brown mountains above Yuno and wondered why no thaw-water flows down their arid flanks: there is plenty of snow on the summits and it must go *somewhere*. Very odd.

At the head of the valley the track finally gave up pretending to be a road; but here the P.W.D. (or someone) has certainly tried hard to improve communications. As our path dropped to river level – it must be partially submerged during summer – we could see the remains of two other paths very high up on the precipitous mountains directly above. Both have been broken in a dozen places by avalanches, rock-falls and landslips, but possibly one is repaired annually for summer traffic.

Soon our path became horrid for Hallam, with round, loose river-bed stones underfoot and a few feet of snow on either side. Then it became horrid for me, with liquid mud inches deep and the nearby snow too soft to take my weight. The Braldu Valley narrowed as we went east and we looked in awe at many massive new avalanches sprawled across the red-brown slopes on our right. These mountains were much more broken and jagged than the neat grey rock wall beyond the invisible river. At last our path curved across the snow towards the Braldu and we saw a racing, pea-soup tinted torrent, hardly forty yards wide. Next a huge outcrop of rock had to be negotiated and Hallam was twice brought to his knees by black ice in the permanent shadow of overhangs. Although Rachel had dis-mounted and the load was piled high he frequently seemed likely to go over the edge. It was impossible to estimate the true width of the path as snow lay deep along the verge; often when I prodded what seemed like solid ground it disappeared in an unsoothing way. Then we turned a corner and just ahead the path could be seen traversing a gigantic avalanche on a steep, snow-laden mountain. I looked at my watch: it was 11.45. We were hardly five miles from Dasso but the sun was very hot and prudence dictated a retreat.

Rachel was furious. 'But we're nearly there!' she protested. 'Why are you fussing now? You don't usually fuss – why do we have to go back today?'

'Because there is a time to fuss,' I replied crisply, 'and in my estimation this is it. Now will you kindly stop talking and get off this mountain as fast as you can!' Which she did, being essentially an obedient child, while I with great difficulty turned a somewhat unnerved Hallam on a boulder jutting out from the narrow path.

When we had re-negotiated the outcrop I readjusted the load and Rachel remounted. Then, characteristically, she pursued her study of the maternal psychology. 'How do you *know* it's time to fuss?' she demanded. '*I* think we've been on much more dangerous paths.'

'We have,' I agreed, 'but not at noon in mid-March on an avalanche mountain. It's time to fuss when survival has nothing to do with personal skill or caution. On a dangerous path one can be surefooted and careful. But one can only die in the face of an avalanche.'

'I see,' said Rachel. And I hope she does.

On our return march we made a detour in an unsuccessful attempt to see the birth of the Shigar, where the Braldu and Basna unite. This involved following an uncomfortable little path over loose stones through deep snow to the edge of the Braldu. As we reached the water six men – the first people we had seen since leaving Yuno – arrived on the opposite bank. They had of course been visible for some time, moving towards us like ants across an immense width of snow, each man carrying a heavy goat-skin sack. They made no attempt to return my greeting but stared at us with that bewildered incredulity which is the normal reaction of the Baltis to the Misses Murphy. Then they took off their *shalwars*, tied them to their loads, and in three pairs, with arms around one another's shoulders and sticks used to steady themselves, began very slowly to cross. The racing torrent was groin-deep and I realized too late that our presence meant their having to endure wet shirts in the cause of modesty. Their main difficulty was not the strength of the current – trying though that must have been – but the shifting stones on the river-bed. Three of the men were elderly and the frailest of these slipped once, briefly submerging his sack. But we discovered that it contained butter, so no harm was done.

When the men had gone on their way we remained by the water, stoically masticating apricots while Hallam enjoyed his oats. He is now much the best-fed member of the expedition; lifting Rachel into the saddle, I notice that she weighs about half what she did three months ago.

The sun was hot and the air sparkling as we continued down the valley. Despite our 'defeat', I count this among the best of many wonderful Balti days; and it emphasized the curious fact that here neither hunger nor lack of sleep seem to matter. Is this owing to the altitude or to the euphoria engendered by Baltistan's beauty? Whatever the cause, it is most convenient to live on a plane so exalted that after an hour's sleep one can effortlessly walk twenty-two miles on three fistfuls of apricots.

When we arrived in Sildi at 5.30 it seemed that we were again going to be ostracized. The first four men I approached either didn't understand my request for shelter or pretended not to – I fancy the latter. Then I went towards an old woman on a roof, with a kindly, very wrinkled and incredibly dirty face. Before I could speak she beckoned me to bring Hallam around the side of her house and pointed to a one-roomed hovel some thirty yards away, which proved to be the residence-cum-shop of her married grandson. This young man's wife and two children, aged three and one, have filthy faces covered with appalling running sores but are cheerful and friendly. Water was willingly provided and sugar was on sale in the shop (at Rs.9 a seer: I notice that most customers buy only a few spoonfuls), so I soon had a kettle of very sweet tea on the boil – the sort of concoction that would revolt me at home but here takes the place of a strong whiskey at 6 p.m. The little room quickly filled up with curious villagers and at first everybody seemed well-disposed towards us. Then a tall, arrogant, handsome young mullah arrived and treated us with calculated rudeness. While he sat by the stove we were ignored, but the moment he went everyone relaxed and our young hostess brought us four hot chapattis from the kitchen across the yard where granny was preparing supper. By the time we had wolfed these, with a second kettle of tea, Rachel was almost asleep on her feet; but there was no room to bed her down until our host, five of his friends and his wife had used the prayer-mat spread in the centre of the floor. When I unrolled her flea-bag the two other children were laid to rest beside her, wrapped in unspeakable shreds of old quilts. Meanwhile, business was brisk in the 'shop' – a home-made cupboard some six feet high and three feet wide containing small amounts of dust tea, rock salt, goats' milk butter, sugar, cigarettes, multi-coloured glass bangles and soap.

The young couple's supper was brought from the kitchen by granny; it consisted of a small bowl of nasty-looking grey liquid, with four very thin chapattis for Him and two for Her. Then it was bed-time (8.30) so our hostess lay on the floor between the children and fed the year-old girl while her husband rolled himself in the only warm quilt and settled down on a narrow charpoy. In Baltistan one gets the general impression that women have the status of talking animals.

SHIGAR. 18 MARCH

It was another restless night. I lay squeezed between Rachel and the three-year-old, whose frequent wretched whimperings in my ear were augmented by his sister's no less frequent spasms of coughing and crying. During the small hours our host summoned his wife, but when no longer needed she returned to the floor. All the time I was being tormented by fleas who have come out of hibernation with appetites like lions, and Rachel tossed and muttered and scratched in her sleep though she never actually woke.

We set out at 7.45 a.m. and dawdled happily over the fourteen sunlit miles back to Shigar. When we paused in a village to look for food one mini-stall was open and on a top shelf reposed a solitary four-ounce packet of desiccated biscuits. Two tiny eggs were also on offer and I devoured these raw on the spot, to the enormous amusement of the assembled villagers.

We saw many more teams ploughing, the majority so reluctantly that it took three or four men to drive two animals; and two pairs of men were themselves pulling ploughs because their dzo had broken away and galloped off with raised tails, pursued by gangs of delighted small boys. In this valley we have seen more pack-ponies than elsewhere – small, sturdy and woolly, not at all like our lean, long-legged Hallam, who is really much too big for Balti paths. (I feel sure he has foreign blood.) To own a pack-pony is a considerable status symbol, because of feeding costs, and most people shoulder their own burdens, pausing often to rest on 'shooting-sticks'. These have a length of wood across the top to form a seat and are very necessary for long journeys through snow, or when a man's load is too heavy for him to sit on the ground or get up again without help.

During one of our halts today, near a long slab of rock used as a regular resting-place, we were joined by three laden men who have unwittingly given me a guilt-complex. They were driving an unusually docile dzo, and leading a billy-goat with a goat-hair rope tied around his horns, and each was in his way a typical Balti. The barefooted old man, with an aquiline nose and an unkempt beard, was tall and thin and clad in rags; the middle-aged, shorter man wore a patched blanket and had a huge hanging goitre and a squeaky voice; the one-eyed young man who led the goat had a broad Mongolian face, a half-witted expression and a slight limp. When they paused beside us the old man mumbled a return to my greeting and all three stood staring at us for some moments in silence, before slowly lowering themselves on to the resting-rock. They then continued to stare in silence, as did the dzo and the goat, and I suddenly caught myself thinking (or rather, feeling) that there was perhaps more in common between them and their animals than between them and us. At once I was genuinely shocked by this involuntary reaction to three fellow-humans, a reaction that outrages the teachings of every religion and code of ethics, not to mention the U.N. charter and my own personal principles. But can it be that on occasions involuntary reactions push one closer to reality than one wishes to be? Ever since, I have been wondering just how equal men in fact are – forgetting principles and ideals. If those three had been transported, at birth, to a relatively prosperous Pakistani or Irish home, and brought up by loving, educated foster-parents, how would they strike one today?

I have come to suspect that in their pre-Islamic era the Baltis were only superficially influenced by Buddhism. The fact that they seem to have abandoned it so readily indicates this; in Tibet proper, neither Christian nor Islamic missionaries ever made any significant number of converts. Like the nomads of West Tibet – their comparatively near neighbours – the Baltis were probably primitive animists below the surface, with only a very vague idea of what Buddhism is all about.

SHIGAR. 19 MARCH

Among the glories of this Rest House is a roll of pale pink loo-paper, left here last summer by one of the two tourists (an American girl and a Frenchman) entered in the Register for 1974. Rachel asked excitedly, 'How did *this* get here?', and when I explained she curled her lip. 'They must've been cissies to put *loo-paper* in their luggage!'

'It doesn't follow,' I said mildly. 'Not everyone has been brought up the hard way, on snowballs and stones.'

Life in Baltistan certainly teaches one to adapt a few possessions to many uses: I can think of no better antidote to the West's gadget-demented sub-culture. Our sack, for instance, is officially a sack – if you follow me – but in its off-duty hours it becomes, according to prevailing conditions, a window-curtain, a table-cloth, a mattress, a pillow, a horse-blanket or a floor-covering to protect new Rest House carpets from my culinary activities. Similarly, the lid of the old Complan tin used as a tea-caddy also serves as a mirror (the inside) and a candle-holder (the outside), while our frying-pan serves as Hallam's grain-dish, and our kettle as tea-pot, and our nailbrush as clothes-brush, saucepan-cleaner, boot-brush and potato-scrubber, and our *dechi* as wash-up basin and, *in extremis*, as chamber-pot. Possibly the time is nearer than we think for the Western world to learn how expendable are most of its newfangled gadgets.

A non-glory of this Rest House is the water supply, despite numbers of sparkling streams nearby. I discovered today, when the chowkidar was missing, why our tea has been tasting so strongly of soap. About ten yards upstream from where he fills our bucket the local women wash clothes, secluded between two large rocks.

We spent the morning meandering around Shigar and taking Hallam for a ten-mile trot. During the afternoon I sunbathed while four friendly boys took Rachel to their various homes to meet their womenfolk. Today I have felt almost sulkily reluctant to return to the duties, labours and manifold complexities of Outside. As I lay in the sun, gazing at the still white glory of the surrounding peaks, I wished childishly that Baltistan were the only world I needed to know for the future.

SKARDU. 20 MARCH

There was an inevitable melancholy about today's return to Skardu – our last trek with the faithful Hallam. Yet it was impossible to feel gloomy for long with the gentleness of spring in the air and the orchards no longer snowy and silent but budding and filled with new bird-song. Tiny shoots of tender green flecked banks that only eight days ago were heaped with snow, and now the valley floor is a smooth expanse of grey-brown sand while the track is firm and dry.

Having crossed the high saddle we stopped for two midday hours near the foot of the solitary mountain. Rachel made one of her elaborate sand-castles and road-systems while I sat against a boulder working for my lunch by breaking apricot stones. Three months ago I as often as not broke the kernel, too; now I give one expert rap and the shell splits neatly. When we got up to go I looked at my 'litter' and reflected that a true Balti would carefully collect that little pile of broken shells and carry it home for fuel. Perhaps I feel so at ease in Baltistan because of my essentially frugal nature, which in Europe is offended every day by our mindless 'consumer society' waste of food, objects and energy.

An hour later we were crossing the young Indus for the last time. We paused in the middle of the bridge to look down at its swift green strength where it swirls between monstrous sleek boulders; when we cross it next it will be a mature river, broad and brown, flowing powerfully past Attock Fort.

Skardu has been transformed by the thaw – this was our first time to see it not completely covered with thick snow. In spring it looks even less like a real town as everyone ploughs their fields, which lie between the bazaars and ramshackle government offices and drab new cantonment areas. Each householder farms a few fields, whatever his other occupation, and people I had connected only with their sedentary winter jobs were out this afternoon, sweating and already suntanned. Some were driving teams of cross-breds, while others scattered seeds from leather pouches or wicker baskets, or dragged crude wooden harrows over the lumpy earth. One neighbour of ours – a little old man with a short grey beard and merry eyes – had improvised a labour-saving device and was looking very pleased with himself. Under a wooden lid, removed from a large chest, he had tied bushes of some strong, thorny scrub – and on the lid sat his beaming little granddaughter, thoroughly enjoying herself as grandad pulled her up and down his new-ploughed field.

This evening I at last brought myself to decide on a departure date: the 24th, Insh' Allah and weather permitting. It is best to go quickly, since go we must.

SKARDU. 21 MARCH

Today is Now Ruz, a very important festival for Shiahs, as it has been for many races and creeds throughout the millennia. It certainly seems a much more rational New Year's Day than 1 January, but unfortunately the weather refused to co-operate this year in Skardu. The morning was grey and chilly, with dark clouds sitting firmly on the mountains as we strolled through the bazaars looking for signs of celebration. Friends embraced smilingly as they met, groups stood about chatting and many were sauntering along holding hands and showing each other eggs painted purple, orange, pink or blue. New garments are traditional for Now Ruz and a few prosperous merchants were dressed in entirely new outfits, including exquisitely embroidered sleeveless leather jackets. A large minority wore nothing new and the rest sported one new garment, usually a shirt or *shalwar* made of some cheap gaudy material. These flashes of colour, where normally only homespun clothes are worn, provided the sole festive touch as one looked around. Many shops were open, though Now Ruz is a Public Holiday, and it struck me that the tortured mourning of *Muharram* appeals more to the local temperament than this joyful occasion. Unlike the Khapalu people, these Skardu folk have little talent for gaiety.

During the afternoon we heard in the distance what might have been a Sousa march before the Baltis got at it, and Sadiq told us that a band always accompanies the annual soccer match between Police recruits and High School pupils. The notion of soccer to music tickled my fancy, so we made for the parade ground and saw a straggle of men and boys drifting around the edges, indiscriminately cheering the inept but well-mannered teams. The Baltis do not yet take their football very seriously. On a short row of chairs along one sideline sat People of Consequence, and when we appeared another chair was at once provided. Yet there was the usual lack of ease in the presence of a 'liberated' woman. This is not a lack of friendliness but a total inability to relax with an unescorted and therefore probably immoral Western woman. A solitary female traveller is almost as shocking to the isolated, orthodox Shiahs of Skardu as a naked woman would be to the average Dubliner. Remembering this, one must commend these people for their tolerance and not complain about their aloofness.

We enjoyed the second half of the match, during which the band quickened its tempo when the game livened up and stopped abruptly when the ball went out of play, as it frequently did. The final score was one all. Then the Police prepared to give a display of Balti folk-dancing, whereupon the spectators became much more enthusiastic and swarmed on to the pitch to form three sides of a square. Our chairs formed the fourth side and the band sat opposite us on the ground – two drummers and a flautist. The dancers emerged from the crowd in groups of two, three or four and were amusing enough but not outstanding, apart from one pair of elderly men who engaged in a mock duel with wooden swords. Two dances struck me as very Tibetan and I discovered these were specialities of the Khapalu area.

All the performances were accompanied by the crowd's rhythmic clapping and I have never before seen the Skarduites in such a light-hearted mood.

For us Now Ruz ended on a sordid note. Rachel was abed and I had just begun this entry when a pathetic small voice said, 'What's biting me doesn't feel like fleas.' I took up my candle to examine the victim and the bites did not *look* like fleas, either. So I lit another candle, the better to hunt, and found Rachel's clothes literally *crawling* with tiny grey body-lice. This was an extremely serious situation. I threw away all those filthy garments we removed before going to Shigar, so at present we have only the clothes we stand up (and lie down) in. Having made sure that the victim's skin was lice-free, I thrust her, naked and shivering, into my flea-bag. Then I stripped to examine my own garments. Mercifully these are not lice-infested, though I caught three fleas, and Rachel is now comfortably asleep in my vest and sweater under her own snow-suit. Body-lice are well named; there was not one louse on her pants, tights and stockings, despite the swarming mass of grey horrors on her upper garments. I dropped the infested clothes in a far corner of the field; first thing tomorrow they must be boiled. I find I react quite differently to fleas and lice. There is something so irresistibly comical about fleas that one can feel no real animosity towards them; a flea-hunt is a form of sport, demanding considerable skill, and one has to admire the creatures' cheeky agility. But those slow grey crawlers this evening really revolted me.

SKARDU. 22 MARCH

This was the day I have been dreading. We sold Hallam for Rs.400 to Sadiq's brother who lives nearby. I was even more upset than Rachel and became excessively snappish, not having her outlet of tears. Therefore when she most needed cheering she got unearned abuse instead. I had not thought it could be so awful: it felt almost as bad as parting from a dog. He was such a gallant member of our team, and in his quiet way such a personality. And now there is only that awful emptiness and silence in the next room . . .

SKARDU. 23 MARCH

Yet another sunless day – the whole valley a study in grey and brown under a sullen sky. Unless the weather improves there will be no flight tomorrow but, just in case, I did all my sorting out and packing up this morning.

At 2.30 we went to the polo-ground to see the first match of the season, between Skardu Town and the Karakoram Scouts. This is the sport (described by Vigne as 'hockey on horse-back') which really fires the Baltis, and hundreds of excited spectators were milling around at the foot of the Rock. Rachel was beside herself with delight at the sight of so many prancing ponies, gorgeously dressed and obviously revelling in the pre-match tension. When the contest started – two hours late, after a thrilling tent-pegging competition – it lacked both the murderous verve of a game I saw years ago in Yasin and the polished skill of polo on the plains. Nor were the ponies in top condition at the end of winter; the civilians' were too thin and the officers' too fat. However, Karakoram polo can never be dull and the final score of six all seemed to please everybody. We then hurried off to a farewell party at which I was most moved to see a cherished two-ounce tin of Nescafé being opened in my honour – the first coffee I have tasted since 18 December.

At sunset a gale-force southern wind began to howl through the valley and just now (9.30) I have been out to look at the weather. The wind has dropped already and after three cloudy days the sky is clear. Alexander Cunningham reported that 'Skardu' may mean 'the starry place', and tonight the glitter of the stars seemed so close I fancied that by reaching high I could pluck them out of the blackness.

It is difficult to accept the fact that we shall probably be Outside in little more than twelve hours' time.

ISLAMABAD. 24 MARCH

We *are* Outside – and pretty frightful it is, too. No doubt the altitude change is partly to blame for my unfavourable reaction. I feel uncharacteristically depressed, my head aches, I might weep if you looked at me too hard and nothing interests me. Also, I am utterly repelled by the luxury of my immediate surroundings, and by the noise, bustle and smells of twentieth-century life. I miss Hallam, I miss the snow-peaks, the silence, the contentment, the thin clear air, the sense of exhilaration and energy and *peace* . . .

It must only be a matter of time before we go back to Baltistan – perhaps for an early autumn trek, when we can leave all jeep-tracks behind and follow small paths over high passes.

List of Equipment

GENERAL

1 lightweight high-altitude tent
1 riding-cum-pack saddle,
   with crupper, leathers and irons
1 compass-cum-pedometer
1 quart water-bottle
1 small kerosene stove
1 two-gallon plastic jerry-can
1 tin kettle
1 tin *dechi*
1 fork
2 knives
2 spoons
2 small plastic bowls
2 large plastic mugs
1 tin-opener
1 scissors
1 small towel
1 tin toothpowder
2 toothbrushes
1 cake soap
1 Boy Scout first aid kit

50 penicillin tablets
1 tube penicillin ointment
50 water-purifying tablets
50 sulphaguanadine tablets
200 Vitamin C pills
200 multivitamin pills
15 yards nylon rope
1 camera
10 rolls of film
4 maps
3 large notebooks
10 biros
20 coloured felt-tipped pencils
1 large sketching pad
6 school text-books
3 exercise-books
1 big canvas zip-bag
1 very large rucksack
1 very small rucksack
2 electric torches
12 batteries

MY CLOTHING

1 husky-suit
1 nylon anorak
1 pair slacks
2 woollen vests
2 woollen underpants

1 sweater
1 pair socks
1 pair hiking boots
1 scarf
1 Chitrali cap

1 pair silk skiing gloves
1 pair leather gloves
1 ex-German army parka jacket
1 astronaut's blanket

1 high-altitude sleeping-bag
1 cotton-padded sleeping-bag
1 nylon cape-cum-groundsheet

MY BOOKS

*The Karakoram and Western
 Himalaya*, Fillipo de Fillipi
The Horned Moon, Ian Stephens
Pakistan, Ian Stephens
War and Peace
Anna Karenina

The Mandarins, Simone de
 Beauvoir
Literature and Western Man,
 J. B. Priestley
*The Seven Ages of
 Man* (Shakespeare Anthology)

RACHEL'S CLOTHING

1 padded snow-suit
2 sweaters
1 pair slacks
2 woollen vests
2 woollen underpants
1 pair socks
1 pair fur-lined boots
1 Viyella shirt

1 pair woollen tights
1 pair sheep-skin gloves
1 woollen balaclava
1 hard riding-hat with chin-strap
1 down-padded sleeping bag
1 inflatable cushion
1 toy squirrel

RACHEL'S BOOKS

The Kingdom Under the Sea, Joan
 Aiken
A Book of Princesses, ed. Sally
 Patrick Johnson

William the Fourth, Richmal
 Compton
Dr Dolittle on the Moon, Hugh
 Lofting

EMERGENCY RATIONS

3 2 lb packets Bachelors dried soup
3 tins Complan
1 kilo Pakistani cheese

4 tins Australian cheese
4 tins tuna fish
4 tins corned beef

Glossary

ATA – wheat-flour

BUNGO – young girl (Balti)

BURKA – long, all-enveloping gown worn in public by Muslim women

CHAI-KHANA – tea-house

CHARPOY – wooden frame bed with webbing, or ropes

CHAPATTIS – thin unleavened bread, cooked without fat

CHOWKIDAR – caretaker, or night-watchman

CHOTA – small

CHU – water (Balti)

DAK-BUNGALOW – government staging house

DAHL – lentils

DECHI – handleless saucepan

DHOBI – washerman

DULA – Ethiopian walking-stick (Amharic)

DZO – yak-cow hybrid (Tibetan)

FERENGHI – foreigner

GHEE – clarified butter

GHORA – horse

HAKIM – doctor

HARTAL – general strike, usually organized from religious or political motives

ID-I-KURBAN – Muslim festival held on varying dates to commemorate Abraham's offering of Ishmael

KHANA – butter food

LATHI – long, iron-bound bamboo stick used as weapon

NULLAH – narrow river-bed in the mountains, often dry in winter

P.W.D. – Public Works Department

PARATAS – thick fried chapattis

PUNIAL-WATER – home-made wine of varying potency from the district of Punial

ROTI – bread cooked in loaves, or in buns

RUPEE – standard coinage, worth about five pence
SEER – measurement of weight; about one kilo
SATU – barley roasted and then ground (Balti)
SHALWAR-KAMEEZ – loose pantaloons and loose knee-length shirt
TSAMPA – dough made of roast ground barley and butter tea (Tibetan)
TAHSILDAR – local tax collector

Bibliography

Ladak, Physical, Statistical and Historical: Alexander Cunningham, London: 1854
Karakoram and Western Himalaya: Fillipo de Fillipi, Constable: 1912
Himalaya, Karakoram and Eastern Turkestan 1913–1914: Fillipo de Fillipi, Edward Arnold: 1932
The Marches of Hindustan: David Fraser, London: 1907
My Life as an Explorer: Sven Hedin, Cassell: 1926
Where Three Empires Meet: E. F. Knight, London: 1893
Where Four Worlds Meet: Fosco Maraini, Hamish Hamilton: 1964
Travels in the Himalayan Provinces: William Moorcroft, London: 1841
Trails to Inmost Asia: G. N. Roerich, Yale University Press: 1931
Travels in Cashmir, Ladak, etc.: G. T. Vigne, London: 1835
Two Summers in the Ice-Wilds of Eastern Karakoram: F. B. and W. H. Workman, London: 1917
Wonders of the Himalaya: Sir Francis Younghusband, London: 1924

Index

William Dalrymple

In Xanadu

A Quest

'A classic.'   *Sunday Express*

'William Dalrymple's *In Xanadu* carries us breakneck from a pre-dawn glimmer in the Holy Sepulchre right across Asia to a bleak wind in Kubla Khan's palace . . . it is learned and comic, and a most gifted first book touched by the spirits of Kinglake, Robert Byron and E. Waugh.'

Patrick Leigh Fermor, 'Books of the Year', *Spectator*

'*In Xanadu* is, without doubt, one of the best travel books produced in the last 20 years. It is witty and intelligent, brilliantly observed, deftly constructed and extremely entertaining . . . Dalrymple's gift for transforming ordinary, humdrum experience into something extraordinary and timeless suggests that he will go from strength to strength.'

Alexander Maitland, *Scotland on Sunday*

'The new Theroux.'   *Today*

'Exuberant.'   Colin Thubron

'Dalrymple writes beautifully, is amazingly erudite, brave and honest, and can be extremely funny.'

Quentin Crewe, *Sunday Telegraph*

'The delightful, and funny, surprise mystery tour of the year.'
Sir Alec Guinness, *Sunday Times*

'Erudite, adventurous and amusing . . . reminded me of Evelyn Waugh.'   Piers Paul Read

City of Djinns

A Year in Delhi

William Dalrymple

Winner of the 1994 *Sunday Times* Young Writer of the Year Award.

Alive with the mayhem of the present and sparkling with the author's ubiquitous, irrepressible wit, *City of Djinns* is the fascinating portrait of a city as has never been attempted before. Meeting an extraordinary array of characters, from the city's elusive eunuchs to the embattled descendants of the great Moguls, from the rich Punjabis to the Sufis and mystics, and investigating the resonances of these people and their modern ways with the India of the past, this is a unique and dazzling feat of research and adventure by one of the finest travel writers of his generation.

'A sympathetic and engaging portrait of this age-old city . . . It is fine, entertaining, well-written stuff, thoroughly researched but with none of the stern academic tone that so many historical profiles adopt. What sustains it, apart from his erudite knowledge of Moslem architecture, medicine, music, military architecture, and arcane religious principles, is Dalrymple's sense of historical adventure. Just open your eyes, he says. If you know how to look, even the empty tombs and abandoned ruins of the past are alive . . .'   *Financial Times*

'Unlike much of modern travel writing *City of Djinns* is informative, learned and funny . . . a lively and sometimes profound book.'   *Economist*

'Scholarly and marvellously entertaining . . . A considerable feat.'
Dervla Murphy, *Spectator*

ISBN 0 00 637595 2

The Crossing Place

A Journey Among the Armenians

Philip Marsden

The Crossing Place is the account of a remarkable journey through the Middle East, Eastern Europe and the Caucasus, a quest to discover the secret of one of the world's most extraordinary peoples. Caught between opposing empires, between warring religions and ideologies – at the crossing place of history – the Armenians have somehow survived against the odds.

'A fascinating journey, a lone and absorbing quest for what stubbornly survives a holocaust – a people, a landscape, a language, a religious vision'　　　　　　　　　D. M. Thomas

'An interest, then an obsession, then a quest – and eventually a book, *The Crossing Place*, in which Marsden's fine and unostentatious travel writing is criss-crossed with traces of politics and cultural history . . . This is a beautifully written book, with enough incident and observation to convey the unpredictabilities of real travel'　　　　　　Noel Malcolm, *Daily Telegraph*

'One of the best young travel writers in search of the elusive, enigmatic Armenians . . . A wonderful journey recounted with knowledge, humour and a beautiful, elegiac sadness'
　　　　　　　　　　　　　　　Nicholas Wollaston, *Observer*

ISBN 0 00 637667 3

Seven Years in Tibet

Heinrich Harrer

Heinrich Harrer, already a famous mountaineer and Olympic ski champion, was caught by the outbreak of the Second World War while climbing in the Himalayas. Being an Austrian, he was interned in India. By an almost superhuman effort, and on his third attempt he succeeded in escaping into Tibet.

After a series of remarkable experiences in a country never before crossed by a Westerner, he reached the forbidden city of Lhasa. He stayed there for seven years, learned the language and acquired a greater understanding of Tibet and Tibetans than a Westerner had ever before achieved. He became the friend and tutor of the young Dalai Lama and finally accompanied him into India when he was put to flight by the Red Chinese invasion.

'Some books, like some mountains, are lonely and unrivalled peaks, and this is one of these.'   *Economist*

'Few adventurers in this century have had the combined luck and hardihood to return with such news as this. Fewer still have rendered it so powerfully unadorned.'   *Times Literary Supplement*

'Like the voyage of the Kon-Tiki, it deserves to take its place among the few great travel stories of our own times.'   *The Times*

ISBN 0 586 08707 9

Rory MacLean

Stalin's Nose

Across the Face of Europe

'A minor masterpiece of comic surrealism.' *The Times*

'The best book I've read for a very long time.' John Wells

'Crazy, charming, a delight.' John Le Carré

Winston the pig fell into Aunt Zita's life when he dropped on to her husband's head and killed him dead. It was a distressing end to a distinguished life of spying. After the funeral Zita, a faded Austrian aristocrat and a vivacious eccentric, refused to remain at home. Instead, together with Winston, she hijacked her nephew Rory and set out in a rattling Trabant puffing and wheezing across the continent on one last ride . . .

'The farce with which Rory MacLean often clothes his narrative is a metaphor for the much blacker and indeed surreal comedy of the Communist years. As an allegory it is powerful and frequently moving. As a tale it is tremendous . . . It is also a thing of beauty.' Jan Morris

'With the unlikely cast of a Tamworth pig, a coffin, two elderly aunts and a battered Trabant, Rory MacLean creates a fantastic tableau that embraces the horrors, betrayals and ironies of modern East European history. *Stalin's Nose* is a dark, sardonic and brilliant book which grows in stature with every page – the most extraordinary debut in travel writing since Bruce Chatwin's *In Patagonia*.' William Dalrymple

'The wittiest, most surreal travel writing of recent years.' Frank Delaney

'At once eccentric, amusing and chilling . . . A Gogolesque tour in a Trabant.' *Economist*

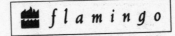 flamingo

Charlotte Du Cann and Mark Watson

Reality is the Bug that Bit Me in the Galapagos

Trips in the Americas

'Oh, you're escaping from reality,' said the Californian in the El Dorado café.

'No,' I said, 'we are not escaping.'

'And anyway,' snarled Mark, 'what is reality?'

'Reality,' she said throwing her leg up into the air, 'is the bug that bit me in the Galapagos.'

In 1991 two friends sold everything they had and went west. From Mexico through Central and South America to the end of the Andes, Charlotte Du Cann and Mark Watson decribe their extraordinary journey and their many encounters with wise women, romantic communists, magicians, lovers and other nomads. All their old cultural maps are challenged as they discover inner landscapes as huge, wild and terrifying as the unpredictable geography they traverse; at once disturbing and intimate in its poetry and vision, this is no ordinary travel book.

From the pyramids of the Yucatan to the roaring Pacific, moving from the quick-silver quiet of Quito to the devil's drama of Bogotá, towards the twilight zone of Practically Patagonia, *Reality is the Bug that Bit Me in the Galapagos* is the journal of their troubadour life, an exploration both of human nature and the open territory of magic and spirit.

ISBN 0 00 654716 8

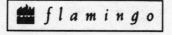 *flamingo*

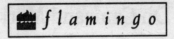

Dervla Murphy

The following Dervla Murphy titles are available in Flamingo:

☐	The Ukimwi Road	0 00 654802 4	£6.99
☐	Full Tilt	0 00 654800 8	£6.99
☐	In Ethiopia with a Mule	0 00 654798 2	£6.99
☐	Where the Indus is Young	0 00 654801 6	£6.99
☐	On a Shoestring to Coorg	0 00 654799 0	£6.99
☐	Eight Feet in the Andes	0 00 654797 2	£6.99

You can buy Flamingo paperbacks at your local bookshop or newsagent. Or you can order them from HarperCollins Mail Order, Dept. 8, HarperCollins *Publishers*, Westerhill Road, Bishopbriggs, Glasgow G64 2QT. Please enclose a cheque or postal order, to the order of the cover price plus add £1.00 for the first and 25p for additional books ordered within the UK.

NAME (Block letters)_____

ADDRESS_____

_____

_____